Sawchuk

Sawchuk

The Troubles and Triumphs
of the World's Greatest Goalie

David Dupuis

Published in 1998 by Stoddart Publishing Co. Limited
34 Lesmill Road, Toronto, Canada M3B 2T6
180 Varick Street, 9th Floor, New York, New York 10014

Distributed in Canada by:
General Distribution Services Ltd.
325 Humber College Blvd., Toronto, Ontario M9W 7C3
Tel. (416) 213-1919   Fax (416) 213-1917
Email customer.service@ccmailgw.genpub.com

Distributed in the United States by:
General Distribution Services Inc.
85 River Rock Drive, Suite 202, Buffalo, New York 14207
Toll-free Tel. 1-800-805-1083   Toll-free Fax 1-800-481-6207
Email gdsinc@genpub.com

03   02   01   00   99   1   2   3   4   5

Canadian Cataloguing in Publication Data

Dupuis, David Michael, 1958–
Sawchuk: the troubles and triumphs of the world's greatest goalie

ISBN 0-7737-60644

1. Sawchuk, Terry.   2. Hockey goalkeepers — Biography.   I. Title.

GV848.5.S35D86 1998   796.962'092   C98-931478-2

Cover Design: Bill Douglas @ The Bang
Text Design: Kinetics Design & Illustration

Photograph opposite the title page: Hockey Hall of Fame

THE CANADA COUNCIL | LE CONSEIL DES ARTS
FOR THE ARTS | DU CANADA
SINCE 1957 | DEPUIS 1957

We acknowledge for their financial support of our publishing program the Canada Council, the Ontario Arts Council, and the Government of Canada through the Book Publishing Industry Development Program (BPIDP).

Printed and bound in Canada

This book is dedicated
in loving memory of my parents,
Bernice and Celestin Dupuis,
to my wife, Marlis, and to my
children, Tanis and Jordan,
for their continued support and love.

Contents

Acknowledgments

*I*N the 28 years since his death, many writers have attempted to write the authorized biography of Terry Sawchuk. I know that I am the first to do so, and most likely I'm the only person who ever will.

I would like to thank Jerry Sawchuk, Terry's oldest son, who gave me the green light and entrusted me with the family's precious memorabilia. Many thanks to you and Laura for your warm hospitality and for opening closed doors. Pat Sawchuk Milford shared unhesitatingly her painful and happy memories of her years with Terry. I am forever indebted to her for her candidness and friendship. I am grateful to Terry's other children: JoAnn, Kathy, Debbie, Carol Ann, Terry, and Mike, for sharing their thoughts and memories of their father. He would be extremely proud of you all.

My good friend Paul Henry, a scout for the Florida Panthers, believed in the project from the outset. When I first told him of my dream, to write a book about my goaltending idol, he connected me with a key person in Sawchuk's life, Marcel Pronovost. I am indebted to Marcel, a hockey legend in his own right, who spoke to the family on my behalf. If Marcel Pronovost trusts you, the Sawchuk family trusts you. Thank you, Marcel, for your faith, honesty, and openness in our many conversations. Without you, this story would not have been told. You truly are Terry's best friend.

I would also like to thank others whose assistance was invaluable: Denise Hayes, my secretarial assistant, transcriber, and friend; my sister Anne Gagne, whose loyalty, love, and editing skills went beyond sisterly duties; my brothers, Pat and Alvin, for their support; Jake and his wife, Victoria, for their unfailing encouragement and enthusiasm throughout this long project; and Bonnie Bradley for her support and for granting me a leave of absence to work on my dream. The many people in various fields of expertise who contributed to the success of this project include: Pat Gignac, a friend, for his photographic assistance; Drs. John Warren and Dikran Abrahamian for spending many hours reviewing Terry's psychological and medical profiles with me; physiotherapists Wanda Nayduk and Sebastian Asselbergs for their expertise and input into understanding the human body and sport injuries; Midland radio station KICX-FM for the use of their equipment and for DJ Aaron Collin's expertise in converting the audio-cassette of the Sawchuk's wedding; Charlie Dyer, Waxy Gregoire, and Thomas Paradis for the use of their libraries and mementos; John Gignac of Hacker, Gignac & Rice and Wayne Logan of Logan & Company for their guidance and legal advice; Donald Bastian and Jim Gifford of Stoddart Publishing for believing in the project; Craig Campbell and Phil Pritchard of the Hockey Hall of Fame for granting me access to the archives; and hockey writers Roy MacGregor and Douglas Hunter for their advice and support.

Writing this hockey book could not have been accomplished without the contributions of colleagues and teammates who knew Terry and were associated with him throughout his career. My sincere appreciation goes out to Alex Delvecchio; Dr. John Finlay; Fern and Jeanne Flaman; Emile Francis; Bill Gadsby; Glenn Hall; Andra and Red Kelly; Art Kras; Ted Lindsay; Harry Lumley; Budd Lynch; Jiggs McDonald; Jimmy Peters; Pierre Pilote; Jim Proudfoot; Leo Reise; Sharyn and Wayne Rutledge; Jimmy Skinner; Art Skov; Johnny Wilson; Lefty Wilson; Randy Wilson; and Danny Wood.

Recording feats of sports figures for posterity is placed in the hands of reporters who love the game of hockey. Thanks to the following notable writers whose work helped me to verify my facts: Jacques Beauchamp, *Montreal Matin*; Jack Berry, *Detroit Free Press*; Red Burnett, *Toronto Star*; Luis Cauz, *Globe and Mail*; Andrew Crane, *New York Post*; Andrew Crichton, *Sports Illustrated*; Marshall Dann, *Detroit Free Press*; M. F. Drunkenbrod, *Detroit Times*; Milt Dunnell, *Toronto Star*; Cy Egan, *New York Post*; Gerald Eskenazi, *New York Times*; Joe Falls, *Detroit Free Press*; Trent Frayne, *Maclean's*; George Gross, *Toronto Telegram*; Bill Libby, *Hockey News*; Vince Lunny, *Real for Men*; Jim Lycett, *Detroit News*; Hugh Mackie, *Hockey World*; Mike Morrow, *L.A. South Bay Daily Breeze*; Andy O'Brien, *Weekend Magazine*; Russ Parham, *Inside Sports*; Jean Pouliot, *Les Sports*; Herb Ralby, *Boston Globe*; Al Silverman, *Sport*; Lewis Walter, *Detroit Times*; and Scott Young, *Globe and Mail*.

Last but not least, I thank Terry Sawchuk for inspiring me. Writing his story has fulfilled my life-long dream. His greatness and weaknesses remind us that we are all human. Here's to you, Uke!

Prologue

SATURDAY AFTERNOON
IN CHICAGO

A fall day in 1996. As Interstate 94 wound down around the base of Lake Michigan and up into the state of Illinois, the cityscape of Chicago, "The Windy City," came into view. Sprawling along the shore of the Great Lake, its skyscrapers stretched towards the sky in all their majestic beauty and elegance. One would think it the most unlikely place to begin the Terry Sawchuk story, but on this particular Saturday, a sunny autumn afternoon in Chicago, the present crossed paths with the most memorable event of Terry Sawchuk's career.

Driving the car was Jerry Sawchuk, eldest child of the great goaltender. He smiled as he entered the city's outskirts. He had come to Chicago to visit his late father's — as well as his own — favourite uncle, Nick Maslak, formerly of Winnipeg, Manitoba.

Obtaining a temporary travel visa around 1938, Nick had come to Chicago to visit his two brothers, Mike and Pete. Fate intervened when he met Dorothy, decided to get married, and landed a job with the Wabash Railroad, and later the Norfolk and Western Railroad Company, where he worked for twenty-eight years until his retirement in 1975.

Nick Maslak's tall, wide frame and loud, powerful voice had always commanded respect, and at eighty-six, he was unbelievably fit and sound of mind. He still had his own apartment, drove his own car, wore a baseball cap and track suit, and could talk about the Chicago sports teams of '56, '66, '76, '86, or '96, Clinton or Dole, or local issues. He bought and read the *Tribune* every day and had many friends throughout the neighbourhood and city. He always spoke respectfully of God, an inherent trait carried from his strong Catholic Ukrainian roots. Nick loved to reminisce.

But after all these years, his favourite topic was still his family, which included his favourite nephew, the late, great goaltender, Terry Sawchuk.

"As God is my witness, I said to my sister, Terry's mother Annie, 'Annie,' I says, 'little Terry's getting to be a pretty good little goaltender. I think we should get him his own set of goal pads.' Up until then he had been using those shin pads, you know, the ones defencemen wear. And so I goes downtown to the hardware store and got Terry a pair of pads. I bring them to Annie's and we put them on Terry. The pads, they came up to his neck!"

Uncle Nick laughed and his eyes sparkled at the memory. He continued, "So I take those pads and we cut them, to fit little Terry. We put them back on him and they fit like a glove. But he didn't like them! He took them off and never wore them again!"

Nick laughed again, but only momentarily. Suddenly his eyes narrowed as he looked at his nephew. Seriousness rose in his voice as he spoke with the fervour of a minister.

"You know, Jerry, there almost was no little Terry. One day your grandmother called me. We lived next door to each other. She says, 'Nick, I don't know where little Terry is. He hasn't come home from the rink yet. It's way past the time he should have been home!' So I go out looking for him and I see his little friend and he said he saw Terry go down this certain path. So I go down there, and heaven help me, there is little Terry in the snow bank with his skates still on, sound asleep. I carried him home and I said to my sister, 'Annie, another hour and there would have been no more Terry!'"

Jerry's look was incredulous. "Uncle Nick! You're kidding! I did that to Dad, too!"

Terry's boy recounted the moment when, as a child, he too had gone to the skating rink and was long overdue at home. A concerned father set out on foot to retrace his son's path and found him, fully dressed in his hockey paraphernalia, sound asleep in a snow bank. History repeated itself as Terry Sawchuk picked up his oldest child and carried him home.

But Uncle Nick's mind had seized on another memory of his goaltending nephew. "Whenever Terry was in Chicago, he'd phone his Uncle Nick and come over for some garlic sausage. He loved garlic sausage. Sometimes he brought some of the team with him and we'd have a big feed, sometimes spaghetti, too.

"I still remember the guys used to say to me after one of his games here, 'Hey, Nick, that nephew of yours, Sawchuk, is some kinda goaltender,' and I'd say, 'You betcha! That's my Terry!' Especially that Saturday afternoon game when Bobby Hull hit him with that slap shot. Boy, he was the best! Unbelievable!"

As Jerry listened to Uncle Nick speak glowingly of his father, he nodded with a smile, but he knew that Terry Sawchuk's story, about to unfold, would be tinged with bittersweet memories.

Despite his pride in his father's accomplishments on the ice, Jerry remained torn with issues left unresolved by his father's premature passing in 1970. Next to his mother, Pat, Jerry had borne the brunt of the abuse heaped upon an innocent family by a husband and father who was incapable of dealing with his personal weaknesses and demons.

Despite it all, Jerry, as representative of the Sawchuk family, was determined that the true Terry Sawchuk story be told. The good parts all came flooding back: running around the Olympia with Mark and Marty Howe; riding atop his father's back like a horse; going on fishing and golfing excursions with his father; organizing outdoor barbecues; and romping with their pet German shepherd. He knew too that the other siblings and his mother could easily recall the good memories incited during their years together.

Dealing with the dark moments would be more difficult. Recessed were the many times when the family would barricade themselves in the kitchen, quietly waiting, and praying, for the drunken tirade from the man of the household to cease, for him to pass out quietly for another night in his favourite chair in the living room. They would have to relive the painful memories of arguments, yelling, and screaming; of the frightening year in Los Angeles before the divorce in 1969; the shock of their father's passing and the debacle that occurred during his funeral.

But, for now, Uncle Nick had conjured up a great memory.

Indeed, that Saturday afternoon in Chicago, April 15, 1967, has been etched in time as the finest afternoon, or evening for that matter, that Terry Sawchuk, or any other goaltender in the history of big-league hockey, had ever relished. It was the cornerstone against which any other goaltending performance, before or since, must be measured.

— • • • —

For Terry Sawchuk, that Saturday started out as the unlikeliest of days for him to unveil any heroics.

It was the day of the fifth game in a gruelling semifinal playoff series between Terry's Toronto Maple Leafs and the first-place Chicago Black Hawks. So far, the aging Leaf team had held their own and to the surprise of everyone, the series was tied at two wins apiece.

Having played exceptionally well, and having faced 138 shots through the first four games, Terry had asked Leaf coach Punch Imlach if he could sit out this fifth game to rest his bruised and battered body. His large frame was gaunt and he sported a bruised shoulder, a bruised calf, a sore elbow, and a sore arm. To boot, because of injuries and a platooning setup with Johnny Bower, the thirty-seven-year-old goalie hadn't played more than two games in one week all season. Now, he had just completed his fourth game in seven days. Towards the end of the last game he had tired visibly and Chicago had tied the series. In fact, the whole Toronto team, whose average age was significantly higher than the Black Hawks', showed signs of tiring and were plagued by injuries.

By game time, Terry had slowly donned his equipment. He was calm and at ease in the knowledge that his teammate, the veteran Bower, had the starting assignment. It hurt even to get dressed, he mused to himself. Thank God he didn't have to play! After the cursory warmup, he contentedly made his way to the end of the Leaf bench to watch the game and rest his wounds.

As he looked up at the three tiers of screaming fans whose cheers only increased during the playing of "The Star-Spangled Banner," Terry thought to himself that this was a hell of a place to visit and play. Chicago Stadium usually had terrible ice, but the warm temperature this afternoon made it even more sluggish than usual.

He sat down after the anthem and wondered if Uncle Nick was somewhere in this boisterous crowd. After all, he had left him tickets. His mind wandered to his family back home in Union Lake, a suburb forty minutes north of Detroit. He wondered if they were watching. He thought of his wife, Pat, home pregnant with their seventh child, and the thought was not a good one. He had gone into a tirade when she informed him she was expecting again. Saying they couldn't afford another child, he had implored Pat to have an abortion.

But Terry knew that the ultimate decision was his wife's, and he knew what it would be, given her love of children and her Catholicism. Though their marriage had often been rocky, it had never been more so than lately. Her refusal to abort the child and his helplessness and anger about the situation had only deepened the rift between them.

Sawchuk muttered to himself, erased the thoughts from his mind, and looked out at the opening face-off.

Though their shooting and passing were a little rusty at first, the Hawks began Game Five with a flourish. But a Chicago penalty to Dennis Hull slowed their attack and, a minute into the penalty, and six minutes into the game, the Toronto power play appeared poised to get its first shot on goal. Rookie Mike Walton snared a slot pass from Pete Stemkowski and fired a low blast past a startled Denis DeJordy at the 6:16 mark to put the Leafs up by one.

But three minutes later Terry was about to see his plans for a restful afternoon go down the drain. At the 9:31 mark, an attempted clearing pass by Bower from behind his net was intercepted by Pierre Pilote along the boards. His shot was deflected by Lou Angotti into the empty Toronto net to tie the game. The Chicago Stadium crowd erupted. From behind the bench, Imlach watched Bower warily. His veteran goalie seemed a little shaken as he settled down for the ensuing face-off.

A minute and a half after their first goal, the Hawks swarmed towards Bower again. The goalkeeper fumbled a Doug Jarrett shot and Billy Hay shuffled the rebound neatly to Bobby Hull, who fired the puck high into the Leafs' net. Twenty thousand fans erupted into pandemonium. Imlach could see it was not Bower's afternoon and he ran to the end of the bench where Sawchuk was seated. Concern was written all over the coach's normally impassive face. Terry knew what he was about to be asked. He could see it coming.

"Ready to go in?" he asked his weary veteran. Terry took a big sigh and answered, "If I have to, I'd rather go in at the beginning of the second." Punch nodded, and then called Bower over to the bench for a talk.

"Whatsa matter?" Punch asked.

"I don't know," Bower answered with an honesty Punch had always counted on. Bower agreed to finish the period, and the Leafs managed to tie the game on a Frank Mahovlich power-play goal. In the dressing room, Imlach was immediately in front of Bower's seat. His clutch goaltender looked up at him, the sweat pouring off him.

"You seem a little shaky. Are you?" Punch asked him.

"Ya, I guess I'm a little shook."

"Want me to make a change?"

Bower looked down at the floor and took a big breath. Sitting beside his goaltending partner, Terry waited pensively, not really looking forward to Johnny's answer. He knew what he would say in this same position and then he heard Bower say, "Well, there's a lot at stake."

With that, Imlach turned to Sawchuk and nodded. Terry nodded back and took a big breath. He had a few minutes to compose himself.

To begin the second period, he slowly glided to the net and scraped down the slushy ice. He lifted the mask down over his face to take a few warm-up shots. He indicated he was ready and got down into the famous "Sawchuk Crouch."

Three minutes into a rough second period, referee John Ashley called a charging penalty against the Leafs' Allan Stanley. Imlach briefly argued the point as the awesome Hawk power play set up to the right of Sawchuk. Terry had faced these guys before. They were the main reason he was aching from head to toe.

Hawk centre Stan Mikita snapped the draw back to defence-man Pierre Pilote, who in turn fed the puck back to Mikita in the corner. The Hawk captain circled near the back of the net and fed a thirty-foot pass to a charging Bobby Hull. Sawchuk quickly charged out as the Golden Jet let go one of his patented slap shots. The puck caught the goaltender on his already aching and tender shoulder and careened off his mask. Sawchuk went down as if he had been shot and lay on the ice as the play was whistled dead. Leaf trainer Bobby Haggert charged onto the ice towards the fallen goaltender. Terry closed his eyes to deal with the excruciating pain. Finally, he was able to lift himself up on his good elbow, as concerned Leafs stood nearby. He felt like his shoulder had been poked with a hot iron.

The Hawks on the ice chuckled to themselves, hoping they might get the shaky Bower back in the net. Pierre Pilote skated through the crease with a grin and sarcastically said, "Stay down, Ukey," implying there was more to come.

As Haggert knelt by Sawchuk, Terry shot back a cold glare at Pilote. His blood was beginning to boil.

"Where'd you get it, Ukey?" Haggert asked.

"My bad shoulder," he answered, holding it with his other hand.

"Think you're all right?" The question jarred Sawchuk. He looked at the trainer with a snarl.

"I stopped the fucking shot, didn't I?"

He could hear the chuckles and sarcastic jibes of the Hawk players nearby. It galvanized him against the pain. Reaching for the trainer, Sawchuk said, "Come on, Bobby, help me up and I'll stone those sons a bitches!"

The Terry Sawchuk that Bobby Haggert helped to his feet was not the same man who had been felled by the Hull blast. He would rise with the confidence, sudden agility, determination, and quickness that he had possessed in 1952 when his star was at its brightest with the Detroit Red Wings. Indicating to everyone that he was set to resume, he pulled down his mask and set to work. Very quickly the Hawks realized that the dynamics of the game had suddenly changed, and they would soon wish that they had kept their big mouths shut.

The Hawks came at Sawchuk with everything they had. For the duration of the Stanley penalty and later during a penalty to right winger Jim Pappin, the Chicagoans peppered Sawchuk with shots that were sure goals, quality chances.

"I remember breaking in towards Sawchuk and throwing the puck back to Bobby (Hull) for a sure goal," relates Pierre Pilote today, "and I braced for and took a hit. I expected to get up to celebrate a goal. There was no goal! I couldn't believe the puck was not in the net!"

With angry determination and razor-sharp anticipation, Sawchuk's goaltending skills gelled this hot, smoke-filled afternoon. With each unbelievable save he made, his confidence and concentration grew. Each time he frustrated the Hawk snipers, he dug deeper, his revenge grew sweeter.

In that second period, the Hawks took fifteen shots at him, nearly all of them sure goals. The goalie took bullets to the body from Doug Mohns, Pilote, Ken Wharram, Hull, and Mikita. The Hawks threw the puck around in a frantic attempt to set up the open player. Each time, Sawchuk was there to turn back the shot with cat-like agility.

At one point, Mikita broke in, blasting a low, screened shot that Sawchuk kicked out with a half-split save. He then bounded back up to his famous gorilla crouch, then made a classic high right-hand blocker stop on Mohns so fluidly that it left the screaming Chicago fans beside themselves in frustration.

As the period ended, perspiration dripped off the bottom of Sawchuk's mask. Leaf players skated over to him to pat his pads with their sticks, a hockey gesture meaning "Well done!" as he skated off the ice.

Sawchuk was pleased with his performance thus far, but was too tired and too sore to show it. Besides, there was still another period to go.

His teammates realized he was giving them a performance that they had to take advantage of. The game was still tied despite the fact that most of the period had been spent in the Leafs' end.

In the Chicago dressing room, the Hawks, though frustrated, figured they had the momentum and the firepower to eventually get one past Sawchuk. And once they got one by him, maybe more goals would follow. As they bounded back out for the third period, the Hawks were full of confidence.

As Sawchuk slowly made his way back into his net, he was also brimming with confidence. The Leaf skaters huddled around the net to quietly exhort him to continue his magnificent play. If he could hang on, they'd try to get him a couple. Sawchuk pushed his mask back down over his face. He bent down in his crouch to face the beginning of the period. He remembered the jeers of the Hawks and the pain of the Hull slap shot in his shoulder, and suddenly felt young again. He ignored the pain. He ignored the swirling cigarette smoke above his head from the twenty thousand screaming fans. He ignored the increasing heat that was warming the stadium and made the drops of perspiration drip from the bottom of his mask even before the game resumed. He ignored everything except the Chicago Black Hawks.

The third period began where the second had left off. Chicago came at Terry with everything in its arsenal. Their defence pushed the play continuously into the Toronto end. The young team that had smashed twelve different scoring records in the regular season looked at the old Frankenstein-masked goalie in the Toronto net and smelled a kill. But Frankenstein was ready. So were his teammates.

With the Hawks pressing in the Toronto end, centre Pete Stemkowski and left winger Bob Pulford converted a Chicago turnover into a dangerous two-on-one. Taking a perfect pass from Pulford, the centre just missed the open upper net over a sprawling and helpless DeJordy and the puck sailed up into the spectators, much to their relief.

Then, at the 2:11 mark, Pulford fed a slot pass to Pappin, who got a quick shot away and then took a whack at the rebound. The puck skimmed away from DeJordy to Stemkowski, who stuffed it into the vacant Hawk cage.

The Leaf goal stunned the home team, and forced them to put their attack into overdrive. Stemkowski drew a tripping penalty at 4:33 and Chicago saw an opportunity. They peppered Sawchuk with shots, but he blocked each with a part of his body and his defence did a fabulous job of clearing the rebounds. Many of Sawchuk's saves were sheer thievery and each drew moans and screams from the crowd.

Stemkowski drew a second penalty just after the ten-minute mark, and the Hawks knew they had to score. Hull blasted a low shot that Sawchuk deftly turned aside before Pat Stapleton rushed up, forcing Sawchuk to make an amazing stop with his blocker. With Hull and Mikita swarming around his net, the goalie's anticipation denied Mikita a sure goal, leaving the Hawks shaking their heads. A Ken Hodge slap shot spun the old goalie around, as he deflected the puck wide.

Then Doug Mohns broke in free with what would turn out to be the Hawks' last hope. Mohns tried to deke a couple of times as he swept across the Toronto net, but the shutout king stayed with him, maintaining his stance. Mohns had nowhere to shoot as Leaf defenders rushed towards him, and his effort bounced harmlessly off the goalie's pads. In the first thirteen minutes of the period, Hull and company had pelted the Toronto goalie with twenty unbelievable shots, but to no avail.

When Chicago's Lou Angotti took a slashing penalty with six minutes left to go, Terry looked up at the clock and took a deep breath. The Leafs could taste victory. They pressed the Hawks, stayed with them, hit them, checked them ceaselessly. The Hawks were a spent force. In the last six minutes, they would manage only two helpless shots, and in the final minutes it was the Leafs who dominated the play, adding a goal by Jim Pappin as insurance.

At the final buzzer, all the Leafs were ecstatic, except for Sawchuk. With the game over the pain finally set in. There were no victory dances as he made his way off the ice surrounded by his jubilant teammates. Just pain, particularly in his throbbing shoulder.

As he sat gingerly in his place, a melancholy feeling came over him as everyone rushed to tell him the unbelievable game he had played. But he didn't have to be told, by Punch or anyone else, that it was the greatest exhibition of goaltending ever witnessed.

He sat for a long time in his equipment, dragging on a cigarette, sipping on a Coke, leaning back with his eyes closed, still taking deep breaths. Slowly he was finding it possible to savour the 4–2 victory. Nearby, his coach was gleefully holding forth on his goaltenders' performance. "I've got the two best fuckin' goalies in the world. Sawchuk was like that guy on the bridge, you know, Horatio. Wouldn't let anything by. He was fantastic!"

With the reporters out of the room, and the adrenaline out of his system, Sawchuk undressed slowly. The players' exuberance ebbed as they caught sight of their battered, swollen, black-and-blue goalie. As he removed his T-shirt and walked towards the shower, his teammates realized just how much he had given of himself in making those thirty-seven saves over two periods. In summing up his performance, he was overheard to say quietly, "I'd like to leave hockey like that. In good style."

1

THEY CALLED HIM BUTCH

MANITOBA, the "land of 100,000 lakes," is today the easternmost of Canada's three prairie provinces. But in 1870, as it prepared to join Confederation, it was part of the territory known as Rupert's Land. When the Canadian Pacific Railroad linked up to the province's capital, Winnipeg, in 1881, it became the gateway to the Canadian west, beyond which lay hundreds of thousands of acres of flat, virgin farmland and the promise of a better life.

When Prime Minister Wilfrid Laurier boasted that the twentieth century belonged to Canada, many heeded his word and Manitoba's population almost doubled between the late 1880s and the mid 1920s. Through Winnipeg's train station came waves of Polish, German, Scandinavian, Dutch, and especially Ukrainian settlers. Amongst this last group was a young boy named Louis Sawchuk, who arrived in this region with his parents from the Austrian Ukraine region. Louis's father was Ukrainian, though his mother was Polish.

Winnipeg, named after a Cree word meaning "murky water," is situated at the junction of the Assiniboine and Red rivers. The hub of the province's land and transportation systems, Winnipeg was a bustling capital in the 1920s when the agricultural, mining, and industrial sectors took off and the economy of western Canada expanded.

At the beginning of the 1920s Louis Sawchuk worked in a factory that made burlap used to bag potatoes, one of the many staples grown throughout the Canadian prairies, especially so around Winnipeg. In this factory, Louis met Anne Maslak, whose family lived nearby and attended the same Ukrainian church as the Sawchuk family. One thing led to another and courtship developed into marriage.

Nick Maslak, Anne's brother and "Uncle Nick" to all the Sawchuks, remembers his sister's wedding well. "The wedding for Louis and Anne was a common, immigrant wedding. After the wedding we went to the little hall that the Ukrainian church had. My sister wore a white common dress and there were tables set up for food and everything. The community came together and it wasn't a big thing, but it was nice. A nice Ukrainian wedding."

The young married couple began their life together on Aberdeen Street in East Kildonan, a northern working-class suburb across the Red River from the greater Winnipeg area. The first house they rented was straight across the street from the Maslak homestead. At first glance, the couple seemed mismatched in a sense. Louis was a quiet man of slight build, with big hands and better-than-average strength in his upper torso. His wife, on the other hand, possessed both a strong, domineering personality and a stout physique. From the outset, even after Louis found other employment and Anne quit the burlap factory to raise children, it would be she who would set the tone and rule in their household.

Louis secured work with the MacDonald Sheet Metal Company. It was a busy time as sheet metal was in high demand. He quickly learned the tricks of the trade as a tinsmith.

Nick remembers Louis as "a wonderful man and a good home man. He was good to the kids, he was wonderful with kids. He was even wonderful with animals. He had a way with them, it was unreal. You could say whatever you wanted to the man and you never could hurt him.

"But Louis was also strong as an ox! One time I'm with him at the corner of Selkirk Avenue and McGregor in downtown Winnipeg, where the horses used to pull the trolley cars. In front of the drugstore there, Louis got into an argument with this guy and then suddenly, bang, Louis knocked him out with one punch. Suddenly this guy named China Pete came along, and he says to us, 'Hey, do you know who you hit? One of my best pals! That's Harry Dillon laying there, the former boxing champion!' I says, 'Good for him, let him lay there!'"

In 1922 Louis and Anne's firstborn arrived. They called him Michael, but they soon nicknamed him Mitch. By all indications he was the apple of his mother's eye and was a well behaved, attentive baby. It was often said that Michael was too beautiful to be born. He was the centre of their little world.

Around 1928 a second son, Roger, arrived. Anne hardly had time to adjust before she discovered that she was pregnant again. This particular delivery followed the crash of the New York, Toronto, and Montreal stock exchanges. When Terrance Gordon Sawchuk came screaming into the world on December 28, 1929, North America was frozen in the grips of the Great Depression.

Louis and Annie somehow made do on the tinsmith's sporadic, and lean, wages. Then one day, when Terry was still in diapers, Roger became listless and his mother watched helplessly as a fever overtook the little boy's body. Despite her best attempts, scarlet fever strangled the life from her middle son and he died quickly. Louis and Anne were devastated. Mitch went over to console his parents. Reaching for him, Anne cried into his shoulder. Thank God she still had Mitch and Terry, she thought. Wanting to leave the memories of their lost son behind, they moved across the street, renting the house beside Anne's parents.

Unlike their first house, which was cramped, Terry's second childhood home was a one-and-a-half storey, wood-sided place with three bedrooms. But the house was stretched to the limit when Anne delivered another baby boy, Gerald, in 1937. Terry and Mitch had to share a bed, but little Terry, who adored his older brother, didn't mind.

The home smelled of smoke, due to the wood stove, as well as cabbage rolls and other Ukrainian dishes, including Terry's favourites, kasha baked with onions and bacon, and jellied pigs' feet and head cheese.

With Louis away from the home working long hours throughout the Thirties, Mitch became the de facto head of the household. He frequently helped his mother with chores around the house and was especially fond of caring for little Terry. Of Mitch and Terry, Uncle Nick says, "You wouldn't think they were only brothers. You'd think they were attached to each other. Mitch was a good boy, loved school. He loved Terry, too. Never seen them without each other. If Mitch went to the store, Terry went with him. Always together."

Little Terry seemed happy, but his stubborn character caused Annie to be more critical and corrective of his behaviour than Mitch's and they clashed often, with mother always winning, of course.

It was clear that Terry loved his mother and soaked up any semblance of praise she gave him. She in turn provided for him, yet her domineering character seemed to create a distance between them.

"We weren't wealthy or anything," Terry would recall, "just average. But I always had everything I ever wanted."

Terry was put on skates for the first time at the age of four, and as a hockey player himself, Mitch encouraged little Terry.

Since East Kildonan, like the Winnipeg area as a whole, was dotted with dozens of small ponds, lakes, and streams, Uncle Nick took a leading role in forging the Sawchuk hockey stars.

"Louis had a nice big yard so we made a bob ski run. We had a larger, wider yard so we made the hockey rink there. Then, when Terry was getting better, we made one big rink, about the length of six houses, right to the sidewalk. It was as slick as you could make it. And we used to play with our shoes, just fooling around. All of the guys in the neighbourhood would come out, too, and we'd play around.

"We used to love watching the kids play hockey. We had a big window in the kitchen and my mother and father — Terry's grandparents — and I would watch them all for hours and hours. In fact, my dad and I strung chicken wire across the window so the pucks wouldn't break the window."

Terry's love of hockey was immediate. "He would get up in the morning, especially Saturday and Sunday, and be on skates with Mitch from the time he got up. You had to beg to get him to come and eat. We'd have to bring him a sandwich outside, honestly, swear to God."

When they weren't playing on the backyard rink, nothing stopped Terry and Mitch from playing from dawn to dusk on the nearby rivers. With a piece of horse dung as their puck and newspapers or cardboard tied with rope around their legs for protection, they played and played until the prairie sun sank slowly over the flat horizon, bathing the playing surface in a golden glow.

On days when Mitch wasn't available, Anne would accompany her young son to the nearest outdoor hockey rink and wait for hours until neither of them could stand the cold anymore. Always they would retreat from the minus-twenty-degree frigid temperatures to thaw, sometimes painfully, by the wood stove.

Uncle Nick remembers Mitch as "a big kid and a good skater. He would come on the ice and he was tough, let me tell you. He was a good kid, and he was good to Terry."

Regularly, this high school hockey goaltender gave his young brother and protégé some tips.

"Terry," Mitch would say, sometimes on an ice surface, sometimes in the family kitchen, "you have to keep your eyes on the puck and have good balance."

The youngster would memorize his brother's instructions verbatim. At this impressionable juncture in his life, young Terry's hero worship expanded from that of his goaltending brother to the exploits of the legendary Maple Leaf goalie, George Hainsworth. At one point Terry traded four hockey cards to get one of Hainsworth. Louis had managed to acquire a second-hand radio and Foster Hewitt's descriptions of Hainsworth on Saturday nights left Terry beside himself in hero worship.

Terry never saw Hainsworth play, but that didn't stop the loyal Leaf fan from strapping on his brother's pads and pretending to be Hainsworth whenever he wasn't emulating his older brother.

"[Mitch] used to take me out in Dad's car and let me drive," Terry remembered in a 1952 interview. "And we played cards together all the time."

At the age of ten, Terry's world was shattered when Mitch was suddenly felled by a fatal heart attack. He was seventeen years old.

A black cloud hung once again over the Sawchuk household. Terry couldn't believe what had happened as he gazed at his brother lying in the coffin. All he could do was cry. The common theme during the wake that was held in the family's living room was that Mitch was too good a boy for this world.

As his brother was carried away out of the house, Terry could hardly bear the thought of going on in this life without him. "I couldn't believe it when it happened. I missed him for a long time afterwards," Terry later said.

For Anne and Louis Sawchuk, the death of another son was almost too much to bear. A part of their soul was ripped out and buried with their firstborn son. Mitch seemed so full of life and goodness, how could God have taken him from them, too?

For Terry, the loss of his brother was compounded as his mother became even more withdrawn. It was as if she were afraid to attach herself to her two surviving sons for fear that she would lose them, too.

A cool, aloof family, the Sawchuks tried to deal with their own pain privately. It was difficult for a ten-year-old to have nobody to help dry his tears. Terry often lay in the bed he had shared with Mitch, trying to understand. Their life went on.

Terry refocused his life on hockey and improved quickly. Anne Sawchuk was continually amazed when answering the door to find kids four or five years older and three feet taller than Terry asking him to come out to play. Old enough to walk to the local ice ponds alone, her son now began to play organized hockey in the Playgrounds League with Hespeler. In this, his first season, Terry played goal, but the next season he was on a team that already had a good little goaltender named Lenny French, one of his best friends. Without missing a stride, Terry took his strong natural skating ability to centre ice, where he proceeded to win the league scoring championship, once scoring eight goals in one game. Terry also doubled as a defence-man with his school team.

But the sudden success Terry enjoyed as a forward did not

dampen his love of goaltending. He often took Mitch's pads and put them on in memory of his dead brother. As he sat with his pads on in the kitchen, he looked at his George Hainsworth hockey card and he dreamed.

As they had done after Roger's death, the family moved to a simple two-storey house on Bowman Avenue, still in East Kildonan. By this time in their lives, Louis had gone into a sheet-metal business of his own.

On the home front, it was clear that Anne Sawchuk continued to rule with an iron hand. Terry loved his mother very much but was resentful of her controlling, aloof nature. He was also angry at his father's absence and abdication of family control.

Terry began playing football in the summers and regularly arrived home with bad cuts and bruises. With his size and his anger, Terry played the game hard, earning the nickname "Butch."

Uncle Nick also remembers Terry coming home from school with a black eye once in a while, but he was never one to hold a grudge.

"He took his salt with his gravy. He'd say 'Mama, I had a fight,' and then forget all about it. But he was a lively little kid, like every common kid, you know, got into a little school fight now and then. But he was also good at sharing. Sometimes he gave too much away."

Terry's mother forbade him from playing football for fear he would endanger his hockey career. But one Sunday morning when Terry was twelve, he was off to attend Mass. Along the way there was a football field that this particular morning was host to an impromptu neighbourhood game. Dressed in his Sunday best, Terry attempted to slip past his friends who were avidly involved in the game. Catching sight of him, they yelled out to him.

"Come on, Butch! What's wrong with you? Don't you want to join us? Are you afraid?" He could not resist the challenge, and he skipped Mass, which, as far as his mother was concerned, was a cardinal sin. He threw himself full force into the play but his participation was short-lived as he injured his right elbow in a thunderous pile-up. His first thought as he got up off the ground was of his mother. He held his elbow with his left hand, the pain almost unbearable, and his arm beginning to shake. Thank God his clothes weren't too dirty, he thought, as he walked slowly towards the church and watched from outside until the Mass had ended and the congregation emerged. Knowing that the timing was right for him to head home, he noticed his arm was beginning to feel a little better. Once home, he quickly went to his room to change clothes. His arm was still very sore but he managed to hide his injury for the next few days from his mother. When asked about his dirty clothes, he told her he fell. He was chastised severely. In time he noticed that his right arm had lost some of its mobility, and he could no longer straighten it. But the pain was gone and Terry quietly adjusted. If anyone ever asked him, he merely admitted that his elbow was "sore."

The Esquire Restaurant in Winnipeg, owned by Max Fanstein, sponsored a boys' Midget hockey club called the Esquire Red Wings. The coach, Bob Kinnear, a western scout for the Detroit Red Wings, helped sponsor Fanstein's outdoor rink and ran a mini minor hockey program. East Kildonan had produced a few NHLers, such as Alfie Pike and Wally Stanowski, and the Red Wings were forever searching for western Canadian hockey talent. The Wings also employed fellow Winnipegger Joe Mandella to help Kinnear recruit prospective talent. It so happened that Bob Kinnear was looking for a goaltender. Kinnear would later recall, "Terry was about eleven or twelve, husky and chubby. He was a defenceman with his school team. He was one of a hundred or so kids who hung around my outdoor rink. We always needed equipment and I recall him saying he had a pair of pads at home so I told him to bring them down."

Kinnear suggested that Terry try them on and see how he could stop a puck. To his amazement, the kid was a natural. He summoned his scouting partner, Mandella, and they both agreed the big kid had potential.

At Prince Edward Public School, Terry left the goaltending job to his friend Lenny French, but at the Kinnear rink, he owned the net, wearing Mitch's pads. Soon his thoughts focused on becoming the best goalie he could, and friends and teammates alike soon realized that Terry *was* the best. Under Kinnear's tutelage, the goalie excelled, helped by his excellent skating ability and balance.

Don Rope, a future Canadian hockey Olympian, recalls, "When Terry's team was far ahead in the second period, he would take off his goal pads and play defence. It was amazing to see him play [out of the net] with those goal skates on!"

A breakaway by Rope on Terry in those early years also stayed fresh in the boy's memory: "I never even saw any part of the bloody net. He had absolutely every angle covered. There was nothing I could do!"

Remembering Mitch's tutoring about the importance of balance to a goaltender, Terry began to slowly develop his unique crouch. Placing his hands out in front of him and bending his waist so that his centre of gravity seemed always to be perfectly above his feet, his stance allowed him to have excellent lateral movement as well as balance.

Come summertime, Terry's competitive drive kept him actively involved in other sports. Uncle Nick says, "One day Terry and a bunch of kids were riding on boards with wheels underneath, like skateboards. He goes flying off one of these and smashes his elbow on the pavement. He hurt it real bad. He didn't say anything, but the next morning he couldn't lift his arm when he got out of bed. Annie took him to a children's hospital. Terry was about fourteen at the time."

The diagnosis was a reinjured dislocated elbow. His football secret had come back to haunt him. The doctors informed his mother that the old injury to the ulna, the large joint bone at the elbow, had caused the elbow to heal in a calcified, deformed fashion, limiting its extension. They toyed with the idea of re-breaking it, but eventually ruled that this procedure could make the elbow worse and opted to place the arm in a plaster cast for two weeks, to keep the elbow immobile and prevent further chipping. Once the cast was removed, the arm continued to be bothersome and took a turn for the worse.

"Right after they take off the cast, poor little Terry is getting the bad fevers and his elbow and arm get hot and are going blue," Uncle Nick continues. "So we put cold towels on it but he still had the bad fevers, and the arm is still blue. A fella I knew told me about the gangrene. He said, 'It's a bad infection, we might have to cut Terry's arm off.' I said, 'God forbid.' So I call my dad's doctor in the church society. The doctor says, 'Yes, he could lose the arm.' I said, 'Don't say that! No! No!'

"So I go over there and he gives me this medicine for Terry. And we kept putting the cold towels on it and everything. Anyways, God bless, we drew out all the poison. The fevers left, and the elbow and the nerves and the ligaments, the colour turned normal and Terry grew with the short arm. It was always bent. He couldn't straighten it anymore but the worst was over. No more fever, no more blue."

Kinnear, as an NHL scout, could smell talent a mile away. He knew he had a find in Terry. During the summer, Detroit general manager Jack Adams read Kinnear's glowing reports about the young goalie and suggested that Kinnear bring him down to the next Red Wing training camp.

In the fall of 1944, having secured the permission of Louis and Anne Sawchuk, Kinnear accompanied fourteen-year-old Terry on the train to Detroit for a workout with the Red Wings. If the young lad was awed by the experience, he didn't let it show on the ice.

He was so good in the workout that All-Star defenceman Black Jack Stewart approached Adams afterwards and said, "That boy is going to be a great one!"

Back in Winnipeg, during the 1944–45 season, Terry moved up to play Juvenile and briefly attended classes at East Kildonan High School before quitting to acquire his working papers, so that he could help out his family by earning a wage. His father helped him secure work at another sheet-metal company, installing, among other things, huge vents over bakery ovens. Each week Terry dutifully brought his mother his weekly paycheque, and she in turn afforded him a twenty-five-cent allowance.

Kinnear kept close tabs on his goaltending prospect as Terry advanced the next season to the Junior A Winnipeg Rangers. Despite the fact that Anne ruled the Sawchuk household, it was Louis who used his business acumen to oversee his son's hockey affairs. Around this time, Louis experienced a terrible fall from a twenty-foot scaffold, and fractured his spine. His recovery was slow, but it enabled him to be at home when interest in young Terry was increasing.

One night during the 1945–46 season, Baldy Northcott, the one-time star of the Montreal Maroons, paid a visit to the Sawchuk homestead. A scout for the Chicago Black Hawks, he had kept a close eye on young Sawchuk as well, and he was offering the Sawchuks a cash bonus if Terry would sign a C Form, rendering him the exclusive property of the Chicago Black Hawks for life. Louis wouldn't allow his son anywhere near a C Form. He fought to keep Terry a free agent. Besides, he told his son, the Black Hawks had no future. Despite the fact that the offer must have been appealing to a family whose primary breadwinner was laid up for an indefinite period of time, Terry passed.

Having heard of Northcott's visit, Kinnear was now under pressure to sign the star goalkeeper. The next day, he visited Terry and his parents in an attempt to finally seal this deal. He knew that other teams would come calling soon enough and perhaps steal Terry right out from under his nose.

Kinnear had a definite advantage. He was a good friend of Terry's and had helped him along. Over time he had been able to sell the Sawchuks on the strengths of the Red Wing organization. Louis knew it was a sound organization with a good team. And it was a team that took care of its prospects. Terry sat alongside his parents, listening anxiously. Finally, Louis agreed and a contract was presented.

As Terry leaned over the table and signed, Bob Kinnear breathed a deep sigh of relief. He shook Anne's hand, then Louis's, then Terry's. He told them they would not regret their decision, and that the money would help them now.

He left hurriedly to get home to a phone to place a call to Jack Adams in Detroit with the news that the Red Wings had just signed the greatest goaltending prospect he had ever seen.

2

CLIMBING THE LADDER

*I*N the fall of 1946, the Red Wings informed sixteen-year-old Sawchuk that he was to report to the Ontario town of Galt, where he was to play for its top Junior A affiliate.

Anne and Louis Sawchuk knew this moment would come, given Terry's hockey abilities. Still, to see their third son leave them could not have been easy. As Terry clambered down the stairs with minimal belongings packed in an old cardboard suitcase, his mother leaned forward to give him a kiss and to put a ten-dollar bill in his hand to help him on his journey. "It was one of the few ten-dollar bills she ever had!" Terry would later relate. On his own for the first time, the young goaltender lost a battle with his conscience during the long ride into southern Ontario as, after much reservation, he became involved in a crap game in the train's smoking car. It was evident that this was not Terry's first attempt at gambling: within the hour he had a hundred dollars sitting at his elbows, having cleaned out every player but one. He wanted to quit while he was ahead, but decided instead to run on his luck while he was hot. He and the last participant rolled for the lot and Terry lost. All he had was his mother's ten-dollar bill, which he'd wisely held back.

In Galt, Terry re-enrolled in high school, taking Grade 11 classes at the Galt Collegiate Institute and Vocational School, and settled into a rooming house. The Wings paid Terry twenty dollars a week, of which twelve went for room and board.

He once related to writer Trent Frayne, "I remember seeing a pair of shoes that I wanted desperately. They were twelve bucks. I faithfully gave the guy two dollars a week for six weeks, staring in the store window every day. . . . Finally, I made the last payment, put on my new shoes and walked proudly out of the store. I discovered walking down the street that I didn't like them anymore, and never wore them again."

Terry played a year in Galt for the Junior Red Wings and quietly returned home to Winnipeg at the end of the season. It was here that Sawchuk came into his own as a baseball player, leading his Morse Place Monarchs to the 1947 Junior provincial baseball championship. His .500 batting average attracted attention from baseball scouts from the St. Louis Cardinals, Pittsburgh Pirates, and Cleveland Indians.

—•••—

In the fall of 1947 Terry had his first contact with Marcel Pronovost. Born in Lac-à-Tortue, Quebec, the smooth-skating defenceman had been playing in Shawinigan Falls in front of future Hall of Fame goalie Jacques Plante.

"Terry and I came into one of the Red Wings' camp, in the old Waterloo Arena, in '47 and then we went to the Common Camp in Detroit. That's where we learned that they were moving the Junior team from Galt to Windsor."

In Windsor, Sawchuk did double duty for the Windsor Juniors and the Windsor Hettche Spitfires of the International Amateur League, where, despite facing seventy-eight shots, he surrendered just two goals in his first two games.

"In my opinion," wrote Ken Johnson of the *Windsor Star*, "the kid is the best goalie in junior hockey today. All predict a bright future for the Winnipeg-born goalie who, at seventeen, stands five-foot eleven inches and weighs one hundred and ninety-three pounds. He's agile, too."

To Windsor coach Jimmy Skinner, Sawchuk seemed a serious young man. "Terry was always thinking, always quiet. He would shake hands with you and then not say a word. He was so serious about hockey that I never saw him clown around."

Things appeared bright for the Spitfires until November 2nd, 1947, when Skinner received a call from Red Wing boss Jack Adams.

"I'm sorry, Jimmy, but I'm gonna have to take Sawchuk away from you. Bruneteau's goalie's not working out like we had hoped." In fact Harvey Jessiman had not panned out as a professional the way Jack Adams had predicted. Despite having been a first team All-Star two years running, a leg injury was reason enough for Adams to sell Jessiman to the Philadelphia Rockets of the American Hockey League.

Oddly enough, three Winnipeggers — Barney O'Connell, Don Thurston, and Jack Kernahan — spoiled Terry's farewell stint as their Toledo Mercuries handed Windsor and Terry their first loss in a 3–1 IAHL game.

Summoning Sawchuk to his office in the Olympia, Adams handed Terry a train ticket for Omaha to leave the next day. After Terry signed his first professional contract, Adams handed him an envelope containing a $2,000 cheque as a signing bonus. Terry was speechless.

As Terry left his office, Adams noted to himself that Sawchuk would soon be eighteen, and remembered his favourite saying regarding goaltenders: "If they don't have it when they're eighteen, they'll never have it." There was no doubt in his or anybody else's mind that this kid indeed had it.

But Jimmy Skinner was not smiling. "I felt terrible. Just because Mud's kid hadn't panned out, I was losing the best goalie in the world. I was very, very down."

Returning to Windsor, Terry made his first stop at a bank, where he not only cashed the cheque but changed it into 2,100 one-dollar bills (the exchange rate then favoured the Canadian buck). Dragging the bag of cash back to his room at the boarding house, he threw the money up into the air and danced in it as he had once played in leaves as a youth. It was more cash than he had ever seen in his life and he couldn't get enough of it. The pain of his past was temporarily relieved, replaced with pure joy.

When he announced the signing, Adams admitted that Sawchuk was quite young to be turning professional, but added, "He is just so good that he would have been wasting his time if he had remained in junior hockey!"

Terry's new home would no doubt have reminded him of his hometown. Like Winnipeg, Omaha is a river city situated in the middle of some of the continent's most fertile farmland. The city was also an important transportation hub and manufacturing centre. And the locals were enthusiastic supporters of their hockey team.

The Omaha Aksarben Knights, a Red Wing farm team since 1945, played in the eight-team United States League against such teams as the Fort Worth Rangers, the Dallas Texans, the Kansas City Pla Mors, the Minneapolis Millers, and the Saint Paul Saints. The team played its home games in the Aksarben (Nebraska spelled backwards) Coliseum.

As Terry prepared for his first game in Dallas, he was visibly tense as he pulled on his new sweater with the logo AK set inside a large O. He didn't feel any better after warmup, nor as he settled into his crouch to begin the game.

Forty seconds into the game, the Texans broke in towards the rookie netminder and took their first shot on goal. Terry froze and the puck easily hit the twine behind him for a goal. Realizing his nervousness, his defencemen came back, tapped his pads, and exhorted him to relax and play his game. He settled down and shut the door the rest of the way for a 5–1 victory.

In Terry's second pro game in Fort Worth's Will Rogers Coliseum, he stopped forty-five shots to lead his Knights to a 2–1 victory over the Rangers. In the last ninety seconds Fort Worth, having pulled their goalie for a sixth attacker, poured it on, forcing Sawchuk to make five unbelievable saves. "We were beaten by goalkeeping," said Ranger coach Tony Savage. "It was the best netminding job I've seen in many years!"

After a Thanksgiving Day loss, Terry moved the Knights into a battle for second place by winning four games in a row, including back-to-back shutouts. His performance prompted Jack Adams to shock some hockey writers in New York by boasting, "You know, we have a seventeen-year-old prospect in our farm system who is better now than when Lumley came to us at the same age. . . . He's Terry Sawchuk down on the Omaha farm. I'd have all the confidence in the world if we had to use him in our nets now and through the playoffs."

Omaha coach Modere (Mud) Bruneteau praised the kid's temperament. "He never sulks after he's been scored on. He doesn't blame the defence. Instead he'll say, 'I made a mistake, Coach. I played the guy wrong.' You can't beat a kid like that!"

Though the Knights were beset by injuries, Terry kept them near the top of the heap through December. Terry would attribute a large part of his success to the special attention paid to him by Bruneteau.

The former Red Wing, whose snap shot had been legendary, had been handpicked by Adams to guide the younger recruits at Omaha. His likable personality and patient dedication to his players struck a positive chord with the ambitious Sawchuk. For half an hour after each practice, the veteran of eleven NHL seasons would tutor his goalie.

"Mud taught me how to block angles better. He would take shots from all angles and I would attempt to save, and this went on until I had it down pat," Sawchuk would remark later.

All was going relatively well for Terry as he suited up for a game in Houston on December 28, 1947, his eighteenth birthday. He was celebrating by doing something he loved to do — playing goal. It was a routine game until a scramble occurred in front of the Omaha net. Terry was about to jump on the puck or block it when the stick of Houston forward George Agar unintentionally flew up towards Terry's face and the stick's blade struck Terry in his right eyeball. In the dressing room, the Houston team doctor mentioned the possibility of serious permanent eye damage.

At the hospital, a doctor removed Terry's eye temporarily from its socket and repaired the damage with three fine sutures. The doctor was frank with the teenager: there was the possibility he could lose the sight in the eye, and there was also the chance that an infection of the optic nerve could set in and permanently damage his other eye as well. Terry broke down and cried. He was too afraid that night to sleep.

The next morning, the doctor removed Terry's eye patch and carefully examined the eye. The news was good: Terry could still see and there was no sign of infection. Barring further complications, Terry was told he could be back on the ice in a couple of weeks, by late January.

Terry spent the next two weeks in an Omaha hospital before returning to the Knights' lineup. He posted a shutout in his first outing.

Terry moved his Knights into third place in the USHL's four-team Northern Divison. Terry registered four shutouts in fifty-four appearances that season and led the league with a 3.22 goals-against average.

As the Knights entered the playoffs against the Minneapolis Millers, Terry was named the league's outstanding rookie and was voted to the Second All-Star team. Phil McAtee was voted as the league's top goaltender and the first team All-Star. Newspaper sports columnists covering the league immediately questioned how Sawchuk, as Rookie of the Year and holder of the league's best goals-against average, didn't win McAtee's awards as well.

The Knights lost the first game of the best-of-three quarter-final playoff, but threatened to walk away with Game Two after building a commanding 3–0 lead. A goal on a long slap shot from the blue line rattled Terry and sparked a Minneapolis comeback to send the game into double overtime. Teammate Max McNab, a proficient young centre and future executive with the New Jersey Devils, scored the overtime winner at 17:23 to tie the series.

In the third game of the quarterfinal, Sawchuk and the Knights were eliminated from the playoffs. Terry collected his $250 Rookie Award and engraved gold puck and headed home to East Kildonan for the summer.

He returned to his second love, baseball. In fact, Terry had arranged a tryout with the Cleveland Indians' Indianapolis farm team of the American Association. Terry was visibly nervous as he awaited his turn at bat. He struck up a conversation with veteran pitcher Chet Johnson, who gave him advice that he would later apply on the ice.

"Listen kid," Johnson said, "don't be scared of anything. I've had it pretty tough in my day and I've been pushed around a lot. But let me tell you, when I go out on that mound, I tell myself I'm the best pitcher alive. You do the same and you'll be okay!"

After taking his swings and completing the workout, manager Al Lopez offered to send him to the minors in New Orleans for some conditioning. Terry thanked him for the offer but decided instead to return home to Winnipeg.

As a first baseman for the Elmwood Giants of the Manitoba Senior League, the two-hundred-pound goaltender led the league in batting after twelve games with an amazing batting average of .418, even though he was still young enough to play junior ball. Terry went on to win the league batting championship with a .376 average despite the fact that his right elbow was permanently disfigured and bothersome.

His Giants team won the Manitoba baseball championship. Terry also played that summer with the Morse Place Monarchs. Unfortunately, their playoff schedule conflicted with the Detroit Red Wing training camp in Saskatoon, and without Terry they didn't fare as well.

—•••—

"In all my hockey I have never seen a young goalie handle himself as well as Sawchuk." Such was the diagnosis of one Tommy Ivan, coach of the Detroit Red Wings, as they broke camp and prepared for their final camp in Detroit. In a move that was seen as a definite promotion, the Wings brass assigned Terry to the Indianapolis Capitals of the American Hockey League for the 1948–49 season.

With Sawchuk in their net, the Capitals won their season opener, 5–1. Stopping twenty-five shots, Terry lived up to his pre-game billing, but had to share the limelight with twenty-year-old Jerry Reid from Owen Sound, Ontario, who scored a hat trick in his first professional game.

With Indianapolis, Terry would encounter another nurturing coach. Ott Heller was a great defenceman who had patrolled the New York Ranger blueline for fifteen seasons. As was the case with Mud Bruneteau, Adams had wanted Heller for his farm system because of his ability to work with youngsters. Heller took a special interest in Sawchuk, and in doing so strengthened Terry's self-confidence. In an era when coaches tended to be unknowledgeable about the mechanics and fundamentals of goaltending and indifferent to goalies' progress, Heller went out of his way.

Heller noticed that Sawchuk covered his angles very well but that he still had a tendency to go down. He worked long and hard with Terry. "When I used to fall, he'd yell for me to get back up on my feet," said Terry. "We worked that over and over again, with me starting to fall and him hollering at me to stand up."

Ross (Lefty) Wilson had come to the Detroit Red Wing camp as a goaltender in 1945, but did not make the grade. Jack Adams took a liking to the former Canadian General Motors worker and navy man, and offered him a job with the organization's Omaha farm club as spare goaltender and trainer. By the time Sawchuk arrived in Indianapolis, Lefty Wilson was there as well. One of his early encounters with the rookie goaltender certainly got them off on the wrong foot.

"I gave him a practice sweater, a brand new one. He took one look at it and ripped it right down the middle. He tore it right in half right in front of me. Boy, was I pissed off! He said he wanted room for his neck and belly pad. I said, 'You son of a bitch, you're gonna wear that same fuckin' sweater until the last goddamn practice.' Which he did."

It was at this point in his career that Terry truly developed his trademark deep crouch. At this level of hockey, he faced more screen shots. With Heller's tutoring about remaining on his feet fresh in his mind, he found his deep crouch enabled him to see screen shots through players' legs, yet still remain on his feet.

Throughout the autumn, Terry kept his team in the hunt for first place. He also began to partake of the good life off the ice.

"When Terry was a seventeen-year-old in Omaha, and the next year in Indianapolis," Marcel Pronovost recalls, "this was the beginning of Terry being associated with older hockey players and having a few beers and carousing.

"After a game when the team went to a bar, the guys could have their pick from twelve to twenty women. If you wanted to, you could have gotten lucky every night of the week. These women all had their own places, their own apartments.

"For young hockey players, the best method of releasing tension was either sex or a drinking binge. Most of the guys chose a combination of the two."

In Indianapolis it became apparent Terry was starting to use alcohol as a release from hidden anger and frustration.

"In Indianapolis," Lefty Wilson reminisces, "when the Uke was on beer, he was all right. But if he ever got into the rye or scotch, he got mean. But back then that didn't happen too often."

In December, Terry experienced a slight groin pull — one of the most painful and most easily aggravated injuries in sport. Groin injuries are especially rough on goalies because of all the lateral movement and stretching they must do game in and game out. Kick saves and split saves are made by extending the medial and posterior thigh muscles. Teams did not carry a regular backup goalie on their rosters, so Terry had to play through the injury. But the workload prevented the muscles from healing, and in fact worsened the injury.

The pain did not apparently hamper Terry's play as he continued to keep his Capitals in the hunt for first place. In late December, just before his twentieth birthday, they hosted New Haven. Terry hobbled out gingerly to start the game.

The score seesawed back and forth and, as the first period progressed, Terry winced visibly each time he had to move to stop the puck. A couple of quick kick saves were particularly aggravating, but he managed to finish the period.

As the second period began, it hurt just to stand in the crease. He leaned on the net to take the weight off his leg at each opportunity. New Haven's attackers sensed a weakness and tried to force him to drop down. Terry was having great difficulty getting back up and the pain was beginning to cloud his judgment. He lost a lobbed puck in the rafters and it dropped in front of his feet and bounced into the net before he realized what had happened.

Later, Sawchuk completely misjudged a rising shot and was struck in the face and knocked unconscious. The trainer rolled him over, revealing a pool of blood on the ice. As they carried him to the dressing room, a hush fell over the crowd of 4,400.

By the time he reached the dressing room, Terry was conscious again and he asked for a cigarette. The front of his jersey was full of blood. The team doctor, Hugh Williams, examined the short, deep cut over Terry's right eye. Preparing the needle and suturing thread, the doctor looked down at Terry and said, "This is gonna hurt like hell!"

Without anesthetic, the needle was stuck into Terry's skin and the edges of the cut pulled tight together. After the fifth stitch, Dr. Williams was done. Sawchuk looked like he had a closed zipper on his upper forehead.

Terry got up off the table and proclaimed himself ready to play, but Lefty Wilson, the team's trainer and emergency substitute goalkeeper, was already suiting up. He looked over at Terry and said, "Let me have the belly pad, kid!" Resigned, Sawchuk removed the piece of equipment and handed it over. Terry was sent to the hospital for observation and a couple of days of rest with heat treatments for the groin injury.

Going into the final week of the regular season, the Capitals had a shot at second place, and Terry had only missed two games, but the groin injury had taken its toll. Dr. Williams advised coach Heller that, unless Sawchuk sat out the final four games of the season, he would be useless to his team come the playoffs.

Caps general manager Dick Miller approached league president Maurice Podoloff about replacing Sawchuk for a week with Detroit's star goalie, Harry Lumley. Podoloff polled the other team owners, but the proposal was defeated.

The Caps instead opted to sit Sawchuk out for one of the four remaining games. He finished the regular season having played in sixty-seven games, racking up two shutouts and a 3.06 goals-against average. Indianapolis ended the season in second place but Terry, although game, was sub-par in the playoffs. The Caps were eliminated, 2 games to 0, in the opening round.

Despite this disappointment, Sawchuk was awarded the Dudley "Red" Garrett Memorial Trophy as the American Hockey League's rookie of the year. He easily outpolled four other candidates, including teammates Fred Glover and Gerry Reid. The league's statistical *Red Book* said, "Sawchuk displayed remarkable fortitude during the later stages of the season, playing with painful injuries, which only forced him to miss one game!"

It was the second straight year that Terry had won a rookie-of-the-year award.

—•••—

After another summer of baseball and golf, Terry returned to the Red Wing camp in the fall of 1949. There was no doubt in anyone's mind that he was ready for the National Hockey League. But there was a roadblock on Terry's route to the big time. A picture in the *Detroit Free Press* showed Wings coach Tommy Ivan sitting on the arena boards, flanked by Sawchuk and Harry Lumley. The caption noted that the Wings had a goaltending problem: too many good ones.

Lumley, known as "Apple Cheeks" because of his appearance, grew up in the small town of Owen Sound, Ontario. He was a seventeen-year-old sensation with the Barrie Flyers Junior team when the Wings acquired his rights from the New York Rangers and gave him a three-day tryout. Recognizing his talent, Adams immediately assigned him to Indianapolis for the 1943–44 season. He spent only twenty-one games with the Caps the next season before moving up to the Wings for good, and he put in a stellar performance in a seven-game Stanley Cup loss to the Leafs in the spring of 1945. Backed by Lumley's great play, Detroit again faced the Leafs in the 1948 and 1949 finals and were swept in four straight games in both years.

Just twenty-two years old in the fall of 1949, Lumley was just coming into his own, having been runner-up for the Vezina Trophy the past two seasons. Impressive as Terry's potential was, Jack Adams had no choice but to relegate him to Indianapolis for another year.

Despite Terry's excellent play, with a goals-against average of 2.69 after 16 games, the Caps were mired in seventh place in the ten-team league. Terry's frustration showed as he began to incur a series of penalties, which had an effect on Harry Lumley in Detroit. One day Jack Adams burst into Lumley's stall brandishing a telegram he was about to fire off to Indianapolis, telling the team to fine Sawchuk $50 for every penalty he took. "And you pay attention to this, Harry, because you're in the same boat!" But even though Terry was having problems in Indianapolis, Lumley began to feel the pressure.

An incident during a midseason exhibition game at the Detroit Olympia would provide Terry with his first brief taste of NHL competition. Harry Lumley explains: "During charity games I used to often take a forward's stick and play the point as a third defenceman if the faceoff was in the other end. Well, the puck got past me and I ended up trying to chase this fella who was about to shoot the puck into our open net. I tripped and fell and sprained my ankle. It was a bad sprain, too!" (For Harry Lumley, it was not a happy time. His biggest fear, as it was for all NHL goaltenders, was to be replaced by an up-and-coming young star.)

On Sunday, January 8, 1950, barely two weeks past his twentieth birthday, Terry Sawchuk stretched Lumley's sweater over his beefy frame and took his place in net in front of 13,294 Red Wing fans. Terry's heart was pounding as the Boston Bruins came after him. The Wings' defence tightened up in an effort to protect the young goalie. They may have been trying too hard: Detroit defenceman Clare Martin twice deflected passes into his own net, past the startled youngster, and a third goal bounced in off another teammate's skate.

Though the Wings lost 4–3, Harry Lumley went out of his way to absolve Terry of any responsibility and to boost his ego.

"Don't worry about it, kid," he said. "I couldn't have done better myself."

Yet the youngster had already analyzed his performance and was looking forward to his next outing three nights later in Boston.

"I won't be jittery Wednesday night," Terry said matter-of-factly. "I learned up here the players don't try the same trick twice. Mistakes like that cost me a few goals tonight, but I won't make the same ones again."

As Lumley's ankle healed, Terry won four games and lost three in his seven-game stint, allowing just sixteen goals. His first NHL shutout — on January 15th, at Madison Square Garden — prompted Ranger coach Lynn Patrick to remark, "There are only three big league goalies around right now and one of them is in the minors."

Sawchuk's play proved his worth to general manager Jack Adams, but it also magnified Detroit's goaltending dilemma and prompted the press and hockey experts to speculate as to when Sawchuk would make a permanent return to the NHL, and with which team.

Upon his return to Indianapolis, Terry continued his stalwart play with the Capitals, despite the fact that for the remainder of the season, his crooked elbow began to truly give him trouble. Floating bone chips was the diagnosis. But surgery would have to wait with the Capitals in hot pursuit of second place and the playoffs nearing.

Terry was fitted with a cast to immobilize the elbow. He had become so accustomed to having a locked elbow that the cast wasn't a hindrance, but only added helpful protection to the tender area. He quickly grew accustomed to the inconvenience, though down the stretch, the elbow remained swollen and left Terry in extreme pain.

For the second season in a row, the Capitals finished the season in second place in the Western Division. American Hockey League fans overwhelmingly voted Terry to the first All-Star team over Buffalo's Connie Dion and Gil Mayer of Pittsburgh. Terry also came third in the Most Valuable Player voting, behind runner-up Ab DeMarco and the winner, Les Douglas of Cleveland, who was the league scoring champ. The Indianapolis media protested that Terry should have won MVP.

Terry was in top form in the best-of-three quarterfinal as the Caps swept the St. Louis Flyers in two games.

Team doctor Hugh Williams had been applying ice to Sawchuk's elbow immediately after each game, and Terry underwent diathermy therapy between games to further contain the swelling. Dr. Williams said that by playing, Terry was actually working some of the swelling out, accelerating his recovery.

In the best-of-three semifinal, Terry was again fabulous, allowing only one goal in each of the two games as the Caps swept aside the defending Calder Cup champions, the Providence Reds.

Indianapolis was the clear underdog in the league final against the Cleveland Barons. With Johnny Bower — the "China Wall" — in the net and the big line of Bobby Carse, Pete Leswick, and Les Douglas, each a first team All-Star, the Barons seemed a cinch.

Prior to the first game, a newspaper ran a photograph of Terry, retouched so that he had four left arms and four right arms. That must have been the way the Barons saw the real Terry as he turned back forty-three shots to lead the Capitals to a 4–1 upset victory.

"We saw too much Sawchuk" was the only analysis Barons' coach Bun Cook could muster for reporters.

Indianapolis broke through the China Wall for six goals in the second game on only twenty-two shots. Sawchuk shone in the 6–2 victory as he faced thirty-seven shots. After squeezing out a third-game 4–3 victory on home ice, the Capitals went for the kill in the fourth and final game. Again Terry was outstanding as he held off the Barons in a 3–2 Calder Cup–winning match before a packed house of 7,000 delirious fans.

In a team picture in the Caps' dressing room, Terry can be seen at the centre of the top row of the assembled players, the large number 1 prominent on the front of his jersey. As the goalie for the first AHL team ever to sweep the playoffs in eight straight, Terry truly felt like *he* was Number One.

3

THE KID HAS IT

AFTER a night of celebrating with his Indianapolis teammates, Terry had to leave the jubilant city to join the
Red Wings. Jack Adams was both pleased and relieved
that the Caps had completed their Calder Cup run quickly,
making Sawchuk available as backup in case Harry Lumley got
hurt. Terry arrived to a hero's welcome from everyone in the
organization.

The Wings were in the midst of a Stanley Cup final that was
deadlocked: tied at one win apiece. Hockey fans and insiders
alike were still in shock from the life-threatening head injury
to Detroit superstar Gordie Howe. Late in the opening game of
the semifinal series against Toronto, Howe collided violently
with Leaf centre Ted (Teeder) Kennedy. Doctors drilled a hole
through his skull to drain accumulated fluid and relieve pressure on the brain. For hours his life hung in the balance, and
hourly updates on his condition were broadcast over the radio
to Canada and much of the United States. When doctors
upgraded Howe from critical to serious condition, the hockey
world heaved a collective sigh of relief.

Without Howe, the Wings were still a potent force, but his
absence required some juggling of the lineup. Marcel Pronovost,
then a defenceman on the Omaha farm club, was called up just
in time for the playoffs. "When Gordie got hurt, hell, I even

played right wing for a while. When you lose a player of his calibre, everybody digs a little deeper and we did!"

From his vantage point in the stands, Sawchuk would witness one of the most unusual playoff series ever. The New York Rangers, who'd finished fourth in the regular season, had already upset the Montreal Canadiens, 4–1, in their best of seven-game semifinal. Entering the finals against Detroit, they had to deal with the prospect of playing all their games on the road — the circus had booked Madison Square Garden, the Blueshirts' home rink. Games Two and Three of the series were played at Toronto's Maple Leaf Gardens, the rest at the Detroit Olympia.

The Rangers were giving the Wings all they could handle, taking a 3–2 lead in the series after five games. Detroit came from behind to win Game Six, 5–4, and trailed the deciding game, 3–2, late in the third period when Jim McFadden tied the score with 4:03 left to play. The teams struggled through twenty-eight minutes and thirty-one seconds of overtime before Terry's Galt teammate Pete Babando fired a wrist shot past Ranger goalie Chuck Rayner.

Terry was again part of a scene of celebration, popping champagne corks, and jubilation. Still, he must have been wondering what the future held for him. He felt ready for the NHL, but he also knew that Harry Lumley had just completed a stalwart year, missing out on Vezina honours by just fourteen goals against.

Adding to his uncertainty, he was scheduled for surgery on his elbow in Toronto in the next month or so, and urgent phone calls home revealed a widening crisis. The Red River was surging over its banks and flooding areas of lower Manitoba. Terry quickly returned home to join 15,000 volunteers in building new dikes and adding to existing ones. On the evening of May 4, 1950, Sawchuk's East Kildonan suburb was under water and evacuation orders were given. The RCMP were patrolling the old neighbourhood in canoes rather than squad cars. When the flood waters finally did recede, 100,000 Manitobans had been forced out of their homes, and the estimated damage easily topped $100 million.

When the crisis was over, Terry travelled to Toronto. He checked into a hospital, and surgery was finally performed on his troublesome right elbow on June 28. Four bone chips were removed. The surgeons could see other chips that would require future surgery, but for now Terry was happy. So was general manager Jack Adams.

Assured that all seemed well after Terry's two-week hospital stay, Trader Jack put into play a plan he'd been working up for some time. The Chicago Black Hawks were looking desperately for a goaltender. Adams offered Hawk president Bill Tobin a deal involving Sawchuk. As Jack had hoped, Tobin was spooked by Terry's recent surgery, and demanded Lumley instead. On July 13, 1950, Adams agreed to a mammoth nine-player deal — at the time, the biggest trade in NHL history. Tobin proudly acquired the proven, Stanley Cup–winning goalie Lumley plus defencemen Black Jack Stewart and Al Dewsbury, centre Don Morrison, and left winger Pete Babando, whose overtime heroics seemed forgotten already.

Adams would claim for the record that he'd been reluctant to make the deal, but secretly he was gleeful about his acquisitions. "Sugar" Jim Henry would replace Sawchuk in Indianapolis. Along with forward Gaye Stewart, Adams received a player he had always wanted, Metro Prystai, and a defenceman among defencemen, Bob Goldham. And most of all, he had made room for Terry Sawchuk.

Harry Lumley still remembers this dark day in his life. "I played softball that summer and we were leaving the summer cottage at Sauble Beach, outside Owen Sound, to drive to a game in Goderich. I was just coming to a washout in the road and was about to slow down for it, when all of a sudden, at that precise moment, I hear on the car radio that I've been traded to Chicago. It was such a shock that, instead of braking, my foot hit the gas pedal! I hit the washout at full speed and put the fan through the radiator!

"I did not have a clue that the trade was coming, I mean after all, we had just won the Stanley Cup. Plus it was upsetting to go from a first-place club to a last-place club. I called Jack Stewart who was going with me and we had quite a talk.

I hated every minute in Chicago. I would have sooner gone to fight in the Korean War!"

For Terry, who was recuperating back in Winnipeg, the news of Lumley's trade was a pleasant shock, but when asked to comment, he still didn't seem certain about his future. "I certainly was surprised. I was figuring on playing at Indianapolis again and I'm still not counting on simply walking into the job."

When Terry reported to training camp he weighed a hefty 217 pounds, which did not hamper his quickness or his performance in training camp.

On October 8, 1950, Terry Sawchuk played for Detroit in the NHL All-Star Game, his debut as the Wings' regular goalie. (In the days of the "Original Six," the Stanley Cup champs faced a team made up of the best players from the other five clubs.) The 7–1 result was the first loss for the All-Stars in four years that the event had been held. Terry made twenty-five saves, while Toronto's Sid Smith spoiled the rookie's shutout bid with ninety-three seconds left in the game. Ted Lindsay's hat trick was a first for an All-Star game. Terry's nifty goaltending won him rave reviews and thunderous applause from the Olympia crowd of just over 11,000.

In Detroit, Terry and Marcel Pronovost, like all single young Red Wings, were billetted in one of the many team-approved boarding houses near the Olympia. Marcel Pronovost remembers fondly, "Terry and I each had our own room upstairs at 'Ma' Tannahill's on Wreford Street. Ma Tannahill was something else. She was a bookie [on the side], and she had customers all up and down the street. She was a 'numbers runner,' not really a bookie. It's just like [the Pick 3 lottery] today."

Terry grew quite fond of his surrogate mother and brought "Ma" to most of his games. It seemed that Terry had quite a way with older women: a news story in October declared that Indiana's most famous fan, the legendary Mrs. A.A. (Auntie) McClamrock, eighty years old, was going to miss her number-one hero and favourite hockey player, Terry Sawchuk. Though she was sorry to see him move up to the big league, she was happy about his advancement.

On October 10, Terry was stunned to hear of the death of legendary goaltender George Hainsworth, his boyhood idol, who was killed in an automobile accident the day before. On the ice, Terry and the Wings flew out of the starting gate in an attempt to catch the Leafs, who'd opened with a 2–1 loss to Chicago but then went on an amazing eleven-game undefeated streak.

After twelve games, Terry was the league's top goalkeeper with a 1.67 goals-against average. By now his unique stance, or "crouch," was also attracting a lot of attention.

Before Sawchuk's arrival, goaltenders tended to bend only at the knees, with their upper body bent slightly forward but still erect. Terry bent over at the waist so far forward that his chin practically touched his knees. It was truly innovative, unorthodox, and not always accepted by Adams, who tried at first to get his goalie to adopt a more traditional style. But Terry was insistent that, with screen shots becoming more and more prevalent, only his style could adapt to the changing game.

"I am able to move much more quickly from the crouch position," he said. "I have better balance to move both legs, especially when I have to kick out my leg to stop a shot. I get low because I can follow the puck better looking through the legs than I can trying to peek over shoulders and around those big backs. It's an easier way to get hurt, I guess, but nothing's happened so far."

With each successful performance, Adams's protests grew quieter, until he too was among the converted. "He (Terry) convinced me that the crouch was best for the modern game. When I looked at his record, I knew he was right."

If Terry's new style was symbolic of the dawn of a new age in goaltending, so it was that his arrival marked the end of an era. The "Forties Famous Four" great goaltenders of the Forties — Montreal's Bill Durnan, Boston's Frank Brimsek, Toronto's Turk Broda, and New York's Charlie Rayner — were at or near the ends of their careers.

The previous season, 1949–50, had been Frank Brimsek's last when, after ten seasons (the last one with Chicago), he retired at age thirty-four. He had won two Stanley Cups, made eight All-Star teams, and collected forty shutouts in 514 games. His string of All-Star selections and two Vezina Trophy wins earned him great respect in hockey circles. In his first four years, he was known as "Mr. Zero."

Bill Durnan, thirty-four, made the '49–50 season his last as well after losing three games to the upstart New York Rangers in the semis. He did not suit up for the fourth game. In just seven years, he had posted thirty-four shutouts, made six All-Star teams, won two Stanley Cups, and collected an unprecedented six Vezinas. He played in only 383 games but his stats and awards — as well as the fact that he could catch a puck with either hand — made him a Canadiens goaltending legend alongside the two Georges, Vezina and Hainsworth.

Toronto's legendary Turk Broda — who, at age thirty-six, was still playing exceptionally well — was part of a platoon with the Leafs' sensational new rookie, Al Rollins. Over a thirteen-year career, he had four Stanley Cups, three All-Star selections, and two Vezinas under his belt; in fact, Broda had denied Durnan a perfect record of seven Vezinas in seven years by taking the 1948 honours.

When Terry recorded back-to-back shutouts against Chuck Rayner and the Rangers in early December, it must have been bittersweet, as the Wings bombed a goalie whom Terry had always admired. Rayner had earned the respect and accolades of his peers for his years of toil in the hapless Rangers net for close to 300 games thus far in his career. Chuck had registered twenty-five shutouts so far and had been voted to two All-Star teams. The previous year, having led New York to the Stanley Cup finals, he was awarded the Hart Trophy as the league's most valuable player — making him only the second goalie in history to be so honoured.

On Thursday, December 28, 1950, the night of Terry's twenty-first birthday, the Wings were all over the Canadiens and had built up a 6–0 lead, allowing the Montrealers only twelve shots over the first forty minutes. Habs coach Dick Irvin was desperate to turn the game around, so he called for a measurement of Terry's pads. Irvin contended that they were beyond the legal width. Between periods, referee Red Storey produced a tape measure and proclaimed them to be nine and a half inches — a half inch under the legal limit. An embarrassed Irvin retorted, "Well, they looked big to me!"

"We'll give Irvin an inch or two of padding, if he needs it, and we won't ask for players — a straight cash deal!" Jolly Jack Adams crowed.

On January 4, the Wings shut out their former teammate, Harry Lumley, 1–0, in the Windy City. Terry was leading the Vezina Trophy race — awarded to the goalie with the lowest goals-against average — and was the favourite for the Calder, the trophy for the league's outstanding rookie.

On January 21, Terry duelled his nemesis for the Calder and Vezina trophies, Toronto's Al Rollins, to a scoreless draw in front of the season's best crowd. It was Terry's seventh shutout, putting him two ahead of Turk Broda.

It was around this point in the season that Marcel returned to Ma Tannahill's after recovering from a broken ankle. He found his roommate was now hitting the town frequently with members of the Detroit Lions football team. The young defenceman was asked one night to drive Terry and a couple of veteran teammates, who had begun to frequent the Paradise Palms, the Lions' hangout. Marcel agreed and believed he had survived the ordeal until the very next morning when, as he headed onto the ice for practice, he was asked to see Jack Adams in his office after practice. Adams was not in a good mood.

"Where were you last night?" Adams boomed.

"Ah, ah . . . well . . . I . . . ah was up by Telegraph Road," Marcel answered in shock.

"Ya! I know!" Jack answered lividly. "Did ya drink?"

"Well, ah, I ah, had a couple of beers, but that's about it," Marcel replied.

"Ah well, beers, that's all right. I'll even buy those for you. But don't hang around with that crowd. Stay away from McFadden and those old bastards, they're all done. You're gonna be a star in this league, Marcel! Stay away from 'em!"

Marcel couldn't believe that Adams knew all about Terry and the older members of his team hanging out with the Lions. Yet Marcel could understand somewhat what his goaltending roommate was going through. "Terry was looking to identify with people who were of the same notoriety as he was and also wasn't worried about trusting them. All of us usually kept our friends only to hockey people, because there could often be someone trying to exploit you or whatever. You never knew."

Veteran winger Jimmy Peters says the problem that Terry had in those early years was shared by the whole team. "Back in those days we had a lot of free time on our hands. We wasted a lot of time. We could have been trying to better ourselves with education or courses or something. Instead we'd be someplace drinking beer, or at a pool hall between games.

"Terry, to my way of thinking, never had a problem drinking in the early years. Heck, we were all beer drinkers. Besides it was my experience that all goalies drank. The pressure gets to them. All the great ones liked their beer — Terry, Lumley, Broda, Durnan, they all did."

Terry's extracurricular activities didn't seem to affect his on-ice brilliance. As February began, the Wings were in first place, setting an incredible winning pace, yet the Leafs were still hot on their tail. The two teams pulled away from the rest of the league, and the battle for the Vezina between the Leaf tandem of Broda and Rollins versus Sawchuk was just as intense.

A local hat dealer, looking for a high-profile publicity gimmick, decided to award a new hat to each Red Wing who scored a hat trick or recorded a shutout. Low-scoring games were the norm in the NHL of the 1950s, so few skaters made good on the offer, but Terry — who, oddly enough, didn't wear hats — was cashing in at an alarming rate. Terry gave the first six hats to trainer Lefty Wilson and each of his five defencemen. After Terry's seventh shutout, the scoreless draw against Rollins and the Leafs, he passed his free hat certificate to captain Sid Abel. "I figured it was time to give the forwards a break," joked the boy wonder.

On February 25, at New York's Madison Square Garden, Terry and the Wings were pummelled for five goals through the first two periods. Phillip Vetrano, a thirty-year-old supermarket manager from Brooklyn, began to heckle Terry from the stands as the second period came to a close. As the players left the ice, Vetrano taunted the Detroit goalie some more. Terry stopped, approached the spectator, and words and obscenities filled the air before Terry was persuaded to head back to his dressing room.

"Terry didn't always take kindly to heckling," remembers Johnny Wilson, "and he didn't give a goddamn! If you got near him and yelled things at him, he'd challenge you without blinking an eye!"

A week later, Terry was issued a summons. Not only was he charged with assault, but both Sawchuk and Madison Square Garden were named in a $25,000 lawsuit.

Back in New York for a March 21 game against the same Rangers, Terry and the Red Wings' lawyer appeared before Judge Hyman Bushel. Vetrano charged that Terry had hit him in the left eye with his goal stick. Terry countered that the man yelled obscenities at him, followed Terry to the dressing room, and that he had only waved his hand at the man. The magistrate dismissed the charges.

Terry and the Wings went into Maple Leaf Gardens on March 7 and beat Al Rollins, 3–0, for Sawchuk's eighth shutout of the season. The win spread the Wings' lead over the second-place Leafs to eight points.

Even though Terry followed up the win with a 7–0 shutout of Chicago on March 11 and a 4–0 shutout against Boston on March 15, the Vezina race went down to the final two games of the season. Terry had a one-goal lead over Rollins.

To a number of hockey observers, the goaltending battle was an unfair one. The Vezina rules at this time stipulated that the trophy be awarded to the goalie who had played the most games for the team that allowed the fewest goals. Sawchuk partisans were quick to point out that Terry had played many more games than Rollins, who was spelled periodically by Broda. Despite entreaties by Detroit players, management, and the press, the Vezina rules remained unchanged.

The Wings took the Friday afternoon train to Montreal to get rooms and rest up for the next night's battle with the Canadiens. But for Terry, some habits were hard to break. With memories of Indianapolis and nights partying with a few members of the Detroit Lions fresh in his mind, Terry quietly brought a few girls into his room after the curfew check to have a private party until dawn. Leo Reise remembers that specific night before one of Terry's two big weekend games. "That is the only time that I was ever disappointed in Terry. Here we were busting our butts to try to win him the Vezina and he goes and parties for most of the night."

Marcel Pronovost thinks of Terry's private party that night differently. "I can also remember Terry partying one night until four o'clock in the morning and my having to get another hotel room and the next night he single-handedly defeated Montreal in the Forum by a 2–1 score and he stopped fifty-five shots. It was Terry's way of relaxing at that time and getting his mind off of the game."

A 3–2 setback in Montreal, combined with an easy 4–1 win for the Leafs over the lowly Bruins — in which Rollins faced only ten shots on net over the entire three periods — left Rollins ahead of Terry by one goal. The Canadiens and Wings embarked on the same train out of Westmount Station a half hour after the game to head to Detroit for the eight-thirty start at the Olympia, while the Bruins and Leafs did likewise down to Boston for their eight o'clock rematch at the Boston Garden.

Terry played the game of his life as he stopped the vaunted Canadiens' attack time and time again. With a boisterous crowd of 13,753 cheering him on, there was no doubt — with the Wings already having locked up first place — as to why the fans were on the edge of their seats.

Meanwhile in Boston, the Leaf defence played so tight a game that Rollins earned a 1–0 shutout win.

Back in Detroit, the crowd's and Terry's hopes were high as he maintained his shutout with five minutes left to go in the game. Suddenly, the public address announcer at the Olympia announced the score of the Boston–Toronto game. The Vezina went to Rollins. The Red Wings looked over at Terry, who had lowered his head. Everyone in the arena felt for him as he completed a 5–0 whitewash of the Canadiens.

The Wings' forty-four wins and 101 points were NHL records,

while the shutout, Terry's eleventh of the season, was a high for the modern era. The Bruins' Tiny Thompson had notched the same figure in 1932–33.

Terry's performance throughout that regular season did not go unnoticed. His goals-against average of 1.99 was slightly higher than Rollins's 1.77, but the kid had played in thirty more games. Sawchuk's eleven shutouts easily topped the five by Rollins, who had played in the fewest games ever for a Vezina winner even in a longer 70-game schedule.

Three days after the regular season ended, Wings vice president James B. Norris announced the club was awarding Terry a $1,000 bonus as compensation for having so narrowly lost the Vezina. Not coincidentally, the bonus equalled the amount given to Vezina winners by the league.

Now the team turned its thoughts to the playoffs. Their opponents in the semifinal were the rookie-filled Canadiens, who had finished in third place, thirty-six points behind the league champions. What could not be ignored, however, was that the Canadiens had entered the playoffs with only one loss in their last ten regular-season games.

Montreal coach Dick Irvin could afford to make light of his team's underdog status while taking a jab at his rival, Jack Adams.

"We're along for the ride," Irvin said, "everything to win and nothing to lose. The burden is on the mighty Red Wings, and what a disgrace it would be if they should lose."

At the outset of the playoffs, the troublesome elbow that had acted up on Terry the previous year was doing so again. One of Jack Adams's favourite sayings, "Boys, what happens in the dressing room stays in the dressing room," was applied a bit more forcefully in light of Terry's injury. Open knowledge of the bothersome elbow might have welcomed opponents to take potshots.

As Gerry McNeil, an early season rookie-of-the-year candidate, prepared to face the "mighty Red Wings," he was understandably unsure of himself. Filling the great Bill Durnan's skates would not be easy, especially in a city as reverent of its hockey heroes as Montreal. Sensing the twenty-four-year-old's dilemma, Habs coach Dick Irvin began rooming with the youngster in an effort to get him psyched up and focused on the enemy.

In the first period of the first game at the Olympia, McNeil faced fourteen shots to Sawchuk's one, but amazingly, the score was tied, 1–1. In the second period, the teams managed a goal apiece, but both sides continued to play tight-checking hockey. In regulation time, McNeil faced only twenty-four shots to Terry's twenty. Deadlocked at 2–2, the game went into sudden-death overtime.

The two rookie goaltenders couldn't be beaten through three overtime periods. In the fourth overtime, Detroit blueliner Red Kelly lost the puck to Rocket Richard, who broke in alone on Sawchuk at full speed. Terry came out to challenge the game's most exciting goal scorer, and suddenly he forgot Ott Heller's most important lesson: the young goalie dropped to the ice, Richard paused, then, with Terry at his mercy, the Rocket fired the puck high into the Detroit net. It was 1:10 in the morning and 121 minutes of hockey had been played. Montreal had drawn first blood in a marathon that had seen a now-confident McNeil face a total of sixty-four shots to Terry's forty-five.

After the game, Adams knew there was only one reason to explain the Detroit loss: "The greatest goalkeeping this team has ever faced," he said of McNeil's performance.

The second game at the Olympia featured the same tight checking and excellent goaltending. There was no score at the end of regulation time. This time it would only take three over-time periods to decide a winner. Montreal centre Billy Reay broke in towards Sawchuk with the ever-dangerous Richard by his side. Terry played the centre perfectly, and was ready when Reay passed it to the open Richard. Terry hustled over and out at the Montreal marksman in an attempt to cut down the angle. Richard fired a low shot that Terry just missed on his stick side and the puck was in the net.

Despite two outstanding performances, as Terry and the Wings headed to Montreal to resume the series they were behind the proverbial eight ball. Terry was clearly frustrated by the Rocket. "When he beat me in the first game, he made me make the first move," Terry explained. "In the second game, I came out a bit to cover the angle and he still beat me with a low shot into the corner. I still don't know how he could have found that corner."

With their backs against the wall, the Wings went into a frenzied Montreal Forum for Game Three still confident that they could get back into the series. The first period was a scoreless draw. As the second period was about to draw to another scoreless close, Gordie Howe, celebrating his twenty-third birthday, broke in alone on McNeil, switched the puck to his backhand, and lifted it into the Montreal cage to snap McNeil's shutout streak at 218 minutes and 42 seconds (more than three and a half games).

In the third period, the Canadiens swarmed around Terry but the young goalie turned back thirty-one shots throughout the game. Captain Sid Abel's sizzling shot put the Wings up 2–0 and deflated the Forum crowd. Terry notched his first NHL playoff shutout. In the dressing room afterwards, sitting between Abel and Howe, Gordie mussed the youngster's hair and said, "Great game, Uke!" Terry was slow to undress as photographers milled around him and had him pose for a variety of pictures. For the first time in the series, Tommy Ivan relaxed visibly.

In Game Four at the Forum, Metro Prystai, Gerry Couture, and Abel scored the go-ahead goals in a 4–1 victory in which Terry faced only twenty-three shots. Ecstatic at having tied the series, Adams held high praise for his rookie netminder.

"It was the kid who pulled us through tonight," Adams boasted to reporters and photographers in the dressing room. As they looked on, Jack told Sawchuk to forget the loss of the Vezina to Al Rollins.

In the other dressing room, Montreal coach Dick Irvin maintained his confidence. He pointed out that, although the Habs had lost two games on home ice, so had Detroit. And the series was returning to the Olympia.

Game Five began in much the same way as the others. Again the teams were evenly matched until the Wings took a 2–1 lead. Then a shoving match between Lindsay and Richard erupted into fisticuffs. Without warning, Richard levelled Lindsay, who fell to the ice, out cold. Suddenly the Canadiens took fire. Late in the second period, Bernie (Boom Boom) Geoffrion converted a Paul Masnick pass into a fifty-foot slap shot that eluded Terry. Geoffrion would call this his first big goal and it ignited the Canadiens, who got third-period goals from Calum MacKay and Richard to ice the 5–2 victory. After the game, Dick Irvin was widely quoted as saying that the Rocket's punch had turned the tide.

Trailing 3–2 in the series as it moved back to Montreal, Detroit must have been hoping the home-ice jinx would hold.

For the first two periods, McNeil and Sawchuk were down-right larcenous, as each produced spectacular stops that had the Forum crowd beside itself in frustration and delight. Both teams played clean, end-to-end, "fire-wagon" hockey. Referee Bill Chadwick called not a single penalty all night.

Finally, at 6:49 of the third, Billy Reay beat Sawchuk to put the Habs up by one. Sid Abel quickly dissolved that lead by scoring less than a minute later. Suddenly, the Rocket got the puck behind Detroit's net and wrapped it around before Terry could get his skate over to the post to block it.

At the fifteen-minute mark of the third, Montreal's Kenny Mosdell got loose on a breakaway and beat Terry to make the score 3–1, Habs. But Ted Lindsay got the puck during a mad scramble in front of the Montreal net and got the Wings back to within one goal with forty-five seconds remaining on the clock. Everyone in the crowd of 14,448 agreed what a hockey game this had been. They were on their feet, roaring and screaming as the Wings immediately made their way back into the Canadiens' end and pulled Sawchuk for an extra attacker. The Habs frantically attempted to keep the powerful Red Wings at bay and were able to get a whistle with just six seconds left in regulation time. Both teams were on their feet at the benches as Abel took his place across from Elmer Lach for the face-off. Lach's stick shot out milliseconds before Sid's and he was able to feed the puck back to defenceman Doug Harvey, who killed the final seconds. At the buzzer, the Forum crowd erupted into delirious pandemonium.

As the Wings reached the dressing room where Jack Adams, unable to stand the pressure of watching, had been holed up for the final few minutes, many of the players were visibly upset, including Terry who was in tears. Adams put his arms around the distraught goalie and said softly, "It's not your fault, Terry. You gave your best."

"Thanks, Mr. Adams," Terry replied.

"I remember Terry crying," Marcel Pronovost recalls many years later. "Terry was very emotional. Also, the old man [Adams] had a real soft spot for Terry — he actually did for a lot of us kids from Windsor. That was a tough loss. And Terry really blamed himself, which was ridiculous. He had played miraculously."

In the Stanley Cup final, the Red Wings watched unhappily from the sidelines as the Leafs went on to win the Stanley Cup. It was a truly memorable series: Toronto beat Montreal in five games, all of which were decided in overtime.

For Terry there would be some consolation. On April 27, 1951, he was selected to the NHL First All-Star team, easily earning the nod over Charlie Rayner of the Rangers.

And, on May 4, Terry was the runaway choice for the Calder Memorial Trophy as the NHL's rookie of the year. In a four-year span, Terry Sawchuk had been named top rookie in three different professional leagues. Bob Kinnear had been right. The kid "had it."

4

THE GREATEST SEASON EVER

FOR Terry, the emotional pain of the Montreal loss was quickly replaced by the physical kind during the summer of 1951 as he was admitted to Detroit's Osteopathic Hospital for a second round of surgery on his troublesome elbow. At the same time, a set of badly inflamed tonsils were removed as well.

"Never again!" Terry said later. "I didn't mind the elbow operation but those tonsils. I wouldn't go through it again if I had to!" X-rays revealed that, although the elbow surgery was relatively successful, not all the bone chips had been excavated. A future operation would still be necessary.

In a 1950 *Detroit News* survey of the Red Wing bachelors, Terry had indicated that he preferred brunettes, and that she'd be good looking. "You can always hire a cook," he said, eliminating a prerequisite that his future mate should know her way around the kitchen. It was not in a kitchen where he met the first real girlfriend in his life. Her name was Dorothy Forsberg, the receptionist at his doctor's office in Winnipeg. True to Terry's preferences, Dorothy was a brunette and beautiful.

As July rolled into August of 1951, Jack Adams sat in his office in the Olympia thinking about the past season and the loss to Montreal. He studied his roster and knew he had the core of a team that had dynasty written all over it. But Adams was always looking for ways to fine-tune his lineup. Ever since his Wings of 1937–38 had come in dead last after having won two consecutive Stanley Cups, Jack had vowed never to leave any roster, champions or otherwise, untinkered with.

On August 20, he sold six players to the Chicago Black Hawks in the greatest cash deal to date: $75,000. Gone were George Gee, Jimmy McFadden, Clare Martin, Clare Raglan, Jimmy Peters, and Max McNab. But Trader Jack wasn't done. He traded Gaye Stewart to the Rangers for small but tough Tony Leswick.

Terry left his best girl in Winnipeg to report to training camp in Sault Ste. Marie, Michigan, and he was somewhat shocked as he tipped the scales at 219 pounds.

"Tilt!" Terry yelled jokingly but with a definite tone of concern. "Something's wrong with these scales. I only weighed 212 when I left home a week ago, and I've been eating like a sparrow since. Unless you count milkshakes." Later that day, Adams was blunt with Terry. "I told him to get down to his playing weight," Adams relayed to the press later, "and quick!"

"I remember Terry coming to camp six to seven pounds heavier than his rookie weight of 212," Marcel Pronovost remembers today. "That whole weight situation with Terry was blown right out of proportion. We all came into camp to get into shape, that's what training camp was for. So it was logical for Terry to come into camp a little heavy. Terry was laid up after elbow surgery and didn't do that much in the summer."

It was rumoured that Adams didn't look highly on plump goaltenders, which was one of the reasons he had dealt Lumley.

Lefty Wilson says, "The Uke in those early years was big in the ass and the hips. When he put weight on that's where it went. One of the stupidest goddamn things Adams ever did was bug Terry about his weight."

Sawchuk was put on a "no-starch diet," which meant no more potatoes, bread, or pastry, but lots of lean meat, milk, and fresh vegetables.

During the seventeen-day training camp, Terry maintained his diet. In addition to their usual rounds of golf, the team played four exhibition games against their farm club, the Indianapolis Capitals, and played a two-game series in Northern Ontario against the Chicago Black Hawks. Terry shut out the Black Hawks, 3–0, in Copper Cliff and Detroit won again, 5–1, in North Bay. The Wings also played an exhibition game in Shawinigan Falls, Quebec, where they introduced Lefty Wilson as "Terry Sawchuk — Mr. Zero" as a gag. Lefty fanned on the first shot and the crowd gave him a rough time all evening.

As Terry's weight slowly inched its way down, he officially weighed in at two hundred and twelve after another 8:00 a.m. practice though Adams continued to growl, "He's got to get down to two hundred and ten before the season starts!"

Sawchuk was sensational throughout training camp, allowing but half a goal per game until he was injured in an exhibition game in Windsor. He suffered a bruised left knee, was forced from the game, and had to rest for four days.

As the season started, management and the press raved about Sawchuk, stating he looked so sharp he was almost superhuman. Some wondered whether Terry would be stricken with the sophomore jinx. A number of players had recently won rookie of the year honours and then vanished from the limelight: Pentti Lund, Jimmy McFadden, Jack Gelineau. The latter was perhaps the most dramatic example. Gelineau had been the Boston Bruins' goaltending sensation of 1949–50. By 1951–52 he was selling insurance back in Montreal.

Terry's doubters were quickly silenced as he opened the campaign with his second straight appearance in the All-Star game in Toronto on October 9 as his First Team battled the Second Team to a 2–2 tie.

Sawchuk started the seventy-game schedule with a 1–0 shutout against Sugar Jim Henry and the Bruins at the Olympia. It was the Red Wing organization's thirteenth straight season-opening win. The Wings lost their second game 3–2 to the Leafs but rebounded against the Hawks in a 6–1 win. Terry got his second shutout of the season against the Canadiens, 3–0. Terry was voted the O'Keefe NHL Player of the Week based on his fabulous performance in the first four games.

Terry didn't rest on his laurels as the Wings headed into the

Montreal Forum for an October 22, 1951, game. He stopped forty-four of forty-five shots to lead the way to a 3–1 Detroit victory. In his 1995 book *In the Crease,* famed broadcaster Dick Irvin — son of the legendary Habs coach — singled out this Sawchuk performance as the greatest display of goaltending he had ever witnessed.

"I have watched a lot of goalies stop a lot of shots since then," wrote Irvin, "but I have never forgotten the Detroit goalie's performance that night. It was the first time I had seen him play and maybe that's why I usually answer 'Terry Sawchuk' when asked to pick the all-time best goalie."

The victory vaulted the Wings past the Canadiens into first place. As they headed to Toronto for a game on Saturday, October 27, they were greeted by some venomous comments from Leaf owner Conn Smythe in the *Toronto Daily Star.* Sports editor Milt Dunnell quoted Smythe as saying that the Red Wings played "kitty-bar-the-door hockey," which unduly magnified Sawchuk's ability.

"You see," the Major said, "they teach a player how to stop the other fellow from scoring before they teach him to score himself. That's the way they do it. I'm not finding fault with the system; I just say that's why their goalies always look good."

Smythe's theory that the Wings concentrated more on defence than offence didn't hold any water. The previous year, 1950–51, the Wings had scored 236 goals, a league record.

Johnny Wilson says the charges were a better fit for his own Maple Leafs. "Smythe wanted to take the emphasis off his own club because that's the kind of hockey his team played. They didn't have the goal-scoring touch that we had or the firepower. He was trying to get under Sawchuk's skin, which he did but it made him play even better."

Terry's attitude about the press began to sour perhaps as a result of the Smythe controversy. "Terry always was a little paranoid of newspaper men but it got that he didn't know how to react to them anymore," recalls Marcel Pronovost. "Most of us Wings did not react very well to a pat on the back in print, and Terry most of all began to treat them very roughly."

Bud Lynch remembers how Terry thought about the press.

"The Uke and I soon developed a system, that after I finished my broadcasts, I'd go down to the Wing dressing room. Now because of the stature he was getting in hockey, he used to get hounded for interviews or quotes but he didn't want to be interviewed. He needed time to unwind. So he'd take his time to undress, and shower and then when he got back to his seat he'd wink at me and I'd go over and we'd talk about anything under the sun, so as the other reporters wouldn't bother him. He didn't want to be interviewed."

Few teams in history could boast the firepower the 1951–52 Wings had at their disposal. In front of Sawchuk was a defence crew without peer.

"Benny Woit was the fifth defenceman who didn't see all that much action," remembers Leo Reise. "He'd play maybe six to seven shifts a night. Red Kelly was a great defenceman who could really carry the puck; sometimes he took chances and lost but Terry could make up for that. Red once rushed up the middle and lost the puck to the Rocket. I never let him forget it!

"Bob Goldham and I started every period and ended every period. Tommy Ivan always stressed defence at those times because early and late goals could kill ya. Marcel Pronovost was my partner during the rest of the game. He was a great skater and I stayed home more at that point in my career."

Up front, the Wings also had a potent offence. Gordie Howe, the league scoring champion, was on right wing of the famed Production Line. At centre was team captain Sid Abel and the left side featured the fearless Ted Lindsay, who was often near Howe at the top of the NHL scoring race. Two years previous, Lindsay had won the scoring championship.

The second line concentrated more on checking and featured Marty Pavelich, Glen Skov, and the hustling, tiny Tony Leswick. The third line included Metro Prystai, with newcomers Alex Delvecchio and spot starter Johnny Wilson.

Marcel Pronovost recollects how the season and the team were shaping up in that 1951–52 season. "Our team had every element: phenomenal goaltending, experience in Howe, Lindsay, and Abel, a great checking line in the Pavelich line. But what made the difference was the kid line of Prystai and

Delvecchio, later joined by Wilson. And overall, this was a very young hockey club."

For some strange reason, despite the fact that Terry had obviously slimmed down extensively from even his rookie-playing weight of 210 pounds, Terry had an official weigh-in in the Red Wing dressing room in front of Jack Adams and reporters in late November.

"See, Jack," Terry yelled out sarcastically to the boss. "Why, these scales say 193 and I didn't think I was an ounce over 192 and a half today!"

"Good work, Terry," Adams answered after making a show of checking the equipment for tampering. "Keep it up, or rather, keep it down."

The Toronto Maple Leafs were in second place, four points behind the Wings, when the teams met on Sunday, December 2 at the Olympia. A vicious check into the boards by Leaf defenceman Gus Mortson against Fred Glover turned into a free-for-all. Jack Adams momentarily forgot his blood pressure and rushed to the penalty box to blast referee George Gavel for only calling a minor penalty against Mortson, whom he thought had kicked Glover. After the dust settled, Toronto had won, 2–1.

Three nights later, the teams met again in Toronto. There was still an undertone of hostility and aggressiveness. On one play, Leaf forward Howie Meeker was sent sprawling into Sawchuk and the Detroit net with full force. Sawchuk was winded on the play and Meeker suffered a painful knee injury. During the second period, Terry was involved in a skirmish with the Leafs Ted Kennedy as the goalie held Kennedy's stick. Hot words were exchanged, and Sawchuk challenged Kennedy to meet him after the game. The game ended in a 2–2 tie and suddenly Sawchuk and Kennedy found themselves eye to eye under the stands on the way to their respective dressing rooms. Profanity quickly filled the air as Sawchuk and Kennedy began shoving each other. Soon both teams spilled out into the hallway as someone yelled, "Where's Mortson the kicker?"

"We heard the commotion and came out into the hallway, but it was all done by the time I got there," Marcel Pronovost recalls. "Terry would fight anyone. He wasn't good at it, but he'd fight anyone!"

A band of ushers led by police sergeant Murray Henderson managed to separate the combatants but took a bit of a jostling from Terry.

As the teams headed back to their dressing rooms, Sergeant Henderson looked down at his shoes to find that someone's skate had sliced them open, ruining them.

On Sunday, December 23, Dorothy Forsberg flew in from Winnipeg to spend Christmas with Terry and to watch her first big-league game as the Wings hosted the Canadiens. Though the first-place Wings were sluggish and the Habs buzzed Terry's net all night, he played a fantastic game, stopping all thirty-three shots en route to a 4–0 win. It was his seventh shutout, five more than any goalie in the league.

Sid Abel, Jack Adams, and the whole team called Terry's performance his best NHL game in the two years he had been in the league.

"That's one shutout that really means something," Abel observed. "Terry had to work like a dog for it. We almost lost the game. He saved it."

The press caught the fact that Terry's Winnipeg girlfriend was in town and asked him about it. He refused to disclose even her name, saying only that he hoped she enjoyed the game. Even among his teammates, Terry would be protective of his personal life.

"I remember meeting his girl from Winnipeg," Alex Delvecchio says today, "and we all went out for a few beers after the game and then that was it. Never heard a peep about her again. She seemed very nice."

Johnny Wilson remembered Terry becoming engaged to this girl that Christmas of 1951, but as quickly as she had appeared in his public life, she was gone.

In one interview Terry revealed the girl's name and the engagement, but qualified the rest by saying, "There are no wedding plans made yet. I'd like to build up my bank account first." No wedding with her ever took place. "The Uke silently dropped the whole thing," a teammate said, "and so did we."

Frank Boucher, general manager of the New York Rangers, attended a testimonial dinner for Jack Adams put on in honour of his twenty-fifth anniversary as Red Wings GM. After witnessing a 2–2 tie in the Olympia the next evening, he offered a powerful endorsement of Terry Sawchuk's ability.

"Terry Sawchuk is the greatest goalie in the history of big-league hockey," Boucher said. "I know the real test of greatness is achievement over a longer period of years and Sawchuk is just a kid, but what a kid! He has introduced a new technique with that low crouch of his and you'll see a lot of youngsters copying that style now."

About Terry's contemporaries, Boucher added, "Compare their records to Sawchuk's. That will speak for itself." Boucher's comments carried extra authority, coming as they did from a man who had seen Georges Vezina, George Hainsworth, Tiny Thompson, Frank Brimsek, Bill Durnan, Turk Broda, and his own goaltending legend, Chuck Rayner. When informed of Boucher's assessment, Terry quietly answered, "Did he really say that? It was nice of him to say so."

In this season, one incident clearly indicated the respect with which young Terry held his goaltending opponents. Goaltending legend Chuck Rayner had just shut out the Red Wings, 1–0. He was swarmed by his Ranger teammates as if he had just won the Stanley Cup. Terry wormed his way through Rayner's ecstatic teammates.

"You were terrific tonight, Chuck," Terry said. "No kidding!"

A warm smile broke out across Rayner's face as he gazed at the honest, modest, young man who was the talk of the NHL, standing before him. "Look who's congratulating who," replied Rayner. "You were the one who did the job tonight, not me!"

Terry later explained the gesture. "Chuck Rayner is the best, that's all. He's got a style all his own. It's a great thrill playing against a man you used to idolize, and when he comes up with that kind of a performance, well, you just feel you've got to say something."

On another occasion, Terry lavished praise upon his five defencemen.

"Red [Kelly] and Marcel keep a lot of heat off me. When they're on the ice, the other team has to worry about them as if they were forwards. Leo [Reise], Bob [Goldham], and Benny [Woit] block a lot of shots which I never have to handle. Goldham is a real master at dropping to his knees."

Off the ice the Red Wings split naturally into two distinct groups: one comprising Howe, Lindsay, Marty Pavelich, Red Kelly, and Leo Reise, the other made up of Johnny Wilson, Metro Prystai, Alex Delvecchio, Marcel Pronovost, Glen Skov, Tony Leswick, Benny Woit, and Sawchuk. "But," says Wilson, "on the ice and in the dressing room, we were one group. That was one of the main reasons for our success. We had a good captain and we were a close-knit team."

Marcel still laughs at the memory of one example of team togetherness that occurred in Boston.

"Tommy Ivan called for a one o'clock curfew. But all the guys decided to go out for Chinese food. So we all went out to this Chinese restaurant. We just get served our food at a quarter past one when Tommy Ivan walks in the door. He looks around, sees that everyone is together, a couple of guys had had a beer but we were behaving, so he comes in, sits down for some food himself, and then picks up the bill. What could he say to us?"

Leo Reise recollects one night with particular relish: "One night we're in Boston and I keep the opposing forward out by the blue line, and he shoots and it's in the net! Later, another guy comes down, I keep him over to the side and poof, it's in the net! I goes back to Terry and says, 'Terry, are your eyes going bad or something?' He says, 'No, Leo, both times those guys should have passed the puck, I took my eyes off the puck anticipating the pass. I outsmarted myself!' That stands out to me all these years later because that's the only time that ever happened with Terry. He was a real student of the game."

In early March, Terry was gashed for a ten-stitch cut on his forehead, but, with a big white bandage covering the wound he continued to play marvellously down the stretch.

"In those days," Johnny Wilson adds, "you had one goaltender. When Terry would get cut in the middle of a game, which would happen often, the game would stop and we'd skate around and wait until he was stitched up, bandaged up, then he'd come back out and the game resumed. And in those days a goalie [couldn't afford to] have a slump. When Terry got into a slump, he had to play his way out. But in '51–52, he definitely had no slumps!"

The Wings streaked to the regular-season finish line with 100 points, twenty-two ahead of second-place Montreal and twenty-six ahead of Toronto, their first-round playoff opponents. The Vezina race was similarly a cakewalk: Terry beat out Toronto's Al Rollins by twenty-four goals, with a 1.90 average to Rollins's 2.22. Sawchuk's forty-four wins tied the NHL record he'd set the previous year, and his twelve shutouts tied the number set by Chicago's Charlie Gardiner in 1930–31.

As the Wings headed into the series with the Leafs, they felt they had much to do. They had heard the whispers that they weren't a playoff club, that they folded when the chips were down. And they were facing the defending Stanley Cup champions in the first round.

Game One at the Olympia was an emotional, chippy affair. Terry and his "Pirates," a nickname given to his defence corp, shut down the vaunted Leaf attack time and again, leading to a 3–0 whitewash before a wildly exuberant Olympia crowd. "Terry and the Pirates," a comic strip created by Milton Caniss, premiered in the *New York Daily News* in October 1934. Its popularity peaked during World War II. Every year the Press took a picture of Terry and his 5 defencemen and titled it "Terry and the Pirates." It became a tradition.

Game Two saw Conn Smythe grasping at straws in an effort to turn back the Wings, calling on Turk Broda to take Rollins's place in the Leaf net. A winner of five Cups, Broda could be relied upon to deliver a standout performance when the money was on the line. But although Broda had only played in one game all season, Smythe felt his presence alone would inspire his teammates to bigger and better things.

The Leafs did play an inspired game, but it was Terry's buddy Johnny Wilson who broke through first, putting one past Broda at the three-quarter mark of the first period.

Detroit lapses in the third period gave the Leafs a two-man advantage for nearly two full minutes. The Wings penalty killers held their own and even forced a face-off deep in the Leaf end. Off the draw, the puck was forwarded to the swift Max Bentley, who sidestepped the Wing defence at his blue line and broke away alongside sniper Sid Smith. Terry came out to challenge the puck carrier, but remained ready for a pass across. Bentley put a quick fake on Terry, then passed the puck across to the open Smith. Smith fired the puck instantly but Terry adeptly deflected the puck wide with his skate. As the Wings got back to pick up the loose puck, the ovation for Terry was deafening. The fans were on their feet cheering, screaming, and whistling. On the bench, the Wing players couldn't believe that incredible save and were themselves screaming and cheering for their young goaltender. The uplifted Red Wings shut down the Leafs the rest of the way. Terry stopped twenty-two shots in all for a 1–0 victory. When asked afterwards about the sensational save, Terry replied, "That was Toronto's big threat. Our men got back before they could do any damage and we won." These were humble words from a young goaltending star who had just racked up back-to-back shutouts.

As the series shifted back to Maple Leaf Gardens, Conn Smythe was hoping that Turk Broda might have still another amazing game left in him, but Broda was pummelled for a 6–2 loss.

Al Rollins suited up for the fourth game. The only winning to be done would be by Terry and the Wings, who were in top form. As the final buzzer sounded for a 3–1 victory and a four-game sweep for Detroit, the only consolation the Leafs could muster was that they had kept league-scoring champ Gordie Howe from scoring.

In the Wings dressing room, boss Jack Adams was beside himself with delight. He always relished defeating the Leafs. When Terry got to the jubilant dressing room, Jack had a special hug for him.

"That's my boy!" he exclaimed. "I'll tell you, it helps when you've got a kid like that out there. The greatest in hockey."

The Wings would wait nine days for the Stanley Cup finals to start, while the Canadiens and the gritty Boston Bruins battled it out in the other semifinal series. The Wings practised and tried to stay fired up at their hideaway in Toledo, Ohio, away from the distractions of their daily lives around friends and family back in Detroit.

The tough Boston–Montreal series went seven games, and was won on a determined effort by none other than Rocket Richard. Having missed part of the regular season due to injuries, the Rocket was knocked out of the seventh game after a second-period collision with the Bruins' Bill Quackenbush. With four minutes left in regulation time and the score tied, 1–1, the shaky, stitched-up Richard skated through four Bruins and fought off Quackenbush to beat Sugar Jim Henry. The picture of a bloodied Richard shaking hands with a black-eyed Henry, who is bowing respectfully, is one of the most evocative hockey photographs ever taken.

An ice show was booked into the Olympia on the date Game One of the finals was to take place, so the series opened at the Montreal Forum. The Wings had not forgotten their semifinal humiliation of the year before and they were set to settle old scores. As usual, nobody hated losing more than Terry.

The first game, on April 10, pitted a tired but determined Canadiens squad against the rusty but vengeful Detroit gang. Terry made at least five outstanding first-period saves to keep the game scoreless. Detroit's Tony Leswick opened the scoring three minutes into the second, assisted by Marty Pavelich. Gordie Howe's playoff scoring drought continued a bit later when he failed to put the puck in the net left vacant by an out-of-position Gerry McNeil.

After Leswick scored his second goal of the night at 7:57 of the third period, Montreal's Tom Johnson finally put the Habs on the scoreboard three minutes later. When the Forum's public-address announcer declared that one minute was left in the game, Habs coach Dick Irvin pulled McNeil for an extra attacker only to have Ted Lindsay score into the empty net. When it subsequently came over the loudspeaker that the time-keeper had made a mistake and that there still remained another full minute to play, coach Irvin was incensed. He claimed the timekeeper had forced him to pull his goaltender too early. The game ended 3–1 Detroit, after which the Forum timer admitted, "I don't know what I would have done if a [Montreal] goal had been scored in the last minute!"

Game Two saw the Wings regaining their form, while the effects on the Canadiens of nine games in nineteen nights were evident. Montreal's last gasp came as Elmer Lach tied the score, 1–1, with just under two minutes remaining in the opening period. They would not score again in the playoffs.

After Ted Lindsay put the puck behind McNeil with not yet a minute gone in the second period, Terry and the pirates did their thing, effectively stopping the determined but tired Montreal attack. Though scoring ace Howe continued to draw blanks, he put Habs defenceman Dollard St. Laurent out of the series by standing his ground against the charging Montrealer and inflicting a lacerated eyeball. The game ended 2–1, with the Wings heading home clearly in command.

On the train ride back to Detroit, the Wings were determined but loose. As soon as Tommy Ivan and Jack Adams were asleep, the guys slipped out to the smoker and had a couple of beers — especially Terry, who had trouble sleeping after big games.

A tumultuous welcome greeted Terry and the Wings as they skated onto the Olympia ice — for the first time in fifteen days — for Game Three. The seating rose in two steep tiers, giving spectators a feeling of being over the ice. Though its seating capacity was officially 14,200, it would swell during the two upcoming games to well over 15,000. For a price, it was said, the fire marshals would conveniently turn their heads the other way.

"The Olympia was a great place to play hockey in," remembers Ted Lindsay. "The people in the first four rows of the balcony were the best hockey fans in the world. The fans at the Olympia always gave us such a boost. They were so loud, and they were right on top of you."

Gordie Howe broke his playoff scoring slump by beating McNeil on a screen shot four-and-a-half minutes into the game.

Then at the nine-minute mark of the second period, Ted Lindsay lofted a seventy-foot blooper towards the Montreal net. The puck took a bounce and McNeil couldn't catch it. If this goal didn't demoralize the Canadiens, Terry's play did. With the middle frame drawing to a close, Terry stopped a burst of four shots from the stick of Paul Meger to maintain his zero.

Howe got his second goal of the playoffs just shy of the seven-minute mark of the third period. Terry recorded twenty-six saves and the game ended 3–0.

As Gerry McNeil sat disconsolately in the Habs' dressing room, the Rocket knew the reason for the Wings' success. "Sawchuk is their club. Another guy in their nets and we'd beat them. It's been like that all year. I couldn't get started. There are some nights you just can't get going."

Stanley Cup fever was at a peak as Terry took to his net for the start of Game Four. Every indication was that the Wings were ready to wrap this up in the minimum eight games but the Canadiens were not done yet. The Habs concentrated on shutting down the Howe line, which had figured in all three goals in Game Three.

Montreal had the better scoring opportunities early on, but the Winnipeg Wonder was up to the task. A save on Floyd Curry from five feet out lifted the roof off the old building.

At the 6:50 mark of the first period, Metro Prystai took a pass from rookie Alex Delvecchio and put the puck in for a 1–0 Wing lead. When Glen Skov scored from Prystai at the end of the second period, Tommy Ivan's uncanny assignment before the game was clearly paying off. Johnny Wilson recalls, "Tommy came up to us — me, Prystai, and Delvecchio — and said he wanted us to win the game for the team, and we were the checking line!"

It was also during the second period that a sign from above — more precisely, the upper balcony — might alone have sealed the fate of Richard and company. An octopus was thrown onto the ice, its eight tentacles representing the eight wins needed to win the Cup. Octopi have hit the ice during Detroit playoff games ever since.

In the third period, Prystai scored unassisted. The crowd cheered wildly, anticipating the imminent sweep and another potential Sawchuk shutout. Terry made back-to-back stops on Dickie Moore that had the rookie banging his stick on the ice repeatedly in frustration. At the buzzer, pandemonium erupted as Terry was mobbed by his teammates.

As captain Sid Abel was presented with the Stanley Cup, it was an emotional moment for everyone.

Dick Irvin could not stomach the victory celebrations and, followed by Elmer Lach and Maurice Richard, hurried to the dressing room without offering his congratulations.

In the dressing room, Terry was hugged by Adams and everyone else in the organization. He was the last to take his equipment off as he was hounded by the press for a quote or two. In the mayhem of this victory party there was no way the normally reticent Sawchuk could dodge them.

Terry was told that his four shutouts tied a record shared by the Rangers' Davey Kerr — who had gotten the four in nine games in 1937 — and Toronto's Frank McCool, who performed the feat in thirteen playoff games in 1945. Terry had taken only eight games. Terry's goals-against average for the eight games was a phenomenal 0.63, the lowest GAA ever for an eight-game playoff series.

"I wasn't worried about equalling the shutout record," Terry told reporters. "All I wanted to do was get this series over with."

Exactly one week after drinking from the Cup, Terry was voted to the NHL First All-Star team for the second year in a row. Life, it seemed, just did not, could not, get any better than this. It had been the greatest season any goaltender had ever had.

5

SHUTOUTS AND SETBACKS

FOR Terry the romp through the Stanley Cup finals had masked the increasingly problematic pain in his right elbow.

In the summer of 1952, Terry went to Detroit's Osteopathic Hospital to be examined by Doctor Donald Sheets, who recommended that this surgery be much more ambitious than the first two. He felt the joint should be cleaned out properly, otherwise the young goalie would require yearly operations. Each operation, Sheets explained, was intrusive, promoted tissue scarring, and increased the chance of infection. Most of all, repeated surgeries would inhibit complete healing of the elbow, tendons, and surrounding tissue and muscles.

Sheets removed more than sixty pieces of bone. He cleaned the broken joint and rounded the jagged edges in an attempt to give Terry greater use of the elbow. He was incredulous to see how the elbow had healed and formed itself from the childhood injury, and decided that the malformation was permanent.

Back in Winnipeg, Terry's elbow healed very slowly, leaving him so worried about its status that he lost his appetite.

Back in Detroit, Jack Adams was having a surprisingly inactive summer. After the Stanley Cup victory, he had boasted to reporters, "For balance, for depth, for anything you want to call it, this is the best Red Wing team I've ever had in my twenty-five years in the NHL. I'll let the figures speak for themselves. Let any other club in the league try to match them!"

By July, only one player had been moved: the Chicago Black Hawks, with Adams's blessing, signed Sid Abel to a two-year deal as a player–coach. The Production Line would need a new centre.

But, as Leo Reise explains, Trader Jack had one move in mind even before the end of the 1952 Stanley Cup final. "We were coming back on the train from that second victory in the Forum. I was sitting with Jack Adams and Fred Huber, our public relations fellow, and we were talking. I happened to mention that I might stay in Detroit year-round — you know, buy a house and settle down. The words were no sooner out of my mouth than Jack looked at Fred and Fred looked at Jack and I knew I was gone. They didn't say a word, but I knew." Normally, Reise would only pack up half his stuff to take back to Canada for the summer. When the '52 finals ended, he packed up everything.

Sure enough, in August of 1952, Adams traded the two-time All-Star to the Rangers for forward Reg Sinclair, some cash, and an amateur defenceman. Reise's independence, salary, and age made him expendable.

Terry reported for the 1952–53 training camp just under 180 pounds. His friends and teammates were taken aback by his thin appearance.

"The year he came into camp skinny as a rake, we thought that he was sick or something," recalls Johnny Wilson. "I also remember Terry coming back to camp saying, 'Ya, they took out some more bone chips.'

"But you could tell there was something bothering him; something we couldn't see was eating away at him."

Perhaps Terry worried himself silly about maintaining his 195-pound playing weight of the previous season and, in doing so, inadvertently shed more pounds than expected. Perhaps the prospects of his elbow not being up to scratch combined with his paranoia about a weight gain — as he'd experienced after his other two operations — triggered his loss of appetite. Nervousness and hyperactivity can lead to weight loss, as can depression. Perhaps the failed engagement with Dorothy

Forsberg also affected Terry. In any event, nobody today knows what happened.

After taking his customary training camp physical examination, a flabbergasted Jack Adams asked Terry to undergo a second round of testing to see if they might find a medical reason for the weight loss. To Terry's relief, the tests showed no physical problems. Also, in early practices Terry's elbow held up well, much to the delight of Wings management. In fact the elbow was the best it had been since his teen years.

On October 5, 1952, the Olympia hosted the sixth annual All-Star game. In his third straight appearance, Terry played the entire game for the First Team All-Stars, who tied the Second Team, 1–1.

Former teammate and fellow First Team All-Star Leo Reise was shocked at the sight of the radically slimmed-down Sawchuk in the dressing room.

"I said to myself, 'Terry, my God! What's happened to you? Compared to what you were, you're almost skin and bones!'"

As the regular season began, Ted Lindsay had taken Abel's place as captain and sophomore Alex Delvecchio was the new centre on the Production Line.

The Red Wings were off to an uncharacteristically slow start, sitting in fifth place after a month. The defence was especially sluggish: Red Kelly's play was inconsistent, Benny Woit was slow to adjust to the added workload of a full-time player, and new fifth defenceman Larry Zeidel was having trouble just fitting in.

Behind them, Terry also hindered his own cause just before a late-October road trip by deciding his old catching glove was shot and asking trainer Lefty Wilson for a new one.

"Sawchuk hated change," Lefty recalls. "He'd wear something till it was rotten. At one of the early camps, he just absolutely needed a new belly pad. So I got this old harness maker to make Terry a new one. Using the old one as a model, the fella made Terry a nice new belly pad with big leather clips and everything just perfect. It took the guy two days and it only cost us fifty goddamn cents. I believe Terry wore that belly pad till the day he died. He hated to change his equipment."

Terry could not get the feel for the new glove, with its smaller pocket. He allowed sixteen goals in the three games on the road, including a very embarrassing shelling in the Montreal Forum on October 25.

Marcel Pronovost recalls that night. His mother was attending her first NHL game, and was seeing her son play as a pro for the first time. "God, do I remember that night. The Canadiens wouldn't let us have the puck! The game wasn't ten minutes old and it was 4–0; after that, it was downhill all the way. It was one of those nights when everything went wrong, just everything.

"At the ten-minute mark, my mother asked the usher to give her a chair so she could sit in the hallway — not because she was embarrassed, but because she knew that when Montreal got so far ahead the game was going to get out of hand with fights. She didn't want to see any fights."

The Canadians won the game, 9–0 — by far the worst shellacking of Terry's career. Sawchuk was going through his first serious slump. His appetite waned and his weight dropped below 170 pounds. In a turnabout from the previous year, he was given a special diet in an effort to fatten him up, but his play, the uncomfortable new catching glove, and the team's weak performance rendered the effort futile.

Upon his return to Detroit, Terry worked feverishly to break in a new glove — a three-fingered first baseman's mitt, with a leather cuff attached to protect the wrist. It was larger than the glove he wore on the road trip and he was anxious to begin using it. Jack Adams was in a mood to change his roster, sending Larry Zeidel back to the minors. He also let it be known that Sawchuk was not to blame. "Terry Sawchuk, called a superman and one of the greatest goalies in history last season, is still tops with me."

Players from the Original Six look back fondly on the days of train travel. It was a leisurely way to travel and a builder of team unity. Ted Lindsay recalls: "The train was a great way to travel. Detroit was like the hub of the NHL wheel. We were four to five hours to Chicago in the west, four to five hours to Toronto in the east. The train usually left at dinner time the night before a game. We'd have the porter keep us a couple of berths 'cause the guys wanted to play cards later, but first the guys would go into the smoker and relax, shoot the breeze. Then we'd hit the sack ten or eleven o'clock at night. If we were going to Montreal, the train would roll in sometime early Saturday morning.

"In Montreal, our game would end at about 10:40 and we had to undress, shower, pack our bags, dress, catch a bus at the back of the Forum and catch the train out of Westmount Station at ten after eleven. Once on the train, we'd all relax in the smoker talking about the game and everything for a half hour, and then Ivan and Adams would each head off to bed, to their compartments, and close the door. Once Adams closed his door, he wasn't coming out till morning 'cause he had his own bathroom in there.

"We weren't supposed to drink but the guys would all sneak a couple of beers in their bag, sit in their berths across from each other, sip on a beer or two, shoot the shit, then go to sleep. We'd arrive back in Detroit at 2:30 in the afternoon for a return game against the Canadiens at Olympia at 8:30 that next night, Sunday night. Often the Canadiens took the same train back with us, but they'd sit in a separate car."

Terry has been branded in the years since his death as a womanizer, but the truth be known, he was never what one would call "smooth" among women.

"Terry was not good with women," Marcel Pronovost says, "nor was he good for women. For Terry to get lucky, he had to be practically set up. He had a couple of girls that would visit him from Indianapolis, but he never had a steady girlfriend. The broads that Terry had in those early years were anybody's broads, who would go to the post with any athlete. But Terry could certainly not hold a candle to many NHLers nor some of our teammates when it came to women.

"But I do remember one time, we're in Montreal the night before a game and in those years we used to frequent this place called The Chicken Coop. Well the next thing you know, Sawchuk has a date with a lady named Gerda Munsinger."

The name didn't mean much then, but Gerda Munsinger

would many years later be implicated in alleged sexual affairs with Canadian cabinet ministers, accused of spying on behalf of the Soviet Union against Canada and would turn out to be an embarrassment for John Diefenbaker's government.

Terry took full responsibility for the Red Wing losses. He was paid to stop pucks, he said, and instead they kept going by him. Marcel Pronovost adds, "Terry accepted full responsibility as a way of taking the onus off of the hockey club. Terry never blamed anyone for his shortcomings on the ice. Unlike others, he *never* pointed at a defenceman. It was always a battle between him and the puck and he'd say, 'I shoulda had it!'"

Terry's frustration between the pipes was evidenced by his behaviour towards some of the hecklers he encountered. Being near the border, the Red Wings drew more than their share of Leaf or Canadien fans from Windsor on the Canadian side. One night a heckler was really giving it to Terry. As the first period ended, Sawchuk climbed up onto the mesh trying to climb it to get at the heckler.

A month into the season, the Wings finally got their act together and began inching up in the league standings. Terry's fragile confidence returned as the Wings began to notch successive victories. A mid-November shutout against Boston and Sugar Jim Henry was a definite morale booster.

On December 4, 1952, team owner James D. (Pops) Norris — Jack Adams's mentor, confidant, and boss — was jolted by a stabbing pain in his chest as he worked at his desk at the Norris Grain Company in Chicago. Before an elevator carrying Norris to a waiting ambulance could reach the ground, Norris was dead.

Almost in tribute to their former owner, who was replaced at the head of the Red Wing empire by his twenty-five-year-old daughter, Marguerite, the Wings recaptured the NHL lead by mid December. It seems fitting that Terry scored a shutout in Chicago days after the elder Norris's death.

The Wings were definitely on a roll as they headed into the Christmas season on a twelve-game undefeated streak. But during an early-morning practice on Christmas Eve, an Alex

Delvecchio shot caught Terry on the instep of his right foot, fracturing a small bone. His foot in a cast, Terry was forced to watch from the sidelines for the next few weeks.

As quickly as he himself had replaced Harry Lumley just three years before, Terry watched young Glenn Hall don his sweater and take his place in the Wings net. Terry, often described by teammates as a "worrywart," fretted about losing his place in the Wings lineup.

"Why did this have to happen to me just when the club was going so good?" Terry wondered to himself and others.

In an echo of his own rise to the NHL, Terry could see that Hall was ready for the big time. The Wings lost only one of six games Hall played in.

No sooner was Terry back in action than, in February, he was cut badly in the mouth as his face stopped a shot by Toronto's Harry Watson. Three upper teeth were broken and it took twelve stitches to contain the bleeding. Terry returned to the action but, as the game continued, he began to spit out more blood and the game was stopped once again so that Terry's sutures could be replaced.

"Terry played through almost anything," remembers his chum Pronovost with a certain degree of awe. "In those days, the loss of a goaltender was critical. One would have to be pulled up from the farm system somewhere, and they weren't always ready for the NHL."

Sawchuk's problem was that his replacement was all too capable of playing in the NHL. He was determined not to let Glenn Hall have a second chance to impress Jack Adams. Terry continued to play excellently, but he also continued to have trouble regaining his lost weight, so at times he would feel weaker and more fatigued after a game than usual.

In front of Terry, Alex Delvecchio was right at home between Gordie Howe and Ted Lindsay, as his forty-three assists would help keep the two wingers at the top of the NHL scoring race. The twenty-one-year-old was also on his way to a fifth-place finish in the scoring race. Alex doesn't recall a change in Terry's character as his weight dropped that season. "His temperament never changed in those years. When he had moments that he didn't want to talk, we just left him be. But it was like that with all goaltenders."

Terry's new glove held him in good stead heading into March. On March 7 he posted his seventh shutout of the campaign against Harry Lumley, now with Toronto.

On March 11, Terry and the Wings went into New York to face the Rangers and their sensational rookie goaltender Lorne (Gump) Worsley.

Born in the working-class northern Montreal neighbourhood of Point St. Charles, Worsley acquired his nickname when a childhood friend began comparing him to the cartoon character Andy Gump because of his flat-top brush cut. Gump had not played goal until his last year of Juvenile, at age eighteen, and he had to borrow equipment for his tryout for the New York Rangers' Junior team in Verdun. At five feet, seven inches tall, the rotund goalie did whatever he had to do to stop the puck and his unorthodox acrobatics were both comical and effective.

Terry recorded his eighth shutout in a 2–0 win over the Rangers, and, four days later, Terry got his ninth shutout of the season as he and his old nemesis, Chicago's Al Rollins, played to a scoreless draw. Heading into the final weekend of the campaign, the Wings had easily locked up first place, and Terry had easily captured the Vezina Trophy, his second in a row. The Wings turned their attention towards helping Gordie Howe, who had forty-nine goals with two games to play, to tie or surpass the fifty-goal record held by Montreal's Rocket Richard.

Howe's run at the record was indicative of the fierce rivalries the six-team NHL conjured up, particularly in its three most successful cities, Detroit, Toronto, and Montreal. A pair of milestones had already thrust each of the number nines into the spotlight: Richard became the all-time leading scorer on November 8, 1952, with his 325th career goal, while Howe notched his 200th goal in February 1953. Now it seemed two vocal, polarized camps had sprung up around the right wings. Richard's detractors pointed out that Richard, the purest goal scorer alive, had never won a scoring title. Howe was more of a playmaker, they said, who in 1953 would win his third scoring title in a row. But Richard only needed fifty games to pot fifty goals in 1944–45, the other side said. Howe had twenty extra games. Sure, the Howe forces countered, but the Rocket played against watered-down competition during World War II.

In the sixty-ninth regular-season game, Gordie played extra shifts and was constantly fed the puck by his teammates, but Sid Abel's Black Hawks shut him down. Next, in an ending worthy of a Hollywood screenplay, Richard and his Canadiens came into the Olympia for the season's final game. Again Howe double-shifted all night but little Gerry McNeil stopped all five Howe shots. Gordie was hindered by the tenacious checking of Habs left wing Bert Olmstead. In fact, Olmstead took coach Irvin's directive to "go where Howe goes" to dizzying heights, even following Howe to on-ice conferences during play stoppages.

"He'd go back to talk to Sawchuk," Olmstead would recount, "so I'd go back with him and there'd be the three of us standing there. They would yell at me, 'What are you doing back here?' I wouldn't talk to them. I knew I was getting their goat."

The 2–1 Canadiens victory and the Howe whitewash was tough on the Red Wings and the Olympia crowd. When the game ended, Irvin rubbed it in by raising the Rocket's arm, the way a boxing referee would signal the winning fighter.

Despite his early-season slump, Terry finished with a goals-against average of 1.90, the same as the previous season, and the third straight year that it was under 2.00. Sawchuk also overcame the layoff his injury caused by leading the league in victories with thirty-two.

As the Wings prepared to meet Boston in the playoffs, all observers expected a mismatch. The Wings had ten wins in fourteen meetings with the Bruins — most of them lopsided. And the first game of the semifinal series was no exception as Terry and company shelled the Bruins, 7–0, before a delirious Olympia crowd.

The second game again saw the Wings attacking aggressively but Bruin goalie Sugar Jim Henry was up to the task. Terry, on the other hand, seemed unnerved and tired and, when Fleming Mackell beat him about eight minutes into the first period, it brought to a close a stretch of 229 minutes of shutout hockey — the equivalent of nearly four full games. The Mackell goal lifted the Bruins to a 5–3 win as Sugar Jim stopped forty-five of forty-eight shots.

"The second game of any series is always the key," Marcel Pronovost points out, "because a loss means you lose home-ice advantage, and the series then becomes a three out of five. If you lose that second game at home, you're in trouble!"

Game Three of the series was played in a sold-out Boston Garden, and it saw the Red Wings again on the attack early. But Bruins winger Ed Sandford was the first to score. The Wings fought back on a second-period goal by little Tony Leswick, then Sawchuk and Henry closed the gates the rest of the way, forcing overtime.

The Wings pummelled the Bruin goalie with fifteen shots in the first eleven minutes of OT, but to no avail. Then, at the thirteen-minute mark, Boston's Jack McIntyre launched a knuckler from his backhand that seemed to mesmerize Terry as it hit him in the back and dropped into the net for a 2–1 Boston upset. The crowd's reaction clearly unnerved Terry as he left the ice.

"We all felt bad for Terry," Johnny Wilson says. "He was in a rut like we all were. We tried to help him to forget. We said, 'Come on, Uke, we'll get 'em next game,' but we all felt like shit."

Ted Lindsay clearly does not blame Sawchuk for the loss. "Sure, Terry should have stopped McIntyre's goal, but we shouldn't have even been in overtime, and even then we should have scored way before Jack had that shot on Terry. But it was typical of the way that series was going!"

In the fourth game at the Boston Garden, Terry was clearly fighting the puck, a feeling that he had never before experienced in the playoffs. Soft goals were getting by him, and he seemed unable to cope. Marcel Pronovost says that Terry's strength had always been coming up with the big save when the Wings needed it most, a faculty that seemed to have deserted him in the Boston series.

Compounding the Wings' problems, their offensive star, Gordie

Howe, was exhausted and struggling against the checking thrown at him by Bruin Woody Dumart.

"Woody Dumart checked Howe well," Johnny Wilson recalls. "Gordie kept running into him. And when Gordie did get his chances, he'd miss the net or the puck would bounce the wrong way."

Sugar Jim Henry turned in another virtuoso performance in Game Four and, although outshot, coach Lynn Patrick's Bruins emerged with a 6–2 win.

Prior to Game Five in Detroit, it was clear to all concerned that Terry was not himself. Jack Adams considered putting in a call to Glenn Hall on the Edmonton farm team, but decided instead to keep a close eye on his young goalie.

"Only Lefty [Wilson] and Jack knew it, but Terry was not well for a couple of those games against Boston," broadcaster Bud Lynch reveals. "He wasn't feeling good and he was hurt, but nobody knew except the three of them. And all three thought that Uke would bounce out of it anytime and have a good game."

In the fifth game, the Wings staved off elimination with a 6–4 win. Howe even got a goal on a breakaway to reassert himself. Still, Boston mounted a charge late in the game and they were the more confident team as the series returned to the Boston Garden.

Game Six opened with a pair of Bruin goals in the first period. Reg Sinclair pulled the Wings back to within one midway through the hockey game, before Fleming Mackell broke down the left wing and let go a rising fifty-footer.

"You could have almost read the goddamned label on the puck, that's how slow it was going," Ted Lindsay recalls. "Sawchuk practically just watched the damn thing float by him on the long side into the outside corner of the net."

The Sawchuk muff fired up Lindsay, who banged a six-footer past Sugar Jim to make the score closer at 3–2 Bruins. But four minutes later, Leo Labine again put the Bostonians up by two.

Fighting to stave off elimination, coach Tommy Ivan pulled Sawchuk with a minute and a half left in regulation time and the Wings went on the attack, throwing the puck around in a frantic attempt to score. Many of the Bruins, who would not even get close to the thrill of winning Lord Stanley's Cup, said that eliminating the powerful Wings came close.

"My biggest thrill in hockey," the Bruins' Ed Sandford would say later, "was upsetting Detroit in the 1953 series. We weren't supposed to have a chance. But we used the 'shadows,' Woody Dumart on Howe and Joe Klukay on Lindsay, and we beat them in six games."

As the Wings retreated disconsolately to their dressing room in the euphoric Garden, all were feeling badly for Terry, whom they knew would take the series loss personally.

"I just missed it, that's all," a dejected Terry said of Mackell's fluke goal. "I thought I had it but it dipped."

"Who's to blame? Not Terry!" adds Ted Lindsay today. "Who the hell looked for blame? None of us looked for blame on anyone! It wasn't his fault, I shoulda scored more goals than I did. It was just one of those things!"

Marcel Pronovost remembers Detroit's two superstars taking the loss personally. "Terry really took that Boston loss on himself. Very much so, and so did Howe. They both sat in the dressing room a long time afterwards. But it was really unfair to both of them really, to take the blame."

Radio announcer Bud Lynch's memory of that night is as clear as a bell. "After that last game, we all went over to Jack Sharky's Bar across the street. We knew Jack Sharky and he put us at the back and gave us free beer and I passed out cigars. We stayed there until one o'clock in the morning to unwind.

"Suddenly Fred Huber, the Wings publicist, shows up to tell us that Marguerite Norris is throwing us a champagne party back at the hotel. We sure hustled our buns over there. She had ordered these very beautiful trays of food, and there was tons of booze, and she thanked each player individually, which was a nice gesture. She made the players feel good to know that the ownership and management was still behind them and appreciated their effort in a very tough hour for them. It was a very late night!"

The next morning, the team woke up to walk the three blocks to the train station. In a moment of comic relief, the Wings put

Tony Leswick, five feet, five inches, into the overcoat of Red Wing photographer Roy Bash, who stood six foot five. "All you could see was this overcoat going down the street," Bud Lynch recalls. "It was so funny, God we laughed."

For the Bruins, Sugar Jim's magic would evaporate in the finals against the Canadiens, who easily defeated Boston in five games to capture the Stanley Cup.

The spring of 1953 was a restless time for Terry. After a quick trip to Toronto to hide out for a week, Terry returned to Detroit to submit to yet another medical exam at the insistence of Jack Adams. Terry did not feel right throughout the Boston series and Adams wanted answers, particularly about Terry's stunning weight loss. The only thing discovered during the extensive testing was that Sawchuk had a low blood count.

The last new business for the NHL in 1952–53 was the announcement of the League's All-Star teams on April 24. Four Wings made the First Team: Terry Sawchuk, defenceman Red Kelly, right winger Gordie Howe, and left winger Ted Lindsay. Centre Alex Delvecchio made the Second Team.

Despite these accolades, Trader Jack Adams had stood pat and been rewarded with a premature exit from the playoffs. With Terry's health a mystery, and Glenn Hall knocking on the door, it was anyone's guess who'd start the 1953–54 season in the Detroit net.

6

WEDDING BELLS

A
S usual, summer meant the annual trek back home to
Winnipeg. First, though, his friend Art Kras suggested
they get in a golf game at his uncle's course. It would
turn out to be the most fateful golf date of his young life.

Josephine and Ed Morey owned and ran a twenty-seven-hole
golf course, clubhouse, restaurant, and riding stable on the shores
of Union Lake, near the Detroit suburb of Pontiac, Michigan.
The place was thriving, and patrons included state senators,
politicians, millionaires, and businessmen. Here the Moreys'
eighteen-year-old adopted daughter, Patricia, filled her
Saturdays and Sundays during the school year.

Patricia was a small, cute, shapely brunette who worked
faithfully, and at times frantically, as the receptionist at the golf
course. She darted to and fro, working the cash register — which
rang in all the receipts including those from the riding stable —
welcomed guests, worked in the pro shop, directed customers,
and helped the waitresses clear tables in the restaurant.

Patricia Bowman — the name given to her at birth — remembered her birth mother as a very loving woman who had to
fend for herself and her four children while her husband was
away the majority of the time sailing on the "Crescent City"
out of Detroit.

Patricia recalled that on rare occasions when her father was home he drank his earnings away. "He made a lot of money on the boats but we never saw it. He was an alcoholic. My mother used to have to take in laundry and the neighbours would come through the back door bringing us food. We ate muskrat, and rabbit."

One night, when Pat was nine years old, her mother had gone into labour with her fifth child. Complications arose and she began to hemorrhage. For some unknown reason Pat's father and maternal grandmother hesitated to bring her to a hospital. Pat still speaks angrily and bitterly about the moment.

"He just let her die. There is this woman lying in bed saying, 'My feet are getting cold.' I can't imagine what kind of a mother [Pat's grandmother] was. My mother should have been put in a hospital."

Before an ambulance and doctor arrived, the children were allowed in to see their mother. In horror the children watched as she was transferred onto a stretcher placed partly through the doorway to the bedroom. The sheets were soaked with blood. She was prepared for a blood transfusion, but before this could be done, Pat's mother died.

After their mother's death, the children were split up. Pat was taken in by one of her mother's friends, Helen Kosty, whose husband was also a sailor. Only a few months later, Mrs. Kosty literally dumped Pat on the steps of the detention home in Detroit.

Pat was terrified at the sights and sounds she witnessed. Placed in a cell with two others, she was so afraid that she could not stop crying and screaming.

During her traumatic three-day stay, however, Pat would experience the first semblance of human compassion since her mother's passing.

"There was this nice lady who never put a uniform on me. She said, 'Honey, you don't belong here at all.' I remember her going through a whole batch of clothes and finding a dress to put on me."

On the third day a female social worker, Adele Ayres, came to pick up Pat. She was then transferred to a Catholic orphanage in Detroit called the Guardian Angel Home, where she stayed until Ayres could place her with an interested couple, Ed and Josephine Morey. On the fourth day of a trial period in the Morey household, Pat found herself in the kitchen drying dishes with Josephine.

"I dropped a dish and I just froze," Pat recalled. "She just looked at me and said, 'What's wrong?' I was just shaking, saying, 'I'm so sorry! I'm so sorry!' She smiled and said, 'Oh, you broke a dish, wow! Let's break another one!' And she took another dish and dropped it. It was her way of saying, 'It's okay!'"

Ed Morey noted that the young girl was quiet and seemed to have a shell around her. In spite of that, they grew quite close and the adoption ran its course. She became officially known as Pat Morey. Pat could, at times, prove to be a handful. She often butted heads with her mother, but in time, trust and compassion broke down the walls. She went on to have a warm, loving relationship and teen upbringing with both parents. Her life soon revolved around school and the Morey business, especially the riding stable. Before long, she became an accomplished rider, participating in rodeos and parades and acting as a "horse trailer" for her father.

"Dad would buy these horses from all over the area but he didn't have a horse trailer, so I was it! I would travel the twelve miles or so on horseback to pick up one, sometimes two horses, and I'd lead them back. I loved it!"

In her teen years, Pat worked at the golf course without complaint and, although memories of her past never seemed far from her mind, she was truly happy to have found a loving home.

On this day in May 1953, Terry Sawchuk, the quiet, reserved star goaltender for the Detroit Red Wings saw in Patricia Morey an interesting, talented, flirtatious young woman. He spent the next three hours at the counter trying not only to have a conversation with her but also to flirt with her in return. He couldn't believe she knew nothing about him, the Red Wings, or hockey. He wanted to know everything about her: her past, the adoption story, the horses, and whether she had a boyfriend.

"I told him I had 'many,' and that I just started dating, not quite two years yet, and I was having a great time. My first meeting with Terry was a little chaotic. Even though I was very busy, he stayed nearby."

"Terry was so taken with Pat," states Art Kras today, "that he never did come out to golf with us. He spent the whole time with her in the clubhouse."

If Terry was smitten that day, Pat wasn't aware of it. And as far as she was concerned, while he certainly seemed nice, good-looking, and down-to-earth, the six-year age difference was too great for her to consider dating him.

After that, Terry made several unsuccessful calls to the club-house to talk to her. Each time, she was either out on a date or running errands for her parents. "That Terry Sawchuk guy called again," Pat's father would say. Each time, Pat would shrug her shoulders, not think much of it, and carry on with her life. Finally, his persistence paid off as he got her on the phone to ask her for a date. Feeling somewhat unsure, Pat invited him out to the lake on her next day off.

"He was a perfect gentleman," she said. "We got along great. We ate, went swimming, visited with my parents, laughed, and had fun. He never talked about his hockey team, his athletic abilities as a goalie, or that he was in fact a celebrity." Even if he had brought up such matters, it's doubtful Pat would have been starry-eyed, as she met many members of Detroit's elite at the golf course.

Terry and Pat saw each other a couple more times before he headed back home to Winnipeg for the summer. If Terry har-boured any real serious feelings for her before leaving, Pat was not aware of them. At this stage in her young life, she was intent on finishing high school and having fun with her friends.

After his arrival in Winnipeg, Terry proceeded to call Pat every day, telling her how much he cared for her and how much he missed her. His calls became more serious and more intense, but Pat remained unsure of her feelings until Terry called from St. Boniface Hospital in Winnipeg on June 1.

He told Pat that he had tried to golf that morning, but returned to his parents' home and later checked into hospital complaining of mild nausea and a stomachache. His family physician, Dr. Joseph Lander, diagnosed a badly inflamed

GRAPHIC

DETROIT FREE PRESS
March 16, 1952

HOW SAWCHUK STOPS 'EM

BY MARSHALL DANN

The Short Ones . . . and the Long Ones

Terry was a cover story at only
22 years of age. The phenom was already labelled
"the greatest goalie in the history of big-league hockey."
– Bert Emanuel, *Detroit Free Press*

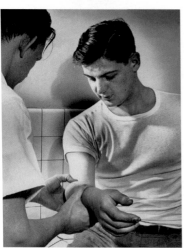

1. Pat Morey, at 16 years old. The future Mrs. Terry Sawchuk had no idea of how her husband would treat her. — Courtesy Sawchuk family

2. In his first year away from home, Terry (front) carried the 1946–47 Galt Junior Red Wings. Fred Glover (left) and Metro Prystai (behind) would later join Terry in Detroit. — Hockey Hall of Fame

3. Terry's deformed right elbow acted up severely during the 1950 AHL playoffs and would bother him throughout his career. — Robert Lavelle/Indianapolis News

4. Terry loved the anonymity of drinking in waterholes such as the Hamtramic Club, and spent most of his spare time in them. — Courtesy Sawchuk family

5. Terry poses for Pat before heading onto the ice in 1953. Going by on his left is Gordie Howe, and behind Howe is Red Kelly. — Courtesy Sawchuk family

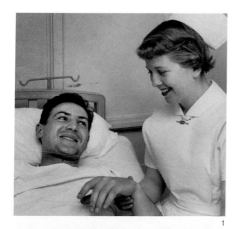

1. This picture, of Terry and a nurse, made Pat Morey jealous. — Courtesy Sawchuk family

2. A rare photo of Terry and his father together, taken on Terry's wedding day in 1953. — Courtesy Sawchuk family

3. Terry never hesitated to accept a challenge from a heckler. In this game at the Olympia in 1954, Glen Skov (#12) and Terry (#1) scramble over the chain-link fence at the top of the boards. Ted Lindsay is already in the crowd. — AP Wireservice

4. Mr. and Mrs. Terry Sawchuk. — Courtesy Sawchuk family

2

3

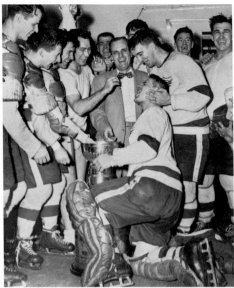

1. Terry sitting out a two-minute penalty during the Marquette Prison game on February 2, 1954. During the penalty, Terry took time to sign autographs.
— Courtesy Sawchuk family

2. Terry at the centre of the victory celebrations in the Wings' dressing room following the 1954 Cup final, won by the Red Wings on Tony Leswick's overtime goal.
— David Bier

3. Legends Rocket Richard and Terry Sawchuk eye the puck.   — David Bier

1. Terry and his son Jerry in the fall of 1955. This is one of the few pictures that show Terry without his teeth.
— Courtesy Sawchuk family

2. Clowning around with two-year-old Jerry in August 1956.
— Courtesy Sawchuk family

3. Carol (front left), JoAnne (back left), Terry, and Pat Sawchuk.
— Courtesy Sawchuk family

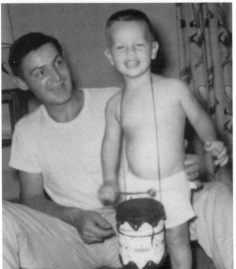

1. The home that Terry and Pat built on Golfside Drive in Union Lake, Michigan, just north of Detroit, as it looked in the early 1960s. Terry had trouble getting a mortgage for this house — he always paid cash and didn't have a credit rating.
— Courtesy Sawchuk family

2. Terry announcing his retirement from the Bruins and hockey on January 21, 1957, in Detroit's Statler Hotel. He returned to hockey the following season. — *Detroit Free Press*

3. Terry enjoying a happy moment at the Oil Can Derby with "Doc" Greene in the early 1960s.
— Lombardo/*Detroit News*

1. Sprawling
in action against
the Canadiens.
— David Bier

2. Terry (upper left)
on the deep sea
fishing trip to Florida
in 1962. He suffered
from seasickness
throughout the
excursion. With Terry
are (clockwise)
Gordie Howe, Marcel
Pronovost, Sid Abel,
and Bill Gadsby
(bottom left).
— Courtesy Bill Gadsby

1

Red Wing Version
of 'Terry and the Pirates'

Terry and the Pirates.
– The Detroit News

appendix and, though it hadn't burst, he recommended its removal. Dr. Lander performed the operation the same afternoon. Pat joked that Terry really didn't have to go to such lengths to make her notice him. The ensuing laughter caused him to hold his side, grimacing with pain.

Pat's feelings for Terry remained in check for a few more days, until he mailed her a newspaper clipping that featured a picture of a pretty nurse taking his pulse. Pat later admitted to a wave of jealousy brought on by the photograph.

Suddenly Terry was back in Michigan, asking Pat on bended knee to marry him. She remembered feeling weak in the knees.

"I've never admitted this, even to myself, but even though I wanted to say no, I said yes. I said yes to this man I hardly knew. I did love him, as only a young girl of eighteen falls in love for the very first time. At that age who really knows the real meaning of love, marriage, and all that life brings with it?"

From there, the nervous young man approached his future father-in-law to ask for Pat's hand in marriage. Ed Morey looked at him with a smile, then boomed, "Yes! Now I can have my bathroom back!" They exchanged handshakes, much to the relief of one young man from Winnipeg.

A wedding date was set for early August. Ed and Josephine Morey were elated that their daughter was marrying someone who could give her a good, secure life even though there hadn't been time for any real courtship.

The wedding plans were on the fast track because NHL clubs forbade midseason nuptials — Leaf boss Conn Smythe had banished at least one player to the minors for running afoul of the unspoken policy.

Invitations were mailed out for what would be one of the most important social events of the year. Showers, presents, and money were given and Pat shopped for a bridal gown. Terry was not forgotten by his friends, who threw him the typical bachelor party.

On the bright, sunny morning of Saturday, August 6, 1953, Pat woke up very early. She'd had to sleep on the floor alongside Terry's visiting parents, his brother, Gerald, and sister, Judy, in order to leave the two bedrooms upstairs free for guests. Pat rushed to take a shower and have the bathroom to herself for a while.

Terry Sawchuk was almost beside himself with nerves. Compared to this, staring down Rocket Richard on a break-away was a breeze. Standing outside St. Patrick's Roman Catholic Church in Union Lake Village, with his Winnipeg pal and best man, Reginald Pearson, at his side, he was visibly tense as *Detroit News* reporter, and father of the maid of honour, Sam Lerner, approached him with a camera.

"May I take your picture, Terry?" Lerner asked.

"Oh, yes. I'm used to that," Terry answered. He had a hard time smiling and he fidgeted.

"Take it easy," Lerner said. "Nobody's going to boo you today."

"Say, that's right!" Terry said, finally smiling. "I forgot, this is a hometown crowd!"

The church was filled to overflowing with an estimated 600 guests on hand, including some of the Red Wings. Almost all was set except for one problem: Terry's parents hadn't arrived yet. Everyone began to fidget as time elapsed. Finally, they arrived. They had gotten lost on the way to the church. Everyone breathed a sigh of relief. Pat felt sorry for them as they were escorted to their pew, at the front of the church, with everyone staring at them.

Three priests participated in the ceremony, including Terry's good friend, Father John Gordon.

During the exchange of vows, the solemn music, and the very long mass, the groom continued to be nervous, serious, and soft-spoken. The bride's voice was clear and calm, though she avoided looking at Terry for fear she'd cry, something all weddings made her do. Except for the delay, everything went off without a hitch.

The reception for Mr. and Mrs. Terrance Gordon Sawchuk was held at the Moreys' golf course. Large tents were set up for dining amidst the impeccably maintained surroundings. A large dance floor had been constructed and the revellers were led by none other than some of the Red Wing players.

At the reception, Wings' broadcaster Bud Lynch recorded

the guests' best wishes to the newly married couple. "I arrived at big Jimmy Peters, who had definitely been into the punch bowl a bit too much, and I asked him to say a few words. He was reluctant. Finally he looked at the microphone, concentrated hard, and said, 'Pat . . . and Terry . . . I'd . . . like to wish . . . you . . . both all the world in the happiness!' I just about died laughing."

Terry hadn't given any thought to the honeymoon, planning merely to go to the Wisconsin Dells.

"Well, we pulled into a couple of driveways, and that's about all I saw of the Wisconsin Dells," Pat remembered. "He hadn't made any reservations. This was the summertime and everything was full! We continued on to Sault Ste. Marie, and he showed me the Canadian side and the falls — it was beautiful. And then we just drove up to Winnipeg."

As they drove, Pat found that Terry got moody. Though he went out of his way to show Pat all the sights as they drove to his hometown, there were many long, uncomfortable stretches, sometimes lasting more than an hour, when her new husband didn't say a word. They stopped overnight for only one night on the road, and made the trip from Detroit to Winnipeg in two and a half days. Pat found it very uncomfortable and tiring.

Unlike their short courtship, when they were getting to know each other and always found something to talk about, they seemed all talked out. Pat was already becoming afraid and insecure.

Upon their arrival in Winnipeg, Terry relaxed visibly, but his eighteen-year-old bride found herself in a foreign country, more than a thousand miles from home, thrust into a strange household, with very few clothes in her wardrobe, and forced to spend much of the time without her husband. For the three to four weeks they spent at the Sawchuk homestead, Terry would usually be out of the house by noon, visiting friends, leaving Pat feeling very much out of place.

Thrust headlong into a cool, aloof household with strangers, Pat was reminded of her early childhood. Still, she tried to make the best of it, helping with household chores. Her efforts at ironing brought chuckles from her new in-laws, making the young bride feel even more insecure. She would often go for walks or spend hours at a local coffee shop to help pass the time.

Yet it wasn't all dreary. Terry did pay her some attention. "When we first got there, we went to a couple of parties around town. I met his friends. Reggie Pearson, Terry's best man, was fine and always made me laugh. The song 'You, You, You' was popular then, and every time he saw me he would get up and dance and go, 'You, you, you.'"

The couple went out to dinner a few times and Terry took Pat to a couple of local baseball games, where he taught her the art of eating pumpkin seeds and spitting out the shells. Another Canadian custom to which Terry introduced her was eating her French fries with malt vinegar on them. She was also astonished the first time she saw fish and chips served wrapped in newspaper. Terry took his young bride to the gravel pits to swim and to Lake Winnipeg.

During their honeymoon, Pat met all of Terry's relatives.

"I loved his aunts and uncles, and his cousin, Jacqueline. She was younger but quite mature for her age. We'd go to games together and we just liked each other. His Aunts Jessie and Lena were a lot of fun."

Pat also got her first insight into the Sawchuk family dynamics. "The family didn't treat their dad with much respect and I wasn't used to that. His dad worked — all that man did was work, and he was a hard worker. He didn't expect much from life and he didn't get it, either. As long as he could pay the bills and have his mashed potatoes, he didn't ask much else out of life.

"I remember," Pat continues, "one time at dinner, when someone got on his case about having a drink in the basement when he got home from work, yelling at him in front of me. Dad was so embarrassed, and I felt so bad for him. I left the table and went upstairs. They treated Terry like a king because he sent money home, but they didn't recognize Dad's contribution."

Nowhere in the Sawchuk household did Pat witness any outward displays of affection. It was a trait that would mar Terry's relationships throughout his life.

The start of training camp drew Pat and Terry back to Detroit. Again Terry drove straight through, stopping only for a rest break or food.

The couple's new home was an apartment complex on Grand River Avenue, directly across from the Olympia.

The location and the price, $125 a month, for the three-room furnished apartments, were ideal for some of the newly married Red Wing players. Pat, however, found the lodgings to be lacking.

"So I get into this place, this breadbox apartment — it was an absolute pit. It was filthy. It was downtown Detroit, exhaust-fume filthy. Grease on the blinds! I had to take them down and soak them in the bathtub. It had an old Murphy Bed with a mattress from hell, this ugly green carpet. The kitchen was like a hallway with cupboards. The sitting room, bedroom, and dining room were kind of like one room before you get to the kitchen and bathroom! And there was no room for a dresser even!

"Terry dumped me in this gloomy, depressing place, and then left. 'Here it is, babe! See ya!' I was all by myself, didn't know anybody, not even the other players' wives, no idea of what hockey was all about. I was petrified!"

Seemingly oblivious to his young wife's insecurities and objections, Terry trekked north to Sault Ste. Marie, Michigan, to begin the 1953–54 training camp.

For the three weeks or so that Terry was at camp, Pat kept busy — cleaning, painting, and repainting — as much to maintain her sanity as to make the place livable. In time she met and became close to the wives of some of the other Wings.

"Cindy Pronovost, Marcel's wife, and Pat Wilson, Johnny's wife, came over and they were sweethearts. Pat Wilson could see what I was wrestling with. She would often take Cindy and me over to her parents' place in Windsor. They helped me adjust a lot!"

No sooner did Terry return from training camp than he dropped another bombshell: he'd invited teammate Benny Woit over for a spaghetti supper the next evening.

Pat panicked. "Why did you do that? You know I just started

cooking! I don't know squat!" Pat responded. She was also aware that Benny's wife was Italian and an excellent cook. Pat's nerves were calmed only slightly by the fact that Mrs. Woit hadn't yet returned to Detroit for the season, so she wouldn't be attending the dinner.

The next day, in her minuscule kitchen, Pat opened her cookbook, *Cooking for Two*. Discovering a natural ability, she prepared the sauce and was ready for Woit's arrival. She served the two hockey players a nice salad and warm rolls. All went well, and Terry was obviously proud of his wife, until she served some spaghetti noodles onto Benny's plate. A sticky, starchy white glob plopped onto his plate.

"It was so incredibly embarrassing, that spaghetti clump!" she recalls. "I rushed back into the kitchen, cooked more noodles using more water this time and stirring it just right. They ate, let me tell you. Even if they lied about the taste, they ate!"

In their cramped quarters, Pat had to adjust to Terry's quirks. His habit the day of a game was to have his steak, salad, and Jell-O before noon and then to sleep until late afternoon. Pat found it a challenge to stay quiet in the same room where her husband slept. Her second challenge was to become acquainted with the game of hockey. It would prove to be easier said than done.

7

ANOTHER CHAMPIONSHIP SEASON

A S the Red Wings' 1953 training camp opened, Jack Adams stunned the hockey world by announcing that the team's goaltending job was up for grabs and could honestly go to either Sawchuk or Glenn Hall, of the Edmonton Flyers, a Detroit farm club. It was virtually unprecedented for Adams to declare disappointment or dissatisfaction with his star goaltender, knowing well how easily Terry's confidence was shaken.

Still, there was no doubt that Adams had been bitterly disappointed by the team's performance in general against Boston the previous spring — and by Terry's play in particular. The pressure made Terry deliver a strong effort in this camp, causing Adams to remark, "If Sawchuk continues like this, of course he'll be our goalie. But I wouldn't hesitate to send Sawchuk to a farm team if Hall does better than him!"

Today, Hall discounts the idea that Terry's job was in jeopardy. "There was never any question in my mind that Sawchuk was the number-one goalie. He was just too good. Mr. Adams might have been sounding off, but there was nothing to it. He also might have wanted Terry to feel insecure before negotiating his contract. But there was nothing more to it than that."

Hall's respect for Terry is exemplified by the fact that he made the Sawchuk Crouch part of his own goaltending style, which would one day be as distinct and influential as Sawchuk's.

If Jack Adams doubted Sawchuk's ability at the beginning of camp, his confidence was certainly renewed by the end.

At the end of training camp, Adams would stage a "show-down" competition. Through a process of elimination, the skaters all tried to score on Terry. The last surviving skater would then try to beat Terry on two of three or three of five penalty shots. The winner would get $25 to $50.

"Nine times out of ten," says Johnny Wilson, "Terry won. He was unbeatable on breakaways. Hell, he was always unbeatable!"

On October 3, 1953, Terry went to Montreal to participate in his fourth straight All-Star game. The All-Stars defeated the Stanley Cup champion Canadiens, 3–1, on two goals by the Rangers' Wally Hergesheimer, and an empty-net goal by Terry's teammate, Alex Delvecchio. Rocket Richard spoiled the All-Stars' shutout bid in the third period.

As the regular season began, Terry felt better than he had in a long while. Marriage seemed to have given him some peace of mind and, with the appendix trouble behind him, his appetite returned and his weight began to slowly inch its way back up.

Terry's renewed health, confidence, appetite, and perform-ance in preseason games led coach Tommy Ivan to predict, "That boy should have his greatest season this year."

The Wings — going with essentially the same lineup as the year before, as Adams again elected to stand pat — jumped out of the gate decisively. By October 25, Terry had allowed just two goals in five home victories, though there were a couple of speed bumps on Sawchuk's comeback trail.

On Thanksgiving Day, a suddenly depressed Sawchuk informed Jack Adams that he was not up to facing the Rangers that night in New York. Terry missed three games, officially because of an "injured" knee. His replacement, Dave Gatheram, allowed only three goals in the three games to keep Sawchuk in the Vezina hunt.

On December 3, after recording his fifth shutout of the season and running his home scoreless streak to 211 minutes and 24 seconds in a whitewash of the Rangers, he expressed wonder at his season this far.

"It's the finest start I've ever had, but I'll be darned if I know why. Maybe it's my weight. I weigh 177 now compared to 165 last season. I couldn't even work up a sweat last season."

In the Ranger nets that night was Johnny Bower, the third of five great goalies to debut and play for a full season in the NHL during the 1950s.

A veteran of eight seasons with the Cleveland Barons of the American league, the "China Wall," as he was nicknamed, was called up suddenly by the Rangers after general manager Frank Boucher mysteriously sent last year's goalie and Calder Trophy winner, Gump Worsley, to the minors in Vancouver.

Born in Prince Albert, Saskatchewan, in 1924, Bower had been in the Canadian army during World War II and, upon his discharge in 1944, played a year in Junior. The next year he caught on with the Barons, where he had been ever since.

In this, his first full NHL season, he would play all seventy games for a weak, inexperienced New York team that would place fifth and win only twenty-nine games. Bower would record five shutouts and post a 2.60 goals-against average. In a twist as bizarre as the one that brought him to the NHL, Bower would spend 1954–55 back in the bushes, displaced in New York by the return of Worsley. The Leafs would make him a big-leaguer for good in 1958.

Pat Sawchuk got a rude awakening when she began attending games at the Olympia and she saw firsthand what her husband did for a living.

"It was nerve-wracking! I wasn't used to any of that stuff. The other wives worried about their husbands being hurt, too, but their husbands weren't as likely to get hurt so severely. My husband wore no mask and pucks were flying at him like crazy, and sticks would be swinging. And he always came home with cuts and bruises. It was awful to watch."

Pat also quickly realized that being a Red Wing meant everything to Terry.

"The Detroit Red Wings were his family. Jack Adams was like

his father. The guys and everything were all close. When he was on that ice, he would have given his life [for the Red Wings]."

For a brief moment it appeared the goalie might do just that. Terry received an anonymous phone threat to either throw a game or lose his life. The scenario was frightening to say the least, and completely out of Pat's control. She watched helplessly as Terry informed management and then left with her for the game. In a typical show of defiance, her husband ignored the threat and put in a stellar performance.

"Terry was really peeved off," Pat said. "I don't know what precautions management took, but he went out and got a shutout that night! That's how he was!"

Though Terry had survived the scare, Pat could have been forgiven if she acted a bit jumpy whenever the phone rang on game days from then on.

Three days into 1954, Terry's battle for the Vezina with Toronto's Harry Lumley hit a new high as the Leafs and Red Wings played to a scoreless tie. Both goalies were sensational. Sawchuk, realizing it was going to be a dogfight for the coveted goals-against award, went on a tear of sorts, recording two more shutouts before the end of January.

As the month of February began, the Red Wings took part in a unique event that provided a nice break from the grind of the regular season.

After the 1952–53 season had finished, the Wings were involved in a promotional tour with Stroh's brewery. In late June, Jack Adams and Ted Lindsay found themselves in northern Michigan. Lindsay picks up the story: "Well, we end up at Marquette Prison – full of lifers and the remnants of the Purple Gang, which was the Jewish Mafia in the U.S. One thing leads to another and the next thing you know there's talk of the Wings going up to Marquette to play a game against a team of prisoners."

Upon their return to Detroit, the Wings scrounged up some old sweaters and equipment and sent them to the prison. A rink was constructed in the prison yard, and the team calling itself the Pirates was formed. They practised until they felt they had improved enough to take on the Wings, then sent word to Adams that they were ready.

At 12:40 p.m., on February 2, 1954, the Wings filed through the prison's steel doors. Lefty Wilson remembers it well.

"It was colder than a son of a bitch. It was so cold [trainer Carl Mattson] and I cut up a bunch of old hockey socks and taped the tops to make toques for everybody. But it was a great day."

The Wings won, 8–2, but highjinks certainly outnumbered serious play.

Terry spent most of the game perched on top of his net and, when the Pirates did come down to his end, he tripped one of the playing inmates and was sent off the ice, where he obligingly signed autographs while he served his "penalty."

Marcel Pronovost can't help but laugh when he remembers the game. "One of the inmates along the boards wanted to give me two bucks to body check one of the prison staff who was playing and who often used to send him into solitary confinement."

"We had lunch with the inmates and the prison team afterwards," Johnny Wilson says. "It was great being with them. They presented us with this trophy, like a bucket or something."

In fact, the inmates presented the Red Wings with a cup that had at one time been a refuse bucket, used in cells without sanitation facilities. Inscribed on the cup were the names of all the Red Wings, all the names of the inmates of the prison team, and the date of the game. Jack Adams good-naturedly hoisted it to cheers from inmates and spectators alike.

Back in the real world, Terry met his challenger in the Vezina race, Harry Lumley, head on. Going into 1953–54, Terry had only amassed three regular-season shutouts against the Leafs in his three-year career. In this, his fourth season, he shut out the Leafs and Lumley five times. This last shutout, the forty-fourth of his career, was another scoreless game, this time at Maple Leaf Gardens. He would also blank the Canadiens five nights later to amass seven shutouts since the start of the new year.

Heading into the final weekend of the '53–54 season, as both teams had two games to play, Lumley led Sawchuk by five goals.

The Red Wings visited the Montreal Forum for a Saturday-night game against the second-place Canadiens, without their top three defencemen, Kelly, Pronovost, and Goldham. All were suffering minor injuries and trying to rest for the approaching playoffs. The Wings were forced to put Gordie Howe on the blue line as Dick Irvin's boys pounded the Wings, 6–1.

More then 350 miles to the west, Harry Lumley's chances looked much better as the Leafs hosted the fifth-place Rangers. Having never won a Vezina in his ten-year career, Lumley hoped to avoid the debacle of 1948 when, as a Red Wing and tied with Turk Broda, he had nervously allowed ten goals in his last two games to hand the trophy to Broda on a silver platter.

Lumley's luck was no better than in 1948 this night, as the Rangers did Sawchuk a favour and humiliated the Leafs, 5–2. As chance would have it, the Leafs and Wings – Lumley and Sawchuk – would face each other in the season's last game, a Sunday-night tilt at the Olympia. Only Kelly was on the side-lines as the Wings tried to atone for letting him down so badly the night before. They would need to win by seven goals to get Terry his Vezina.

From the opening face-off, the Wings poured it on. Lumley soon realized he was in for quite a night as Gordie Howe ripped a shot that deflected off a skate past the startled Leaf goalie. Bill Dineen made it 2–0 Wings just four minutes later. Johnny Wilson made the Olympia crowd roar by knocking in a Dineen pass with his chest. But referee Red Storey called the goal back, maintaining that Johnny had directed it in with his arm. The Wings' bench was incensed.

Lumley seemed unnerved as the second period began, and little Tony Leswick didn't help his cause, banging a wobbly rebound into the Leaf cage to cut Lumley's Vezina lead to only three goals. There were still almost two full periods to go.

The Wings continued to drive for the Leaf net while, at the opposite end of the ice, the man for whom nearly everyone in the arena was pulling, was quite inactive. The Leafs converted very few rushes into scoring chances and Terry could only watch. Though his team led, Terry didn't like this type of game. It was very difficult for a goaltender to stay sharp, physically or mentally.

Lumley's fortunes improved when Leaf defenceman Jim

Thompson crossed centre ice towards the end of the second period. Terry felt uneasy as he saw the opponent lift a high floater into the air towards him. He was suddenly unsure about his timing and, with blue shirts rushing towards him, he opted to stay back in his net and play the bounce. Terry would make this same judgment on the same type of shot many times over the course of his career always with the same result. If Sawchuk had an Achilles heel, this was it.

The puck took a crazy bounce towards Terry's glove side. He reached to snare it, to no avail. The Leafs were ecstatic. Lumley breathed a sigh of relief in appreciation of the young defenceman who had scored only his second goal in almost four seasons. It set the stage for the third period, which began with Lumley up by four goals.

The Wings came out determined to throw everything they had at Lumley. Just two minutes into the period, fellow breadbox apartment–dweller Johnny Wilson scored. Exactly nine minutes later, Ted Lindsay potted another to put Terry just two goals back of Lumley. Not two minutes later, Howe fed Lindsay who made good to cut Lumley's lead to just a single goal. There were still seven minutes to go. Maybe, just maybe, Terry thought.

If Pat Sawchuk began the season not knowing a thing about hockey, she sure did now. Everyone around her was encouraging her, and she could barely watch when the play swarmed around Terry. Nor could she watch as the Wings swarmed Lumley.

With memories of 1948 fresh in his mind, Lumley bore down. He stopped one shot, then another, and another. The Leaf defence tightened up and their forwards backchecked like crazy.

With 1:04 left, Tommy Ivan made a move that was normally unheard of in a 6–1 game — he pulled Terry for a sixth attacker. The race for the Vezina was completely out of Sawchuk's hands. From the bench, Terry urged his teammates on.

The Wings could not penetrate the Leafs' defensive shell. The seconds wound down — three, two, one. The buzzer sounded as everyone in the Olympia let out a simultaneous, anguished groan.

The Leafs swarmed Lumley, who was ecstatic despite having

allowed eleven goals in two games. Despite having lost the game the Leafs were in a festive mood. As Terry bravely made his way towards Lumley, the Leaf skaters congratulated him on a fine effort. A couple more minutes, they conceded, and the Vezina could have been his.

"I guess the better man won," Terry said when he reached Lumley.

In the stands, Pat got consolation hugs from those around her. As she looked down at her dejected husband, she wiped the tears away from her cheeks.

"What a way to lose $1,000!" Terry lamented to the press, referring not only to Thompson's fluke goal but also to NHL President Clarence Campbell's edict that Lumley and Sawchuk both would have received the full bonus if they'd ended up tied. Terry had to be pleased with his 1.92 goals-against average, as he finished below 2.00 for the fourth straight year. His strong performance in the second half boosted him to the Second All-Star team, again behind Lumley.

The Leafs and Red Wings were paired off in the playoff semifinal. Conn Smythe's charges felt secure in the knowledge that they were no slouches, either. They had finished only ten points behind the Wings and three behind the Canadiens. Defenceman Tim Horton and centre Ted Kennedy had made the Second All-Star team.

But the Wings had placed Kelly, Howe, and Lindsay on the First All-Star team and had scored thirty-nine more goals for the season. "They have too many guns for us," Conn Smythe conceded after his Maple Leafs were shut out, 5–0, at the Olympia.

After Toronto took the second game, 3–1, and tying the series heading home, the Wings avenged Terry's Vezina loss with wins of 3–1, 2–1, and 4–3 in double overtime.

Ahead of Terry loomed the Montreal Canadiens, who had easily disposed of the Boston Bruins in four straight. Despite being hampered by injuries all season, the defending Stanley Cup champs had stayed close to the Wings in the standings.

Besides the Rocket, the Canadiens' offence, which had outscored Detroit 195–191, boasted Bernie (Boom Boom) Geoffrion and Bert Olmstead. The trio had placed second, fourth, and fifth in the league scoring race. Also on the team were the fiery Dickie Moore and a pair of rookies who would one day need no introduction, centre Jean Beliveau and goalie Jacques Plante.

"You could see the Canadiens getting stronger with each year," Johnny Wilson recalls, "and we knew we'd have our hands full. But hey, we weren't chopped liver. That '54 regular-season title was our sixth in a row!" The Wings felt the Stanley Cup was Detroit's to lose, not Montreal's to win.

Plante received the Montreal goaltending chores for Game One. Though he'd played just seventeen games during the regular season, the rookie had done so well that he wrestled the playoff assignment from veteran Gerry McNeil. It was a fact of life for NHL goalies that they had to watch their backs lest they get replaced.

Game One was nine minutes old before Terry faced his first shot. Doug Harvey fed Rocket Richard and Terry smothered the backhand drive with his belly pad. The Wings drew first blood as Ted Lindsay deflected a Dutch Reibel shot past a helpless Plante.

In the second period, with Glen Skov in the penalty box, Geoffrion took a pass in the crease from Doug Harvey and stuffed the backhander past the crouched Sawchuk on his stick side. Dutch Reibel regained the lead for Detroit in the third period, sailing a long shot from the right point that went over everyone's head, over a screened Plante's shoulder, into the Montreal net. With Marcel Pronovost in the penalty box, Red Kelly made a short-handed rush into the Montreal end in a classic give-and-go play with Marty Pavelich and backhanded the puck past a falling Jacques Plante for the insurance goal. Terry had an easy night in this 3–1 Detroit victory as the Wings limited the Canadiens' attack to just eighteen shots.

Game Two was a different affair as the Canadiens turned the key on their fire-wagon style of hockey. A first-period shoving match between Beliveau and Skov threatened to turn into a free-for-all and had referee Red Storey struggling to maintain order. Arenas in those days had only one penalty box and comical scenes such as the one that ensued, in which the combatants were separated by a burly, uniformed game attendant, were common.

Beliveau later threatened to open the scoring as he broke in on Sawchuk from the right, but his backhand drive went just wide on the far side.

Later in the first period Howe was penalized, and was joined seventeen seconds later by Leswick. Detroit would play the next minute and forty-three seconds two men short. The potency of the Montreal power play would eventually force a rule change, but at this time in NHL history, penalized players remained in the penalty box for the duration of their sentence no matter how many goals their opponents scored. What followed on this power play was a textbook case. Dickie Moore took a pass from Geoffrion, who cut to Sawchuk's left, crowding and screening him. Terry didn't even see Moore's shot go by him and he vehemently argued a Canadien had interfered, to no avail. Twenty-one seconds later, after Terry robbed Richard of a sure goal, the Rocket ended his 1954 playoff scoring drought with a blast to Terry's stick side. Thirty-one seconds on, Richard made a switch to his backhand in the slot and slipped another one by Terry to stoke the Canadiens lead to 3–0.

A second-period screen shot by Delvecchio brought the score to 3–1, where it remained for the rest of the game.

Game Three switched the series back to the Montreal Forum as Terry was at his best. Early saves on the Rocket, Eddie Mazur, and Tom Johnson enabled the Wings to take a 1–0 lead after Alex Delvecchio took one of Terry's rebounds up the full length of the ice and put the puck by Plante after a give-and-go play with Howe. Terry then made a brilliant save on the Rocket, who burst through the defence on the right side as Terry fell and held the loose rebound.

With three minutes to go in the first period, Red Kelly passed the puck to Ted Lindsay who, while he fell to the ice, slapped the puck high over Plante's glove for a 2–0 lead.

Plante was clearly struggling. Johnny Wilson put a fifty-foot wrist shot through Jacques' legs, and Metro Prystai later scored on a wraparound that left the future Hall of Famer flat-footed.

The Wings won the game, 5–2.

Game Four was a physical, defensive affair in which nerves still seemed to get the better of Plante. In the second period, with Richard in the penalty box, Johnny Wilson launched a long backhand from the top of the crease that the Montreal net-minder missed as it went through his legs. Detroit took the game, 2–0, putting the Wings one win away from the Cup.

Canadiens' coach Dick Irvin had seen enough of Plante and called upon veteran goalkeeper Gerry McNeil to start Game Five. McNeil was up to the task as he and Sawchuk battled for three scoreless periods. At 5:45 of overtime, Montreal centre Kenny Mosdell skated the length of the ice, spun himself around in front of Goldham, and fired a backhand that left Sawchuk guessing — wrongly. As the Canadiens celebrated, Terry was slow to get up, disbelief written all over his face.

Montreal's use of four forward lines to Detroit's three paid dividends in Game Five and again in Game Six, which the Canadiens won, 4–1. Terry seemed shaky and the Wing offence was listless.

Game Seven took place on April 16 at the Olympia. The Wings poured on the offence in the first period, outshooting the Habs, 12–5, forcing McNeil to make a number of great saves. At the other end of the ice, about halfway through the period, Sawchuk was screened and did not see all of Floyd Curry's point shot.

At 1:17 of the second, Red Kelly got the equalizer in the dying seconds of a Wing power play. His quick low shot to the goaltender's glove side found its way in. Detroit continued to check tightly, again allowing only five shots in the period. Terry robbed former Wing Gaye Stewart, coming out to cut down the angle and briefly losing the puck in his pads. At one point a frustrated Rocket Richard swatted the puck into the Detroit net with his glove.

The third period was scoreless. Sawchuk had to be partic-ularly sharp with a minute left to play, as Montreal got a breakaway. Terry came out to meet the attacker as the Olympia fans roared, but the shot went just wide, glancing the twine at the side of the net.

For only the second time in league history, the seventh

game of a Stanley Cup final would be decided in overtime. Coincidentally, the last time this had happened — in 1950 — it had been a Red Wing, Pete Babando, who had produced the heroics. In the stands, Pat Sawchuk had that same nerve-wracking feeling that she'd experienced the night Terry almost won the Vezina.

The Canadiens got the first chance to end it, as Terry was forced to make a great stop on Bert Olmstead. Then, four minutes in, Montreal defenceman Doug Harvey stood behind the Habs net, then threw the puck blindly around the boards towards the blue line. Near the Canadiens' blue line, Tony Leswick lobbed the puck into Hab territory so Detroit could change on the fly.

In a classic Stanley Cup moment, Harvey reached up to bat the puck down to the ice — a routine manoeuvre. But Harvey misjudged the innocent puck's trajectory and it ricocheted off the end of his finger, over McNeil's shoulder, into the net. McNeil stood frozen in disbelief as the Olympia crowd screamed and the Wings mobbed Leswick.

As they had done after Detroit's 1952 win, some of the Canadiens, including coach Dick Irvin, headed straight for the dressing room without congratulating the victors.

Tommy Ivan took off his fedora, wiped his brow, and shook his head in disbelief. NHL president Clarence Campbell walked onto the ice to present the Stanley Cup to Wings captain Ted Lindsay, who stood with an arm around Jack Adams. Lindsay and Marcel Pronovost leaned forward to softly kiss the Cup as two fans carried a large banner onto the ice that read "The New World Champions."

Terry watched the events from the fringes of the hysteria, smiling but calm, and no doubt relieved at the outcome. He could easily imagine himself in McNeil's skates. "Boy, were we lucky!" he mused.

8

THE DYNASTY ENDS

AFTER the 1954 playoffs, Pat and Terry moved out of their tiny apartment into a small log house Terry had bought during the season.

On July 11, Terry golfed with friend Earle Mudge and was driving home to Union Lake that evening on a gravel road when an oncoming car, trying to pass a slower vehicle, entered Terry's lane. Terry veered into the ditch to avoid the errant car, and ploughed into a nearby tree. Terry and his friend were rushed to hospital in Ann Arbor. Mudge suffered a fractured hip, and Terry was treated for cuts on his knees and hands and was hospitalized with a collapsed lung. The car was a write-off.

Terry, perhaps with a certain degree of justification, sighed out loud about his fifth off-season hospitalization in a row, however brief this time was going to be.

"I wish there were no summers," Terry lamented. "The only summer sunshine I ever seem to see is when I'm looking out of a hospital window."

At about the same time, coach Tommy Ivan became general manager of the league's perennial doormats, the Chicago Black Hawks. The move had been engineered between two branches of the Norris clan: James Norris, Jr., president of the Hawks, sought and received Ivan's release from his sister, Marguerite, president of the Wings.

Jack Adams's choice to replace Ivan was Jimmy Skinner, who had just completed a very successful season coaching the Wings' Junior team in Hamilton, Ontario, prior to which he'd enjoyed a five-year tenure with another Detroit-sponsored Junior team in Windsor.

"It took me two or three times to believe Jack when he said I was the next coach of the Red Wings," Skinner says today. "I took a plane down there the next day for a press conference. But I was green as the dickens. I didn't know what to think of it all."

On August 5, 1954, Terry was golfing on his father-in-law's course when Pat felt the first pangs of labour. As they loaded Pat into the back of the car, Terry's mother, who'd flown in from Winnipeg, remarked, "Oh, we have lots of time."

Pat remembers the forty-five minute ride to the hospital. "Terry drove all the the way to the hospital holding my hand and the contractions were getting stronger, and with each one I was squeezing the crap out of Terry's hand.

"Terry had this ring on and it had a big stone. When we finally got to the hospital I saw Terry's hand. I had squeezed Terry's ring right into his finger and there was blood all over his hand. But he never let on I was hurting him one bit during the whole trip."

Pat delivered a five-and-a-half-pound baby boy. When the news reached an anxious Terry, he picked his mother up and gleefully swung her around in the air. "It's a boy! It's a boy!" Anne Sawchuk had never seen her son so happy. The Sawchuks named their child Gerald Thomas, after Terry's younger brother.

The newborn was colicky and cried almost nonstop, proving to be a handful for his mother and grandmother. One day Anne went to check on him. Sitting back on a chaise lounge with her grandson draped over her lap, she rocked Jerry to sleep.

Suddenly, Terry burst into the room and went berserk, screaming, "What are you doing holding my son like that? What kind of woman holds a child like that?"

Anne Sawchuk was taken aback by his rudeness. She handed the awakened baby to Pat, turned to her son with a hurt expression as she left the room, and said, "Do you think that's the first baby I ever held or took care of? Are you an expert? How many have you held?" Anne went to her room, crying.

Anne Sawchuk packed her bags and left the next day. According to Pat, Terry and his mother didn't speak for quite some time after the incident.

Shortly after this explosion of anger, Terry moved back to the breadbox apartments near the Olympia before going to training camp. Pat and Jerry would join him later in the season as Terry inexplicably sold the little log house.

"We were in that same pit," Pat recalls, "only a different apartment. Again, more scrubbing, more painting. Whoever got our old apartment got a good deal!"

Even though he was anxious to get the season underway, new coach Jimmy Skinner was in a tough spot, taking over a team that had just won six consecutive league titles and three Stanley Cups in five years.

Fortunately for him, the Red Wings were essentially the same squad that had captured Lord Stanley's mug the previous spring. Many players, Ted Lindsay among them, believed it really didn't matter who coached the team.

"Everybody on that Wing team and most players in the NHL were professionals," Lindsay says. "We were all the best at what we did. By the time we got to that level, a coach couldn't teach us anything else. We were all self-taught. The game wasn't that complicated; we could almost change the lines ourselves."

Prior to the 1954–55 season, Jack Adams predicted, "Somebody is going to catch up with us one of these days!"

That somebody was the Canadiens. At thirty-three, the Rocket was still a potent force. Jean Beliveau, Boom Boom Geoffrion, Bert Olsmstead, and Kenny Mosdell added depth to the offence while Doug Harvey anchored the defence.

Jacques Plante took his place in the Canadiens' net on a permanent basis, succeeding Gerry McNeil, who'd retired at age twenty-eight.

Born in 1929, the same year as Sawchuk, in Mont Carmel, Quebec, Plante grew up with his parents and eleven siblings in Shawinigan Falls. He advanced enough as a goaltender that he brought home fifty cents a week playing for a factory team in the 1944–45 season. After playing Junior in Quebec City, he turned pro with the Montreal Royals of the Quebec Senior League. In 1952–53, he played for the Buffalo Bisons and was called up for three NHL games with the Canadiens. In the play-offs, he relieved McNeil for the last two games of their semifinal win against Chicago, allowing only one goal.

Plante got into seventeen regular-season games in 1953–54, but his indifferent play in the finals sidelined him in favour of McNeil.

Like all goaltenders, Plante was eccentric. A loner, he often sat away from the rest of the team and knitted items such as toques, mittens, and long underwear.

The 1954–55 season began on a familiar note for Terry. He participated in his fifth All-Star game, a 2–2 tie between Detroit and the NHL All-Stars. Next he recorded his earliest shutout ever, blanking Gump Worsley and the Rangers, 4–0, on October 9. Between November 20–25, Terry strung together three consecutive shutouts, including the fiftieth of his career against Chicago.

Players who lived in the Russell apartments often got together after a game or a practice. Alex Delvecchio remembers: "We'd have dinner nights, or spaghetti nights, and drink a case of beer. I never much thought of it one way or another, and I really didn't give a shit, but at the breadbox apartments, we were never invited to Sawchuk's. Never. It was odd."

Pat Sawchuk recalls her husband taking a definite turn during their second tour at the breadbox apartments.

"That was a very bad year. He often came home drunk after a game or practice, and being a young, naive Catholic girl, I thought, 'If we have a child, and with love and nurturing, he'll change!' But Terry got mixed up drinking with the Detroit Lions football players. I didn't know it at the time but they drank until they threw up and then they drank some more. Apparently there were lots of women at these parties and Terry started staying away more and more to go to these parties. It all came to a head at Christmas time."

It was Christmas 1954. The tree was up and nicely decorated. Pat and baby Jerry were asleep. Terry came barging through the door at four o'clock in the morning, so drunk he could hardly stand up and in an ugly mood. Pat pretended she was still sleeping. The apartment was so cramped that Pat had piled diapers on a small divider. Terry saw them and knocked them off yelling, "Why do you have these diapers on here for?" The baby was now crying as Terry attempted to go to the washroom, but was so drunk he urinated on the bathroom walls. Terry staggered around the apartment yelling about anything and everything. He saw the Christmas tree and went berserk, throwing the tree and ornaments all over the small apartment, then staggered back out into the night.

Still in shock, Pat tried to calm her frightened baby while she surveyed the scene of destruction. The next morning, she called Ma Tannahill, Terry's former landlady, who came over and helped Pat clean up the mess. Ma's reaction upon entering the apartment was, "My God! The guy is mad!"

Terry would regularly leave early in the morning for practice and not show up until late that evening. But although he had returned drunk before, this had marked the first time that he was in an angry, violent state.

When Terry finally came home, he was sheepish and unapologetic, claiming he couldn't remember his tirade. Pat refused to talk to him for a couple of days, but Ma Tannahill didn't hesitate to read him the riot act. Terry's response was to pretend it hadn't happened at all. Though it was a wonder the whole apartment building didn't know about the escapade, the secret was kept between the Sawchuks and Ma Tannahill.

As the new year began the Canadiens stood in Detroit's usual perch atop the league standings, four points up on the Wings. Gordie Howe and Ted Lindsay had been slowed by injuries, and the new year brought a new set of challenges for the dynamic duo. Howe had a seventeen-game slump in which he registered a mere four points. Lindsay's spotty season would be interrupted twice by league suspensions for fighting with fans.

In January, however, Detroit picked up the slack and even deposed the Canadiens briefly. Terry again went on a shutout binge, recording four in a span of sixteen days.

But by late January, with Howe mired in one of the worst scoring slumps of his career and Lindsay hurt, suspended, or ineffective, the third of the Red Wings' spark plugs was burning out.

"Terry continued to drink that year staying away more and more. He would come home and he'd be so obliterated that he wouldn't know where he was, or who he was. How he got home sometimes, I don't know. He still was partying with the Lions and you could see it taking its toll, he was getting run down. Jack Adams knew about Terry drinking and he was not impressed!"

On Saturday, February 5, Terry was bombed by the Boston Bruins, 8–4. It was his worst performance since the 9–0 shellacking in Montreal two years previous. The next night the Bruins tied the sinking Wings on a last-minute Don McKenney goal from ninety feet out. The puck plopped to the ice in front of Terry, who tried to field it with his glove but instead saw it slide unimpaired into the cage.

At this point in the season the Wings had won only one of their past six games. Adams, hoping to head off the situation at the pass, benched Sawchuk and recalled Glenn Hall from Edmonton. Then he secretly ordered Sawchuk admitted to hospital for testing and psychiatric counselling.

"Terry did not take this very well," Pat recalls. "Terry told [the psychiatrist] to get out of his room, that he wasn't gonna talk to him, to get the 'f' out of there. Terry was peeved that Jack would even attempt such a thing."

"Do you know that Jack sent a psychiatrist in to see me and would you know that his goddamn name was Dr. Catchem?" an irate Terry related to Pat afterwards.

There was no doubt that Jack did not mince words or actions with his star goaltender: either smarten up or you're gone.

"Jack Adams had a feel for Terry," Pat remembers of this time. "He knew Terry had problems and he wanted to help him but Terry was not one who liked to be helped."

For public consumption, Jack announced that Sawchuk was being rested for three games. It was the first time in his five-year career that he missed games for reasons other than injuries.

"We're giving Terry a rest — nothing more," Adams told reporters. "We figured this move was both for the best interests of the team and the best interests of Sawchuk.

"Terry can take some needed rest and come back much sharper. We will get another look at Hall, who has been playing well. And while Terry is out, some of the other players on the club may appreciate his efforts more than they have part of this season."

Adams continued, "I've known Terry since he was a youngster. I could see the strain was starting to tell. This is in no way a disciplinary move."

And how could it be, for Adams knew that despite Terry's alcohol problem and the fact the Wings as a group had not been playing as well as expected, they were still neck and neck with the Canadiens in the race for top spot. Despite his recent bout of instability, both on and off the ice, Terry was still having a magnificent season: after fifty-four games, he'd allowed only 109 goals for a 2.02 average, close behind Toronto's Harry Lumley.

In today's sports circles, the off-ice problems of such a prominent superstar would have been front-page news. But at the time, it was reported only that Jack was displeased with Terry's recent performances on the ice. It was speculated that Terry was either beginning to slip as a big-leaguer at the tender age of twenty-five, or that he was being rested for the impending playoffs.

Today, teammates Johnny Wilson and Marcel Pronovost and trainer Lefty Wilson maintain there was another factor in the Sawchuk benching of February 1955: mononucleosis. Early symptoms of this acute infection include a fever and headache followed by swelling of the lymph glands in the neck, armpits, and groin, accompanied by a severe sore throat. Jaundice occasionally sets in indicating swelling and mild damage to the liver. Later signs include depression, lack of energy, and lethargy.

Lefty Wilson recalls: "Terry had mono for certain, but it was never publicized and he never sat out any games. Christ, I didn't even know how to pronounce 'mononucleosis' at the time. We never thought of resting him at the time, but then finally we had to. Adams kept it quiet, didn't let on."

Johnny Wilson concurs. "I remember Terry having it that last year before he was traded, but not too many people knew. I'm not even sure if Pat knew. They (management) kept it pretty hushed."

Pat Sawchuk has trouble believing these reports today. "Jack Adams was a good family man," she says. "He would have told me if I or my children would have been at risk. Mononucleosis is an infectious disease." However, given Jack's disdain for players' wives, it is entirely possible that he would have kept this a secret.

It is also a possibility that Terry was suffering from alcoholic hepatitis. Like mononucleosis, acute alcohol-induced hepatitis begins with a flu-like illness, swelling of the liver, and jaundice. Heavy drinkers also display vague feelings of fatigue. In such cases rest, a nourishing diet, and abstinence from alcohol are recommended. Recovery usually occurs after a few weeks. Although Terry's medical records no longer exist, it is plausible that this was the "mono" that Terry's teammates remember Terry having. And as this condition is not contagious, it would explain why Jack Adams never told Pat Sawchuk about the diagnosis.

All that can be said for certain today is that Adams knew Terry had a problem, dealt with it, and kept mum. It is also clear in retrospect that Sawchuk's fate as a Red Wing was sealed at this time.

Glenn Hall performed admirably in his two-game stint, beating Toronto, 2–1, on Saturday night and coming out on top against Chicago, 5–1, the next evening. Hall had been slated to play a few more days but an urgent call from Edmonton had Hall flying home where his wife had been hospitalized. Terry seized the opportunity by the throat and played magnificently in a 2–2 tie with Chicago. Sawchuk knew he had something to prove. He had witnessed Hall's performance and was aware of rumours, now stronger than ever, that he might be traded to another team.

Terry's return coincided with a Red Wing resurgence. For

the first time all season, Sawchuk, Howe, and Lindsay were playing like their former selves.

In mid March, the Wings had lost only one game of their past fifteen, putting them just two points back of the first-place Canadiens. On March 13 Montreal visited the Boston Garden for a game against the Bruins. In that game the league's leading scorer, Maurice Richard, his sights set on his first-ever Art Ross Trophy, was cut on his head by a high stick from the Bruins' Hal Laycoe. A vicious stick fight ensued, during which the Rocket punched linesman Cliff Thompson.

Richard had struck a linesman earlier in the season, and had paid a $250 fine. On March 16, the league president Clarence Campbell ruled that the Rocket was hereby suspended for the duration of the regular season. And because only three games remained in the regular season, Richard was barred for the playoffs as well. The entire province of Quebec screamed foul, while throughout the rest of the league it was felt Richard was reaping his just rewards for his behaviour.

The same day, Detroit beat Boston, 5–4, to pull into a tie for first place with the Habs. And as fate would have it, the Wings — for whom Richard's absence seemed all too convenient — were scheduled to play the Canadiens on St. Patrick's Day at the Forum. Campbell, who attended all the Habs' games, stubbornly insisted on attending this game as well. The already tense atmosphere in the Forum grew worse as the Red Wings jumped to a 4–1 first-period lead. A fan threw a punch at Clarence Campbell and, during the first intermission, someone set off a tear-gas bomb.

The arena was evacuated, after which a mob wrought havoc outside on Ste. Catherine Street, looting, breaking windows, and turning cars on their sides. The Wings made a run for it as soon as word reached them that the game had been forfeited and on the books as a 4–1 Detroit win. The Wings bus was a moving target for the mobs as it made its way to Westmount Station.

On Saturday, March 19, Montreal regrouped to beat the Rangers, pulling them even with the idle Red Wings. First place would be on the line the next night in Detroit as the Wings prepared to host the Canadiens.

Terry's hunt for his third Vezina Trophy was also at stake. Going into this night, the Leafs' Harry Lumley, slated to play the Rangers at seven o'clock, held a two-goal lead over Sawchuk, whose tilt with the Habs began at eight-thirty.

With scores of police on hand and everyone in attendance searched for weapons or trouble-making utensils such as tear-gas canisters, the game began.

The Canadiens quickly fell behind the Wings on goals by Dutch Reibel, Tony Leswick, and Ted Lindsay, who had been sidelined by injuries for three games. Halfway through the game it was announced that the Rangers had defeated Toronto, 3–2. A shutout by Terry would earn him the Vezina by the same one-goal margin that Lumley had won the award by the year before. But none of Terry's eleven shutouts to date this season had been against the Canadiens.

"When we knew that Terry had a shot at the Vezina," Marcel Pronovost says, "we all dug down deeper and, because it was against the Canadiens, we dug a little deeper still."

Lindsay added two more markers and Alex Delvecchio notched one for a 6–0 lead. With the crowd cheering and everyone on their feet, Terry and his defence shut down the Canadiens' attack and the forwards backchecked hard. The Red Wings stayed close to the Canadiens.

As the final seconds ticked down, Terry began jumping up and down. When the buzzer sounded, it was a double celebration: seven consecutive league championships for the Wings and the third Vezina for Sawchuk. Marcel Pronovost was the first to congratulate him and was one of two Wings to hoist him up on their shoulders to carry him off the ice to the deafening roar of the crowd. Terry's twelfth shutout of the season gave him a goals-against average of 1.96 — his fifth straight season below 2.00.

In the semifinals, the Wings easily swept aside the third-place Maple Leafs in four straight, winning 7–4, 2–1, 2–1, and 3–0. Meanwhile, the Canadiens disposed of Boston in five games to put themselves into the Stanley Cup finals for the fifth time in as many springs.

In the third period of Game One, Floyd Curry gave the Habs

a 2–1 lead. With Dollard St. Laurent off for tripping, Lindsay fed Vic Stasiuk in the slot to tie the game. Then Terry took over. A stupendous two-pad slide against Dickie Moore, a terrific grab of a Calum MacKay backhand, and then three point-blank saves with Gordie Howe in the penalty box kept the Wings in there. Pavelich then broke loose and beat Plante on the glove side. Lindsay's empty-netter sealed the 4–2 victory.

Montreal coach Dick Irvin made a goaltending switch for Game Two, starting twenty-one-year-old rookie Charlie Hodge in place of Jacques Plante. The two had alternated in the Boston series, but the strategy backfired as the Wings surged to a 4–0 lead after the first twenty minutes.

In the second period, Howe banked a shot off the boards behind and to the right of Plante who was now in the Montreal net. The puck bounced back out to a rushing Lindsay, who slammed the puck through Plante's legs. The Red Wing linemates had mastered this play in practice. The Wings stretched their lead to 7–0 after the second. At 12:32 of the third period, Kenny Mosdell spoiled Terry's shutout bid, but the Wings prevailed, 7–1.

Back at the Forum for Game Three the Frenchmen were flying as Boom Boom Geoffrion, vilified by Montreal fans for edging out the idle Rocket in the scoring race, won them over as he fired in two goals twelve seconds apart. The game featured great saves by both Plante and Sawchuk, but the game's outcome was typified by the Habs' Jackie Leclair's golf shot from a poor angle that eluded a surprised Sawchuk standing too far back in his net. Despite being outshot, 37–26, the Habs won, 4–2.

Forty seconds into the fourth game, Terry made dazzling point-blank stops on Kenny Mosdell and Doug Harvey before Callum McKay beat him to open the scoring. Despite a Dutch Reibel first-period tally that tied the game, the second period featured unanswered scores by Geoffrion, Beliveau, and Johnson to put the Wings behind the eight ball heading into the third period. This was Plante's night as the Wings outshot the Habs, 40–30, but lost the game, 5–3. Heading back to the Olympia, the series was tied at two wins apiece.

Gordie Howe's hat trick in the fifth game gave him a new

record for postseason points with nineteen, and helped Detroit to a 5–1 win.

Back in Montreal for Game Six, Terry had his hands full with the Hab sharpshooters. The pattern in this final series continued as the home team won yet again. Final score: 6–3, Canadiens.

The largest Detroit crowd of the season, 15,500 fans, packed the sports palace on Grand River Avenue for the decisive game of the 1955 playoffs. Both Plante and Terry were unbeatable for twenty-seven minutes until Alex Delvecchio stuffed in a Red Kelly pass to put the Wings ahead, 1–0. At the end of the second period Howe deflected a Marcel Pronovost shot to send the Wings to the dressing room with a 2–0 lead and only twenty minutes to go.

Three minutes into the third period, Delvecchio again broke through the Montreal defence, firing a high shot over a diving Plante to pad their lead to 3–0. With five and a half minutes to go, a Geoffrion point shot knocked Terry's stick out of his hand and Floyd Curry knocked home the rebound, to make the score 3–1, Detroit.

That was the way the game ended. Terry was mobbed by his teammates, the first being Gordie Howe, who'd finished the playoffs with a record twenty points. This year the Canadiens did not storm off to the dressing room. Instead they exchanged warm handshakes and hugs with the Wings. Terry talked for a long time with Kenny Mosdell.

There was a moment of comic relief as the Wing players and officials gathered at centre ice for Clarence Campbell to pre-sent the Cup. The public-address microphone became tangled on its descent from the rafters and, to the delight of the crowd, six-foot-one-inch Glen Skov was boosted onto the shoulders of two teammates to untangle the wire. The players stood calmly listening to the NHL President, their arms on each others' shoulders. Howe and Sawchuk exchanged pleasantries, and Howe jokingly patted Terry's head.

In the weeks that followed, there was criticism from the Canadiens' camp that the Wings only won because the Canadiens didn't have the Rocket. "The Rocket's absence may or may not have made a difference," Marcel Pronovost says. "I believe in his absence the Canadiens actually turned it up a notch; some of their players played better than if the Rocket had been there. It will always be a 'what-if.' In our defence, down the home stretch at the end of the season we were by far the winningest team, even before the Rocket's suspension. We entered the playoffs very strong, very strong."

Years later, defenceman Bob Goldham was asked to comment on the 1955 Stanley Cup victory. "The key for us," he said, "was Sawchuk. He was the greatest goaltender who ever lived. We could always count on him to come up with the big save. When I look back on those Stanley Cup series [of 1954 and 1955], what I remember is Ukey making one big save after another."

The Red Wings were on top of the world as they celebrated that night at the Sheraton–Cadillac hotel. They had won seven consecutive league titles, and four Stanley Cups in six years.

But the elation must have been mixed with uncertainty. The Wings and Habs had finished one–two in the standings the past four years, but Detroit's margin of victory shrank from twenty-two points in 1952 to just two points this year. And the Wings' struggles during the absences of Howe or Lindsay had revealed a lack of depth in Detroit's lineup.

The stage seemed set for a housecleaning by "Trader Jack" Adams. And with Glenn Hall knocking on the door, Terry Sawchuk must have wondered if his days as a Red Wing were over.

9

EARLY DEPARTURE

THE spring of 1955 should have been idyllic for Terry Sawchuk. He was a member of the Stanley Cup champions, and by winning the Vezina he had again established himself as the best goalkeeper in all of hockey. For the first time in years he was injury-free, and his young family was growing: the Sawchuks were expecting their second child.

But fate intervened not long after the couple's return to Winnipeg for the summer. Pat Sawchuk began hemorrhaging heavily one day and an ambulance was quickly summoned. Leaving little Jerry in the care of his parents, Terry accompanied his wife to the hospital, where Pat not only had a miscarriage, but was also in a fight for her life. Her blood loss was extensive and her condition was critical for hours, before the bleeding finally stopped.

While Pat convalesced, Terry would frequently take his young son out in his carriage on strolls through the neighbourhood. Then, on May 28, the Sawchuks were dealt another blow: Trader Jack Adams had dealt Glen Skov, Benny Woit, Tony Leswick, and Terry's buddy Johnny Wilson to Chicago in exchange for Dave Creighton, John McCormack, Jerry Toppazzini, and Bucky Hollingworth. Terry's regret at the departure of his teammates, particularly Wilson, must have been overshadowed by his relief at having been spared from the trading block.

When the phone rang five days later, he was caught completely off guard. "Put the radio on," he was told by a friend in town. "You've been traded to Boston." Terry waited half in shock for the word to come over the airwaves so he could hear it for himself. Terry was going to Boston along with Marcel Bonin, Lorne Davis, and Vic Stasiuk. In exchange, the Wings were getting forwards Ed Sandford, Real Chevrefils, Norm Corcoran, defenceman Warren Godfrey, and a rookie goalie named Gilles Boisvert.

"I think it was the darkest day of Terry's life," Pat Sawchuk says. "He cried and cried. I mean, the guys were all so close and then to have to hear about it on the radio . . . it just ripped him apart. He gave everything for that organization and he felt like a piece of meat afterwards. All the trust he ever had in management or team spirit just went."

It took Terry a couple of days to come to grips with the fact that he was no longer a Red Wing. When the Bruins phoned him to make it all official, Terry was able to collect himself and say all the right things to a few reporters outside his parents' home. He was a "bit sorry," he said, about the trade, but added that it was still an honour to play in the NHL, "especially under a coach like Milt Schmidt."

Jack Adams called Terry later, much later than the Bruins. With the goaltender still "peeved" about the deal, their conversation was without a doubt strained. And Terry, true to form, was blunt about how betrayed and angry he felt, especially since he didn't have to kowtow to Jack anymore.

Undaunted, Jack Adams later told the press he knew exactly what he was doing in trading away hockey's best goaltender.

"We let Sawchuk go because we found ourselves with two top goalies. Hall is more advanced now than Sawchuk when he joined us and all the players insist Glenn has been NHL material for the past year. It was a case of trading one of them and Sawchuk is the established player. Consequently, he brought a better offer."

Marcel Pronovost disagrees that the Wings got fair value for Sawchuk. "Adams got shit in return when he traded Terry away, and the others. He got nothing in return, and only Godfrey was still around at the end of the 1955–56 season. He traded away homegrown players who had Red Wings tattooed on their butts; in return, he got players who weren't that dedicated to the organization."

Pronovost argues Jack's intention was to move Terry — whom he considered damaged goods — by any means necessary. He suspects Adams may even have thought he was putting one over on the Bruins.

Whatever Adams's motives, they were clearly rejoicing in Boston.

"In our wildest dreams," exclaimed Bruins' general manager Lynn Patrick, "we didn't think we could pry loose a guy of Sawchuk's status." Jack Adams had told Boston he was willing to trade "a goaltender," but didn't specify *which* goalie until just before he pulled the trigger on the deal. Until then, Patrick thought he'd be getting Glenn Hall.

"As soon as the news got out that we had acquired Sawchuk from Detroit, my office was flooded with telephone calls," Patrick announced. "They'd ask how to get season's tickets. [We'd] never had so much off-season interest in the Bruins before!"

Terry felt odd as he headed to Hershey, Pennsylvania, rather than Sault Ste. Marie, Michigan, for training camp. Outwardly he went out of his way to reassure his new team that his loyalty lay with them.

"Milt," Terry said to his new coach a few days into camp, "I'm looking forward to having the best years of my career with the Bruins."

Milt Schmidt couldn't help but smile as he related the conversation to the press later. "I can't say enough about Terry's attitude during our training period at Hershey. To say the least, it has been wonderful."

There was apprehension mixed in with the Bruins' elation at having Sawchuk in their midst. It all seemed too good to be true. Could Sawchuk be damaged goods? Was his eyesight indeed failing, as had been whispered around the league last year? To put the Bruins at ease, their star goalie passed an eye test with flying colours.

One exam Terry failed was his army physical. Sawchuk had received a couple of draft notices and ignored them, believing that his Canadian citizenship excused him from the U.S. draft. When a third notice arrived, someone pointed out that, because he lived more than six months of the year in the United States, he was draft-eligible. Terry dutifully reported to the local draft board, where doctors took one look at his deformed elbow and declared him physically unfit.

As the Bruins broke camp, defenceman Fern Flaman helped Terry get settled in Boston.

"My first impression of Terry was that he was very nice really, very nice," Flaman says. "A little quirky, but that can be said for all goalies. I picked him up every day to go to games or practices, so I kind of got to know him better than anyone else on the team. And at that, Terry was a hard guy to get to know."

Having secured a place to stay in Westwood, a Boston suburb, Terry placed a phone call to Pat in Winnipeg, to have her and Jerry join him in Boston.

"It was the most terrible plane ride in my life," Pat remembers. "I had a layover in Chicago, then another in New York. I had all these parcels, and a twenty-eight-pound kid who wanted to run all over the place. After a three-hour wait in New York, I finally got on the plane and I had this drunk behind me. Then we ran into the worst turbulence I ever experienced. It was very scary. And we had to circle Logan Airport for forty minutes. What a way to start life in Boston!"

Terry's first order of business for the 1955–56 hockey season was to appear in his sixth straight All-Star game, which took place at the Olympia, against his former teammates, the Stanley Cup champion Red Wings. As the All-Stars skated out for their pregame warm-up, he saw the arena lined with many welcome back signs held up by fans, and it made him feel good. Many yelled out his name as he took shots and he looked down at young Hall now in "his" net wearing "his" uniform and he sighed, yet he left the ice to a smattering of applause. Toronto's Harry Lumley played the first half of the game for the All-Stars, who fell behind, 2–0.

As Terry made his way towards the net to play the second

half of the game, the crowd of 10,111 stood and let out a deafening roar of appreciation for the man who had been their
goaltender for five great years. As he got to his crease and the
ovation increased, Terry choked back his emotions. In the final
minute of the game, with the Wings ahead of the All-Stars,
2–1, coach Dick Irvin signalled Terry to the bench for an extra
attacker. Sawchuk was again given a warm ovation.

NHL president Clarence Campbell was on hand for Terry's
second home game on October 12 to present him with the
Vezina. Terry reacted in kind to the fans' warm reception as he
shut out the visiting Maple Leafs, 2–0. Ten days later, he went
into Detroit and battled Glenn Hall to a scoreless draw. A week
later, he shut out Gump Worsley's New York Rangers in a hard-
fought 1–0 battle.

Sawchuk's presence boosted Bruin attendance — crowds at
the Boston Garden were up 27 percent over the year before —
and his 1.55 goals-against average after nine games certainly
lifted team morale.

"You know what they say," Fern Flaman says, "'a winning
hockey club is a happy hockey club.' Off the ice Terry wasn't
exuberant or anything, but he showed his stuff on the ice."

Surprisingly, Terry's new surroundings had a settling effect
on him. He professed to be happy to be a Bruin, and there was
quite a change on the home front as well. Pat Sawchuk Milford
remembers that first year in Boston today.

"Terry was still gone a lot, such is the life of a hockey player.
But when he was home, he was pretty good. He certainly
wasn't down and out drunk like he had been the year before,
in Detroit. We would go to the rink together, for the games at
the Boston Garden. Then we'd often go out to dinner or something after the games."

As the Bruins got off to a great start, the Red Wings won
only three of their first seventeen games, their worst start since
1938, and they temporarily occupied the NHL basement. But
by mid-November, their fate was reversed as the Wings finally
began to win and the Bruins, riddled with injuries and lacking
in scoring punch, began a slow but sure descent into last place.

Despite the team's slump, by Christmas Terry had accumulated five shutouts, including a second scoreless tie against Glenn Hall and the Red Wings. Alex Delvecchio remembers these early encounters against his former teammate.

"We had a heck of a time against Terry that year. It was a real advantage for him, you know, because he could get psyched up. He was tough to beat."

Jeanne Flaman, Fern's wife, became close to Pat Sawchuk that first year in Boston. She frequently took new wives on the team under her wing in an attempt to make them feel at home in Boston.

"Pat was a real sweetheart," she recalls. "She was just a young kid really but a real pet. She lived near a good friend of mine so I saw her frequently. If there is one thing I'll never forget, it's that Terry would often leave her without money. He'd be gone on a road trip for days and she would have no money, except for this drawer they had in the house which had money in it, but she wouldn't touch that money. She'd borrow money from us to buy stuff or groceries for the kid, you know, but she would not touch a cent of money that Terry kept in that drawer. I found that so odd."

This personality trait certainly strained Terry's relationship with his wife. Pat continues, "Terry always had to control 'his' money. If I touched a cent of the money in that drawer, he would go livid, berserk. He wouldn't hit me, nor did I feel physically threatened, but boy, would he go on a tirade. And in later years, it only got worse."

Jeanne Flaman recalls Terry's frugality could be taken to some unusual lengths.

"We often had team parties at our house and Terry and Pat would come over. I thought Terry wasn't very close to his wife. I remember him bringing some beer to a party once and taking home what he hadn't drunk. I didn't like that."

The Bruins began to show signs that they had no intention of staying in last place as Terry notched his sixth shutout of the season on January 20. The Bruins' resurgence coincided with the return of key players from injuries as well as a trade with the Wings that saw former Bruins Real Chevrefils — whom the Wings had acquired in the Sawchuk trade — and

Jerry Toppazzini rejoin the lineup. The deal paid immediate dividends as the duo netted six goals in their first four games, of which Boston won three.

The Bruins passed fifth-place Chicago and would briefly overcome a ten-point gap on fourth-place Toronto. Things looked promising for Milt Schmidt's boys as they chalked up back-to-back victories against the first-place Montreal Canadiens. In the first, on March 10, Sawchuk scored his eighth shutout of the season, and the sixty-fifth of his career, in a 4–0 decision at the Forum.

During the second win, at the Boston Garden, Sawchuk allowed one goal but thereafter refused to yield to the mighty Habs' attack. From his perch in the press box, Montreal general manager Frank Selke turned matter-of-factly to those around him and commented, "Mr. Sawchuk has made up his mind, there'll be no more goals scored on him tonight, and when he does that, there are no more goals."

The late-season surge would not be enough, however. On the final weekend of the season the Maple Leafs slipped past the Bruins into fourth place. It was the first time Boston had missed the playoffs since 1949–50, though Terry's gritty performance and nine shutouts kept the Bruins closer than they might have been.

Three of Terry's shutouts came against his former team, the Detroit Red Wings, and their Calder Trophy–winning goalie, Glenn Hall.

Hall, a native of Humboldt, Saskatchewan, finally escaped from under Terry's shadow in 1955–56, having toiled in the Wing organization since 1951 with the AHL's Indianapolis Capitals and the Edmonton Flyers of the Western Hockey League. Like Terry before him, Glenn entered the NHL with a unique style. Called the "V", or "butterfly" style, Hall regularly dropped to his knees with his legs and feet spread out to each side. This style, even more unorthodox than Sawchuk's, encountered stiff criticism from Adams.

Yet Hall had a great rookie season, compiling twelve shutouts, a goals-against average of 2.11 — second only to Plante's Vezina-winning 1.86. In addition to winning the Calder, he also made the Second All-Star team. But Hall and his weak-ened Wings were no match for the Canadiens, who outscored Detroit, 18–9, en route to a five-game Stanley Cup final romp.

Terry received the hockey award at the annual B'nai B'rith Sports Lodge Awards Dinner on May 6 at the Sheraton Plaza Hotel in Boston. With a host of dignitaries and sports legends in attendance, Canadiens centre Jean Beliveau presented Terry with his engraved silver platter. Later, the two took in a Red Sox game at Fenway Park and met Ted Williams afterwards in the clubhouse.

The Sawchuks moved back to Union Lake for the off-season, to the small house where they had stayed the previous summer, while they awaited completion of a bungalow adjacent to the Morey Golf Course. They were to take possession around the Fourth of July, but the construction site was vandalized, delaying the move.

As she had done before Jerry's birth, Annie Sawchuk came down from Winnipeg to help Pat during her final weeks of pregnancy. On July 7, 1956, Pat and Anne decided to go and buy things for the new baby. Terry dropped them off, then went to play golf.

Pat remembers: "I started having pains at the store but I didn't say anything because I wanted to finish shopping. But Terry's mother had him paged off the golf course. He came and picked us up, and we went back for my belongings. I didn't feel like going to the hospital. So, I sat down. I had a robe that had had a button fall off it, so I wanted to sew that button back on before I left."

Terry paced frantically, getting angrier by the minute.

"Couldn't you do that at the hospital?" he asked angrily.

"No!" Pat answered stubbornly. "I'm doing it now."

Terry continued to pace. Finally he turned to his mother with worried, pleading eyes.

"It's okay, Terry, it's okay," Anne Sawchuk replied matter-of-factly. "It's not like it was before."

And it wasn't. Terry was very relieved when Pat finally decided to get into the car, but the labour was slower, more nat-ural this time and JoAnne Marie Sawchuk's arrival was greeted much more calmly. The five Sawchuks, including Terry's mother, moved back into the little house briefly before finally moving into their new home.

Set on an acre of land, the home boasted a two-car garage, three bedrooms, a large country kitchen, living room, den, fireplace, and master bedroom. For the first time since leaving home, Terry felt like he had roots, even though he currently was employed in another city.

Terry didn't have much time to enjoy his new home before training camp beckoned. As he prepared to head to camp, he unilaterally decided that he would go to Boston alone this season. He informed Pat that she was staying home and he took the train to Boston. To ensure his players' minds remained on hockey, coach Milt Schmidt made it mandatory for all of his players to stay in the Hotel Manger beside the Boston Garden. A strict 11 p.m. curfew preceded a 7 a.m. wake-up call and a full breakfast before the morning workout. Such was the new, tough, regimented style of the Boston coaching staff.

On October 9 in Montreal, Terry participated in his seventh straight All-Star game, playing alongside Detroit's Glenn Hall.

"What I remember about that game," Hall says today, "is sitting beside Terry in the dressing room. I picked up his stick glove — you know, his blocker — and it weighed ten tons. I said, 'Terry, how in the hell do you lift that thing to block shots?' and he said, 'I don't. I stop the high shots with my elbow, and because my elbow is so weak, the heavy blocker helps keep my stick on the ice!' I couldn't get over that."

As the Bruins' 1956–57 season opened, it was clear that the new work ethic was going to pay off. After their fourteenth game of the season, the Bruins sat in first place.

During his second season in Boston, Terry shared a house in Newton, a Boston suburb, with five other Bruins: Jack Bionda, Allan Stanley, Bob Armstrong, Jack Caffery, and Don McKenney. He rarely called or wrote Pat back in Michigan, not that Pat minded.

"It sounds awful, but it was more of a relaxed time," she says. "We missed him but we didn't miss him, if that makes sense. I was busy, painting the new house, taking care of the kids. It was a nice release, not to have somebody coming home drunk all the time. He had started to do that again during the summer before leaving for Boston."

Though Terry shut out Jacques Plante's Habs on October 27 at the Forum and the Black Hawks in Chicago on November 29, Terry's stalwart play in the Bruins' net increasingly betrayed the state of the goaltender's health, both mental and physical. Terry was finding it harder and harder to get up in the morning, and he could hardly wait to lie down at the end of the day. During games he began to notice his legs tiring a little too early. But the Bruins were in first place, so Terry tried to disregard it all and play on.

By December, he could no longer avoid the fact that something truly was wrong.

"Then I got knocked out against Montreal," Terry would relate later, "and the game was delayed while I went off for a rest. The doctor came to examine me and I told him my neck was so stiff I could hardly turn it. He felt around and said my glands were swollen. He said I should go to the hospital, but you know how I [felt about] hospitals after all those other times."

Terry finished that game, but two days later he could not get out of bed and he missed a team practice. To his roommates, this was the first indication to them that Terry was not well. Sawchuk then contacted team doctor Edward Browne, indicating that he was feeling "kind of sluggish." The next day, Dr. Browne saw Terry and the symptoms left no doubt: fever and headache; swelling of the lymph glands in the neck, armpits, and groin; jaundice indicating mild liver damage. Dr. Browne ordered a final blood-smear test that confirmed his original diagnosis: mononucleosis, an infectious blood disease that attacks white blood cells, for which the only true cure is rest. Browne ordered Terry hospitalized and broke the news to Lynn Patrick that his goalie would be sidelined at least two weeks, and more likely a couple of months. The Bruins were devastated. When coach Milt Schmidt got the news, he told reporters, "It was like being hit between the eyes!"

For Terry, always pessimistic, this was a particularly dark time. He felt so tired and worn out that he didn't feel like leaving his room. He hated hospitals, yet it seemed as if he was always in one. Pat called from Union Lake, concerned about this turn of events. Terry put on a brave face and reassured her that everything was fine and all he needed was some rest and relaxation.

Terry's hospitalization made headlines and struck a chord with fans. Soon the hospital was swamped with more than a thousand letters, get-well cards, and messages. Schmidt, Patrick, and his teammates dropped in on him. There were so many well-wishers that Dr. Browne ordered strict bed rest with no visitors. He was not to expend any energy — even to walk around. Nurses and nuns wheeled him to morning mass or anywhere he wanted to go.

In Chicago, former teammate Johnny Wilson's thoughts were with his buddy.

"When Terry took ill in Boston and was put in the hospital, all of his old Red Wing teammates were all very concerned about him. He had been our number one goalkeeper and we couldn't forget that. All the guys really cared about him, called him up."

After the first few days, Terry began to feel more restless and energetic but it was a false alarm. This is a common feature of mononucleosis. The truth was that it was absolutely necessary for Terry to continue resting so that his body's immune system could build up antibodies to combat the mono virus.

Norm Defelice, a twenty-three-year-old from Boston's Hershey farm team, was in the Bruin net starting with their December 13 game against Chicago. From his hospital bed, Terry listened anxiously to the Bruins' games and, as his strength seemed to return, his restlessness to return to the ice increased. Defelice held his own through a six-game stint — winning three and tying one — but as Terry's condition improved, the pressure for him to return increased.

Sawchuk pushed Dr. Browne for a return to the lineup. He was feeling better every day, he insisted. And Bruin management, no doubt sympathetic to Terry's condition but increasingly worried about their on-ice prospects, must have forced the issue.

In any event, Dr. Browne pronounced Terry Sawchuk fit to play against Detroit on Thursday, December 27, just fifteen days after his hospitalization.

Terry emerged happily from Carney Hospital on Christmas Eve, visited the Garden to see his Bruins lose to the lowly Black Hawks, 4–2, the next night, and practised on the twenty-sixth. He proclaimed himself ready, much to his team's relief.

As he stepped onto the ice at the Boston Garden for the Detroit game, he was given a deafening welcome from the capacity crowd of 14,000. The ovation lifted his spirits as he got in his famous gorilla crouch. But by the start of the third period, Terry began to feel the effects of the long layoff as he fanned on three long shots to allow the Red Wings to take over first place with a 5–3 victory. After the game, Terry said, "In the third period, I knew what to do, but couldn't do it."

On three days' rest, Terry skated onto the Olympia ice before Detroit's largest crowd of the season and played magnificently in a 4–2 victory to reclaim first place for the Bruins. Over the next three games, however, Terry would allow ten goals. No one could deny Sawchuk wasn't himself.

Terry was on the edge of a downward spiral. Rest was essential for a full recovery, yet the self-critical Sawchuk began to fret about his performance — in turn caused by his fatigue — to the point that he began to suffer from insomnia. Terry was worried about his health. He worried about the team. He worried about his family. He worried about his hockey career. The situation clearly threatened to undo any good that his hospitalization had achieved.

Playing against his old team seemed to be a tonic. In Detroit on January 10, he turned aside seventeen shots in the first period alone, leading the Bruins to a 2–1 win. The two points brought Boston into a second-place tie with the Wings. Afterward, Terry was slow to undress and he felt very weak. He received permission from Milt Schmidt to stay overnight at his home in Union Lake instead of returning with the team to their hotel. Pat remembers this night.

"I waited for him and after the game we drove back home. On the way we had to stop at The Twelve High Bar for a couple of drinks, of course. He could hardly drive the car, he was that drained. He could hardly walk."

Pulling into the driveway, Terry could not get out of the car. It took fifteen minutes before he could gather enough strength to walk into the house, and even then he needed Pat's help. He could barely make it in the door before his legs gave out and he had to sit. He was emotionally distraught by his weakness and he began to cry. Pat held him and tried to console him.

"Terry was a physical and emotional wreck that night," Pat remembers. "He was so weak it was pathetic. And of course being the worrywart that he was, he was scared that his career was finished, and I couldn't tell him otherwise. I finally got him settled down, but he thought he was through, and so did I."

Terry rested for the next two days before a Saturday-night game at the Montreal Forum. He made a gallant effort in a 4–1 loss, though he continued to worry and had trouble sleeping on the train back to Boston. The next night held a return engagement with the Canadiens at the Boston Garden. Terry played bravely, facing thirty-four shots, but the Bruins lost again, 3–1. Terry left the arena physically and mentally drained.

The situation came to a head on Tuesday morning, January 15. For reasons he couldn't explain, Terry woke up in a hotel room somewhere in downtown Boston. He had evidently cashed his $3,000 paycheque the day before — his pockets were full of cash — but he didn't remember any of it. He was in a complete fog.

"Terry told me later," Marcel Pronovost relates today, "that he had completely blanked out. He couldn't remember a damn thing. That was his wake-up call!"

Terry gathered himself together and, instead of suiting up for practice that morning, he walked into the office of Bruins' president Walter Brown to inform him of his decision to resign.

"The pressure is getting to me," Terry said to his boss, who was sorting his mail at the time. "I'm not doing a good job. I'm letting the team down and I want to quit!"

Brown was stunned. Fern Flaman, the Bruins' captain, recalls, "When Terry went to see Mr. Brown, told him he was lonely, that he wasn't feeling good, not playing well, Mr. Brown was a tremendous person and he sympathized with Terry and said, 'Well, Terry, you know what's best for you. Your family comes first. You do what you think is best.'"

The goaltender left the arena, went to the house he shared with the other players in Newton, packed his belongings, and went to stay with friends in a nearby suburb.

Coach Milt Schmidt, home in bed with the flu, got a phone call from Brown at noon, telling him of his meeting with Sawchuk. Schmidt immediately dressed and headed to the Garden. He tried all afternoon to reach Terry by phone, finally doing so early that evening.

"When I finally reached him," the coach would tell the press the next day, "he said he had no reason for quitting. He was just 'fed up.' He said in his last eight games, he'd only played two good ones and concluded he was finished.

"I told him, 'You'll have a black name all over the country, and you'll never be able to escape it. And your family, your wife and kids, will pay for the name you give them. You're not sick, your nerves are not shot. You're just quitting, walking out on your team and your name. Well, you're the one who's going to suffer the consequences. As far as I'm concerned, a quitter is the lowest animal.'"

There was no doubt that Terry gave it right back to Schmidt during the conversation. By calling into question Terry's allegiance to his team, and his loyalty to his family, the tough-talking Schmidt no doubt hardened Terry's resolve. The tense conversation ended with an ultimatum: Sawchuk would be suspended indefinitely if he didn't show up the next day for practice and an examination by Dr. Browne. Schmidt's attitude towards Terry left little doubt that he did not believe his star goaltender was ill at all.

Terry's decision was a shock even to his wife.

"I had no idea he was thinking of quitting," Pat says. "He never discussed it with me. I never heard from him, but I certainly knew he wasn't well."

Terry's resignation made headlines in all six NHL cities, nowhere more so than in Boston, where Schmidt's "quitter" label was repeated extensively by the same reporters who had so recently hailed the goalie as a hero.

"Terry was no quitter!" Fern Flaman says. "He was not a quitter by any stretch of the imagination. When he was branded a quitter, I think he felt cornered, and it was hard to retract from his position. It was so out of context and Terry was so stubborn, [that he] finally said, 'To hell with it, I'm going home.'

"Maybe if management hadn't said things in the heat of the moment, it could have been resolved much more calmly between coach and player."

On the same day he announced he was quitting, the midseason All-Star selections were announced, and Terry was the first team's goalie.

The Wednesday practice and the appointment with Dr. Browne came and went with no sign of Terry. Milt Schmidt made good on his threat and suspended Sawchuk.

"I think we've gone far enough with him," he explained. "Now he has only one out — if he is really mentally sick.

"I'd be the first to apologize to him if he is sick but I wish to goodness he'd let us know."

Any trust that Terry had in Bruins' management or the team physician was shattered the day of his suspension, when Dr. Browne denied in print that Terry's bout with mononucleosis had anything to do with his leaving the team.

"He had mononucleosis before Christmas," Dr. Browne said, "but he was fully recovered when he went back to work."

All Terry knew was that if he kept on going the way he was, he could very well end up dead. All he knew was that he had to get off the Ferris wheel.

How could he trust Schmidt, who suggested Terry had something "mentally wrong" with him, or Dr. Browne, who stated Terry was "fully recovered" when he'd returned to action?

For the rest of the week, the press had a field day with the Sawchuk controversy. Stories were printed about how another goaltender, like Bill Durnan and Gerry McNeil before him, had lost the battle of the nerves. On Terry's side were countless medical experts who said that Sawchuk had not been rested adequately, that he had come back too soon. Doctors faulted Dr. Browne and the Bruins for not easing Terry back into the lineup, perhaps letting him play only home games till he could build up his strength.

Hours after imposing the harsh suspension, Milt Schmidt and Lynn Patrick assessed the situation, which to say the least was grim. The permanent loss of the greatest goalie in the universe would hurt the team's Stanley Cup chances as well as their box office fortunes. Schmidt met Sawchuk at the house in Newton. The two-hour talk between the goaltender and his coach went well: Schmidt finally saw for himself that Terry was not well and acceded to Terry's request to go home for a month or so to rest. He also left open the possibility of Sawchuk's return to the lineup.

Lynn Patrick predicted that Terry would be back in a month, as soon as his confidence could return, and "as soon as everybody gets off Sawchuk's back."

As he made his way through the train station on Thursday afternoon, Terry was surprised by the media attention he had generated. A phalanx of reporters waited for him.

"I'm not talking," he said, but they were hot on his heels, firing questions at him. He finally stopped and turned. "Look, I've quit. I'm mad. And I've got news for you. I'm going to sue four Boston papers for what they said about me after I get home."

Shutting the door to his private compartment, Terry tried to sleep through the night as the train wound its way north to Albany, where he changed trains for the swing north and west through southern Ontario towards Detroit. On the second leg of his trip, Terry was hounded by two young Windsor reporters who waited in vain for hours outside his door.

Arriving at the Detroit station just after 7 a.m., Terry was shocked to see twenty more reporters awaiting him. He made a futile attempt to escape them. Terry brushed them all aside until reporter James Y. Nicol of the *Toronto Daily Star* asked him if the "quitter" label was deserved. Terry stopped, looked the reporter in the eye, and said menacingly, "All you'll get is a punch in the nose!"

Finally, Terry agreed to talk in the station coffee shop. He still didn't say much as he sipped on a coffee, but he did answer one of the first questions.

"You fellows ought to know that the Boston club treated me good, maybe too good. I never caught hell once from them in two years and I deserved it a few times." He vowed to answer their questions at a press conference in his home at noon Monday.

"When Terry finally arrived home, he was really down in the dumps, and mad at me for not writing him," Pat Sawchuk recalls today. "I was mad at him for not ever calling, especially about this last situation. Father Gordon was there because he was concerned, as we all were. You could see [Terry] was almost on the verge of a nervous breakdown."

That night, Terry and Pat appeared live on the CBC television program, *Graphic*. The fifteen-minute show, that interviewed celebrities in their homes, must have garnered huge ratings, given the circumstances. To his credit, Terry carried through with the commitment he had made months before to do the show. As the cameras rolled, he apologized to hockey fans for his departure, saying he would explain everything at Monday's press conference. He then went on to say that he would "recommend professional hockey as a career to any young fellow of sixteen."

The next day, Saturday, Terry saw Dr. Clarkson Long, one of the Red Wing specialists, who concluded that the twenty-seven-year-old was suffering from complete exhaustion and was on the verge of a nervous breakdown. Never did he mention Terry still having mononucleosis — perhaps at Terry's request, so as not to further implicate or embarrass the Bruins. Dr. Long did conclude that Terry should rest for "at least" a month.

On Monday, January 21, 1957, the first press conference ever called by an NHL player took place in the Presidential Suite of the Statler Hotel in Detroit. Given Terry's disdain for the media, this was a most ironic twist. Originally planned for the Sawchuk living room, the venue was changed due to the tremendous interest in the story. The large room was easily filled by a battery of newsmen and TV cameras, none of them from Boston.

Terry waited patiently in his suit and tie, tapping his fingers restlessly until all the reporters were ready. The bright TV lights accentuated his deep-set eyes, his worn appearance, his slight jaundice, which still indicated mono-instilled liver trouble, and the dark circles that ran low into his sunken cheeks.

Sawchuk read from a prepared 350-word statement.

"Since my illness in December . . . I certainly have not felt in the right frame of mind, though I have tried to adjust myself to continue playing for the Bruins. I haven't been getting the proper sleep . . . I've lost my appetite . . . my nerves are shot . . .

"I'm still under contract to the Boston Hockey Club, which has always treated me very well. But my health, for my family's sake, is certainly more important than any monetary consideration . . . I promised Milt that if I felt better later on, I'd discuss my future with the club . . ."

As the hot television lights beat down on his forehead, Terry agreed to answer questions. When someone asked him if he would take in any games at the Olympia, he smiled ruefully, answering, "No, that might aggravate my nervous condition."

The reporters were apparently touched to see Terry in such a state, and they resisted the urge to ask controversial questions. The room was quiet as everyone watched the superstar struggle with the moment.

Afterwards, in a further show of goodwill, every single member of the press lined up to shake his hand and wish him a speedy recovery. It was a sharp contrast to the fiasco at the train station, and Terry was clearly moved.

Terry was the first out of the room. In his friend Vince Gordon's car, Terry took a deep breath, thankful to be out of the spotlight. He looked forward to a quiet period of rest and recovery. It was certainly time to try and forget all about hockey. For Terry Sawchuk, it would be the biggest challenge of all.

10

THE LONG ROAD HOME

*I*T was a long ride home to Union Lake for Terry Sawchuk, whose self-imposed exile had begun in earnest. He had threatened to quit before, but those times he had just been floating trial balloons or sounding off when things weren't going well on the ice. He had never truly abandoned the game he loved. But this time, things were different.

Terry's quitting wasn't an act of defiance or frustration with the game, but one of self-preservation. It was a testament to Terry's resolve that he was able to carry out this decision, to walk away from his status as the best and highest-paid goaltender in the NHL. One of the most driven competitors hockey had ever known was forced to watch from the sidelines.

Back in Boston, Lynn Patrick, Milt Schmidt, and company were regrouping. Norm Defelice was called up once again from Hershey. "It's entirely up to Defelice now," Schmidt said. "His play will determine whether he will be our regular goalie for the duration of the season." Following his first game, a 2–2 tie at the Garden against the Wings, the twenty-three-year-old rookie remarked, "I hope my nerves can stand it."

They couldn't. When the Bruins dropped the next two games, general manager Lynn Patrick went shopping for a new goalie and acquired Don Simmons from Springfield of the American league. In his first assignment, Simmons lost to the Rangers, but then he and the Bruins were undefeated over a string of seven games.

Patrick, who had predicted the afternoon of Terry's press conference that the Bruins would win the Stanley Cup that season, "with Terry Sawchuk [back] in our net," quickly changed his tune with each impressive outing by Simmons. Soon, he was calling Simmons the Bruins' number-one goalie, adding that he hadn't seen or spoken to Terry in weeks and that he had no intentions of doing so. As far as he was concerned, it was up to Sawchuk to make the first move. "If he comes back and says he's sorry, that he made a mistake, I'll be glad to talk to him, but he'll have to come to see me."

The impasse continued as the Bruins felt Terry wasn't needed anymore with Simmons playing well down the stretch.

A statement by Lynn Patrick would cement the schism: "We, and I'm sure I'm speaking for Milt and the players, don't want him back on our club."

Fern Flaman says today that the Bruins' general manager didn't speak on behalf of his players.

"Through that whole period, I never heard any player utter anything negative about Terry. Heck, we'd have taken him back in a second."

In Michigan, Terry, perhaps haunted by the fallout from his premature comeback in December, entertained no thoughts of a return to the ice.

After a while Terry felt healthy and rested enough to look for a much-needed job. The suspension by the Bruins left a void in the Sawchuk finances. He caught on at a tool-and-die firm three days a week but that didn't work out. Next he got an equally ill-fated job selling cars.

"Terry worked as a car salesman for about three weeks," Pat Sawchuk Milford recalls. "I don't know if he was selling secondhand cars or what, but he said he just couldn't lie or sell cars to little old ladies."

The ex-goalie's next stop was a job with an insurance company, but he felt it involved too much socializing, something for which he was ill equipped. In fact, Terry seemed unwilling, or unable, to use his celebrity to his advantage. It wasn't uncommon for ex-athletes to find careers in a field such as public relations, where the goodwill their names and images generated opened many doors. "He didn't look at himself as a commodity," Pat recalls. "He just didn't see himself in that way."

Terry's next job-seeking strategy was both comical and indicative of how stubborn he could be. "Terry wanted *me* to ask my father to give him a job. So I go to my dad and he says, 'Sure, when Terry comes to ask me for a job, I'll give him one.' Now I thought that was a fair answer. He just wanted Terry to come and talk to him man to man. So, I told Terry what my father had said, and . . ."

At this point Pat begins to laugh heartily, though she confesses it wasn't funny at the time.

". . . so Terry says, 'Well, if he's not going to offer me a job, ask me to work for him, to hell with him.' My father was the easiest person in the world to get along with. He would have done anything for me and he would have done anything for Terry, but he was a man of principle. Terry could be so gosh-darned stubborn and so what did he do? He went and got a job as a bartender across the street from my Dad's golf course at a place called The Little Brown Jug. And so that hit the papers: 'Terry Sawchuk lands job across street from father-in-law's.' It was terrible. Everybody thought that they had a fight. Had words. But the real problem was that they had *no* words."

The 1956–57 NHL season proceeded without Terry Sawchuk, but events were in motion that would influence his future. The much-improved Bruins, with Don Simmons in goal, took a real run at the NHL pennant but ended up third, eight points short of the Red Wings, and two behind the Canadiens.

Those who had criticized Jack Adams for gutting his Stanley Cup–winning team of 1955 looked like they might have to eat crow as the Wings resumed their usual perch atop the league standings. Howe and Lindsay finished one–two in scoring, and Glenn Hall missed the Vezina Trophy by only two goals. But Detroit fans expecting a cakewalk in the semifinals against Boston would be disappointed

"This is the strangest playoffs I can recall," Adams said. "Boston has more hungry players. They're aggressive and they're always digging." Indeed they were. The Bruins shook off a 7–2 drubbing in Game Two to take a 3–1 lead in the series. Then in Game Five, Boston overcame a 3–1 deficit, scored three unanswered goals in the third period to eliminate the Wings.

Jack Adams found the loss a bitter pill to swallow. He was displeased with his team's performance, and goalie Glenn Hall was a scapegoat. Despite the fact that Hall had won the Calder Trophy as outstanding rookie the previous season and had been a Second Team All-Star that year and a First Team All-Star this season, Hall's days were numbered for reasons other than his on-ice performance.

Hall had been close with Ted Lindsay, who, with Montreal's Doug Harvey and others, was trying to form a players' union in that 1956–57 season. "I liked Ted Lindsay," the man they called Mr. Goalie recalls today. "He used to come over when I was a Junior in Windsor and talk to us in the dressing room and encourage us. Adams told me not to talk to Ted and I told Adams I would talk to whomever I wanted. He didn't like that.

"Jack Adams was everything that I disliked in a person. I enjoyed my time in Detroit but I certainly didn't abide by the rule which was never to say certain things to the general manager. If he had a problem with Ted Lindsay that was one thing, but I'll talk to whomever I want to talk to, don't be putting any ideas in my head."

Trader Jack had felt betrayed that one of his players — his former team captain — was leading the way in trying to form an NHL players' association. His unhappy gaze came to rest both on the "ringleader," Ted Lindsay, and the goalie who wouldn't bow to his authority, Glenn Hall.

In April 1957, shortly after the Canadiens had easily won their second Stanley Cup in a row by disposing of the Bruins in five games, Adams phoned Terry Sawchuk to discuss the possibility of Terry returning to the Red Wings. The prospect pleased Terry, who quickly — and secretly — submitted himself to a barrage of tests by Red Wing doctors. He passed with flying colours.

At the league's annual meetings in Montreal in June, Adams approached the Bruins, who had let it be known that they would entertain offers for Sawchuk. Chicago's Tommy Ivan had already voiced interest in Terry, but he let it be known that he coveted Glenn Hall even more. Trader Jack was all smiles as his plan fell into place.

The Wings closed a deal that brought Sawchuk back to Detroit in exchange for young left wing Johnny Bucyk and cash. Bucyk, who had netted only ten goals this past season, was considered by Skinner and Adams to be an underachiever, lazy, and a poor two-way player.

Then, in July, Adams shipped Lindsay and Hall west to Chicago for goalie Hank Bassen, Terry's old buddy Johnny Wilson, William Preston, and Forbes Kennedy.

To his delight, Terry was a Red Wing again. But, Pat Sawchuk remembers, "He never again trusted Jack Adams."

"Jack began to change even in the few years before he traded me," recalls Ted Lindsay today. "Personality clashes with Jack began to override his hockey judgment. In the Canadiens' organization, if you had talent and performed on the ice, you stayed there, no matter what. In Detroit, if you ticked Jack off, you were gone. To me, that's not the sign of a good hockey man. I was the NHL's second leading scorer behind Howe when he traded me and Hall to Chicago. And it was mostly because of my trying to form the Players' Association, which was badly needed at that time."

It is safe to say that Sawchuk's distrust of Adams was symptomatic of a league-wide breakdown in trust between the players and team owners. Ted Lindsay and Canadiens' defenceman Doug Harvey spearheaded a movement to form a player's union, or "association," which was fiercely opposed by the team owners. As the most vocal, temperamental opponent of the movement, Jack Adams had gotten rid of one troublemaker and was prepared to take on the other ringleader.

"We had a deal worked out with Montreal to get Doug Harvey," Jimmy Skinner recalls. "He had been a troublemaker to the Canadiens' brass, and Jack was going to take him. I happened to be in Jack's office when Frank Selke phoned to say the deal was off. 'Jack,' Selke said, 'I know we had a deal but I have to call it off. If I trade Harvey away, they'll crucify me here in Montreal.'" Adams could understand Selke's predicament. The Wings' front office had been deluged with irate phone calls and letters protesting the Lindsay trade.

Under Harvey and Lindsay's direction, the Players' Association sued for bigger pensions and a share of TV rights fees, then filed an anti-trust suit, but support for the fledgling union crumbled, beginning in Detroit. Marcel Pronovost recalls: "[Detroit's players] were the last in the association to hear any of the details. We were not totally convinced of all of the facts so Red (Kelly) got us, the Red Wing players, our own lawyer. When our lawyer contacted the association's lawyer, he wouldn't give us the information we wanted to know. This delay created a window of opportunity for the owners to try to squash it.

"Gordie Howe was not to blame, nor was Red Kelly. We as a team wanted more information but it was too late in coming. There was nobody to blame except the lawyers for the Players' Association, from our point of view here in Detroit."

In an effort to quash the insubordinates, thirty-two percent of the NHL's players were moved. Many players were sent to the minors, and a large number of rookies made their debut in 1957–58. Only the Montreal Canadiens refused to tamper with their roster. GM Frank Selke must have smelled another Stanley Cup when he surveyed the confusion around him, particularly the once-mighty Wings.

It's not clear where Terry Sawchuk stood on the union issue. He'd been on the sidelines during its early days in February 1957. And at training camp, Terry appeared both grateful to Adams for bringing him back to Detroit but resentful for having been traded in the first place. His support of the association's actions, if any, was remembered by nobody, so it must be assumed that he stayed out of the fray.

Marcel Pronovost remembers the Terry Sawchuk who came back home to Detroit that fall of 1957.

"Terry and I began to room together on the road, and this is where we really became close. He had matured, and there was an affinity that had built between us, that took over.

"A quote was once attributed to me that I would say 'Good morning' to Terry in the morning in French and then in English to see if he would talk to me or what kind of mood he was in. That was all said tongue-in-cheek! What the hell would I be doing saying anything to Terry in French? When we got up in the morning, if we were rooming, I can guarantee you 'Good morning, Terry' was never said. Neither of us was a morning person."

As the Wings began the season, it was painfully clear that the Red Wings weren't what they used to be. They still had a talented core of veterans — Howe, Delvecchio, Sawchuk, Pronovost, Johnny Wilson, and Kelly — but, as Marcel puts it, "the supporting cast couldn't always remember their lines! You could tell that things weren't going to be the same."

One thing that had changed for the worse was Sawchuk's reputation among his peers. When the Wings headed into New York on October 30, they were greeted by a newspaper article in which Bill Gadsby implied that Terry just might crack again under the strain of another season.

"If he sees too much rubber, Terry might go 'tweet, tweet, tweet' again in midseason," Gadsby said. Terry answered the New York quote by whitewashing the Rangers, 4–0. He clearly was still fuming about the comment — and reporters in general — after the game.

"When you win a game, these guys start coming around," Terry said loudly within earshot of the reporters. "I had enough of you guys last year. Why don't you leave me alone?"

Sawchuk's performance turned the Rangers' jeers into cheers. "I told you, Terry Sawchuk was the best goalie in the league!" New York coach Phil Watson said prior to a rematch with the Wings on November 5 at the Olympia. "I said the same thing about Terry when he was with Boston and the records prove it, but it takes more than goaltending to win hockey games!"

Indeed, after the first eleven games, the Wings were mired in fifth place, a measly point ahead of Toronto. Terry's thirty-five goals against were the most in the league, but his play continued to earn him accolades. In back-to-back losses against Montreal and Boston — in his return to Boston Garden — he faced 101 shots on goal, stopping ninety-one.

From the moment he stepped on the ice in Boston, he was

booed heavily, even having garbage thrown at him. The gallery gods roared with delight and derision as the Bruins handed Terry a 4–0 pasting. Terry later accused some of the Bruins of laughing at him.

"In the rush of the game," Marcel Pronovost says, "you really don't hear the fans that much. All players kind of tune out the crowd as you get into the game. Any garbage thrown at him wouldn't have bothered Terry!"

On the home front, Terry's parents and sister Judy were leaving Winnipeg to join Terry in Detroit.

"Judy was about eleven at the time and her parents wanted her to start school at the beginning of the school year, so she came down first," Pat recalls. "Terry had found his parents a nice little house not too far from us and he was going to move them down to Detroit."

Pat was expecting the couple's third child, due in December. The sun had not risen on the morning of Tuesday, October 22, when Pat awoke, feeling uncomfortable. She walked to the bathroom at the far end of the house so as not to disturb anybody and turned on the light to discover blood everywhere. She was hemorrhaging.

"I cried all the way to the hospital figuring the baby was dead, and Terry was really scared, too. It was six or seven weeks early, so they tried this needle that had just been developed to stop labour, but there was no stopping it!"

The premature baby came into the world blue and not breathing due to a complication called "placenta previa." It meant the placenta — the spongy structure in the mother's womb through which the baby derived its nourishment from the mother — was located near the birth canal. Once delivered, the baby was placed in intermittent "shock baths" — put alternately into hot and cold water to stimulate the baby's central nervous and respiratory systems. The procedure worked. Katherine Mary Sawchuk took her first breath and weighed in at four pounds, two ounces.

Pat was sent home after five days, but little Kathy was required to stay in hospital for three weeks. Pat thought all was fine as Terry picked her up at the hospital, but then she walked through the front door. After all of these years, her voice still rises incredulously when she remembers that day.

"While I was in the hospital, Terry had left his sister Judy, an eleven-year-old, in charge of Jerry and JoAnne — a three-year-old and an almost two-year-old — during the day, when he was gone to practice and stuff. An eleven-year-old taking care of these two kids! Judy really did a fine job for her age. [But] the house was like a pigsty. My God, I could have killed him right then and there. I came in and started right in cleaning."

For Pat, the episode was another reminder that life with Terry was never easy. After three or four days, her house was restored and she gladly re-immersed herself in the daily lives of her children. After three weeks, her now-healthy newborn was brought home to her on a snowy night by family friend Rose Jolly, JoAnne's godmother, as Terry was out of town on a road trip and Pat had to stay to watch the kids.

Coach Jimmy Skinner recalls that, about this time, Pat was becoming aware of Terry's extramarital activities.

"I remember Pat Sawchuk coming into Jack's office upset at Terry's behaviour. She was threatening to do something, leave him or something. Jack suggested that maybe we could give her Terry's paycheques instead of him getting them. I remember she didn't think that this was a very good idea.

"So not knowing what else to do, Jack called Terry into his office. He gave him quite a talking-to, you know, about his drinking and his carousing. I remember we threatened to put a tail on him, to keep tabs on him if he didn't smarten up. Jack told him he had a wife and kids at home and that he had better shape up. But it didn't work.

"But you also have to know that Terry wasn't the only one on the team who was seeing other women. I'd have to say Terry was mild in comparison to some of the guys we had. But Terry's wife knew about it."

Marcel Pronovost concurs. "Terry was not discreet, that was the whole goddamn problem. A lot of other Red Wings screwed around on their wives a lot more than he did, but they were discreet. He'd get caught the few times he ventured!"

"Ya, I went into that bar twice," Pat adds, "and he was with this girl and I thought, after everything that has gone on, why do I have to take this anymore? I don't need this! I don't deserve this!"

Pat filed for divorce on February 6, 1958. Terry was informed of the suit moments before he left for a game at the Olympia against the Canadiens. He played brilliantly that night in a 1–1 tie, but in the dressing room afterwards, he was distraught and crying. News of the suit had leaked to reporters, who were uncustomarily barred from the Wings' dressing room until the goaltender was dressed and ready to leave with his brother Gerald. As he left, he shouted at the frantic newsmen, "Leave me alone. I don't know anything about it. Ask my wife!"

"Pat wanted to give Terry a wake-up call," Marcel Pronovost says. "A proverbial shot across the bow. He talked to me about it. He felt it was all unjustified and that he could work things out. It certainly opened his eyes!"

Pat continues: "We got together and talked. Terry was truly remorseful. He was sorry. He didn't want to lose me, didn't want to lose his family. In my heart of hearts, I knew he was sorry, truly sorry. I was a Catholic girl and Catholics don't have divorces and I was prepared to work at my marriage, and so we tried to fix it, and we did. Things went along great for quite some time."

Two days later, Pat accompanied Terry to the Olympia for a game against New York. The press were waiting, wanting to know why she'd dropped the divorce suit.

"The reporters were awful after that game," Pat says. "Terry dressed quickly so we could get out of there, but my stomach was just upside down."

With the campaign almost half over, the Wings were mired in fifth place and the winless situation took its toll on coach Skinner.

"I began to get these awful migraine headaches, had trouble driving, sleeping. Jack Adams made me have an eye exam but my eyes were fine. I stepped aside and recommended Sid Abel who was around town doing TV telecasts, and I stayed on in the Wing organization handling the farm system. Maybe it was all just getting to me. I haven't had a migraine since."

Under Abel's tutelage, the Wings rebounded, finishing in

third place, a point ahead of Boston and twenty-six points behind their first-round opponents, the first-place Canadiens.

Before the first playoff game was three minutes old, Rocket Richard — back from a career-threatening Achilles tendon injury that forced him to miss December, January, and most of February — scored the first goal of an 8–1 Canadiens rout. Game Two was all Montreal again, 5–1. The Wings forced overtime in Game Three before losing, 2–1, and the Habs completed the sweep by a 4–3 score. The Rocket scored more goals, seven, than the entire Detroit team in the series.

"The Rocket was at the tail end of his career," Marcel Pronovost recalls, "but I have always said there is not one hockey player today, yesterday, nor perhaps tomorrow who could electrify a crowd the way the Rocket could. When he grabbed the puck, the crowd came alive, whether he was in Montreal or anywhere else in the league. And it seemed that he always saved his best for Detroit."

The early exit from the playoffs meant an early start to the summer, which left Terry feeling restless. There was a lot of time to reflect on the season just past, but it had been a troubling one. He had played all seventy games, but the team had allowed 207 goals, the second-highest total in the league. His three shutouts were his lowest output for a complete season ever, and his 2.96 goals-against average was his highest to date, almost a full goal higher than his previous Red Wing season three years before. His playoff stats were even more garish: nineteen goals against in four games for a 4.52 average.

Insecure and overly demanding of himself at the best of times, Terry could only remember all the goals that had gotten by him. He felt even more anxious about himself, his job, and his ability to provide for his family.

"Terry developed a daily routine from the time a season ended until it began in the fall," Pat recalls. "He would get up in the morning, drink a hundred coffees, smoke a thousand cigarettes, read the newspaper, do the crossword puzzle, be dressed and out of the house by noon, and head down to the local VFW. Sometimes the kids and I wouldn't see him until later that evening."

The VFW, or Veterans of Foreign Wars, was an organization set up for veterans to socialize, reminisce, or help each other adjust to civilian life once again. Its Canadian counterpart is the Royal Canadian Legion. Union Lake had its own branch, and Johnny Wilson recalls that Terry was drawn there because he could relate to the blue-collar working people he encountered there. He didn't mind the ten-cent beers, either. ·

During the past season Louis and Anne Sawchuk moved with son Gerald to Detroit to be near Terry and Pat, who had picked out a nice home close by. Pat took advantage of Louis's presence to keep Terry home and busy.

"The field behind our house used to be like a racetrack. There were always motorcycles racing around back there and I used to worry about our three kids wandering around, so Terry and his Dad put up this real nice fence to keep the kids in the yard. They did a really nice job on it. It was well built and kept the kids safe. I believe it is still up to this very day."

The Red Wings opened the 1958–59 season on the road being shut out, 2–0, by the Canadiens at the Forum. Terry came back in the next game, Detroit's home opener, to blank the Rangers, 3–0, in a game which saw Gump Worsley carried from the ice on a stretcher after Gordie Howe was pushed into him by New York defenceman Bill Gadsby.

Terry's play was so magnificent early on, that there was talk of a "new" Sawchuk. Jack Adams was generous with his praise. "I've never seen Terry this sharp so early. It is remarkable. The kid has grown up . . . he's matured . . . he's working relaxed."

On November 12, while Terry practised with the Red Wings at the University of Michigan rink in Ann Arbor, a mishap occurred at home involving his thirteen-month-old daughter, Kathy. Four-year-old Jerry and two-year-old JoAnne were playing hockey with wooden spoons, using a little ball of plastic wrap as a puck, in the family's kitchen. During the game, the puck went under the refrigerator. Jerry and JoAnne rescued it, but also knocked into the open a deadly button of ant poison, which little Kathy put into her mouth.

"Little Kathy came to me," Pat recalls today, "and opened

her mouth, and it was all green and I could see the little button. Oh my God, I'll tell you I just freaked!

"I grabbed her, threw her in bed, ran to the kitchen, and gave her milk. I knew that she had to get her stomach pumped. I phoned my doctor but he was in surgery, so my neighbour drove us to the nearest doctor."

Dr. William Robinson immediately pumped the child's stomach, gave her oxygen, and rushed them all to the hospital. One more hour, it was said, and the tragedy could have been fatal. Terry rushed to the hospital to spend the next seven hours with Pat and Kathy before leaving with the Red Wings for Boston. Kathy was kept overnight in hospital, but the worst of her ordeal was over.

In Boston the next night, the Wings led 3–0 with six and a half minutes remaining in the second period, when Don McKenney fired a shot that Terry let go but which hit the post behind him. When the goal judge flashed the light indicating a goal and referee Dalton McArthur confirmed the verdict as a goal, Terry completely lost his temper.

Racing to centre ice, he argued vehemently with the officials, slamming his stick loudly on the ice. Then he raced back behind his net to yell at goal judge Louis Reycroft, and McArthur assessed him a ten-minute misconduct penalty. Terry then rushed back to centre ice and bumped the referee, who narrowly escaped falling to the ice. Remarkably, McArthur did not eject Sawchuk from the game.

The incident clearly demonstrated Terry's increasing volatility. In his first five NHL seasons, he had accumulated a mere nine minutes in penalties, but in the ensuing six years he had accumulated over 115 minutes.

Terry frequently began to take four-year-old Jerry to the rink with him for practices. A comical picture in the *Detroit News* on February 8, 1959, showed the younger Sawchuk in the net, only his head visible behind his father's pads, with three-year-old Mark Howe and four-year-old Marty Howe on either side of him, each poised to shoot the puck.

Terry's play was so stalwart that he was voted to the First

All-Star team at the season's halfway point, joined by his defence buddy, Marcel Pronovost.

But the Red Wings would slump badly in the second half. Detroit won only two games in nearly six weeks between December 10 and January 20. In the end, the Wings had sunk to the bottom of the league, six points behind the fifth-place Rangers. It was the Wings' first time in the cellar since 1937–38. The Wings allowed fifty-one goals more than they scored and Terry's average went up to 3.12 goals per game, the first time ever that it had gone over 3.00.

Terry still managed to notch five more shutouts, including the seventy-fifth of his career on February 12 against the Rangers.

Oddly, the last-place Wings dominated the Second All-Star team, of which Sawchuk, Pronovost, Howe, and Delvecchio were all members.

That spring, Terry handed out the awards at a minor hockey banquet sponsored by the Walled Lake Junior Chamber of Commerce. He showed films of the 1958 Stanley Cup finals, signed autographs, and made a donation towards the construction of a new rink. Though Terry had often been criticized by Jack Adams for his reluctance to do more public appearances, visit hospitals, or even sign autographs, it was clear that Terry did do these things when he was in the right frame of mind.

Art Kras remembers one such moment.

"A friend of mine had some athletes who would come down to St. Heddrick's High School on Mother's Day to talk to the kids, and one time they cancelled at the last minute, so I called Terry. He was running a gas station in Pontiac in the off-season that spring, and I told him the situation. He said he'd meet me at my bar. He closed the gas station for the afternoon, came down, sat with every kid, talked with them, signed all their certificates, and when he got finished, he said, 'Thanks for asking me out.' He really enjoyed it.

"Terry also went to the local Boys' Club of America once in a while at Christmas. Nobody ever knew but he was really nice to those kids. He enjoyed being with them, and they never forgot it either. That was a side of Terry I'm not even sure his family ever knew about. I know he didn't ever want it publicized."

A more mature Terry Sawchuk hit the golf links early. He must have wondered what lay in store. Despite his excellent play, the Wings had missed the playoffs for the first time in 21 years. As he contemplated the past season with the boys at the VFW, he had little doubt that the Wings' fall from grace had been his fault.

11

MR. RELAXATION

"I guess Terry didn't love himself enough, didn't have enough faith in himself," Pat Sawchuk says. "Terry needed his ego fed constantly by the boys, you know, and that was sad. He seemed to have to drink all the time, and he was never really happy. But he drank day in and day out in the off-season."

It was tough for a wife to stand idly by, but there was nothing she could say or do to stop or help him.

Terry's problem with alcohol was obviously a progressive one. In the beginning stages, drinking with his teammates after games, practices, and rounds of golf was strictly a social practice. Even now, as he'd spend day after day at the VFW hall, Terry's drinking centred around companionship. And even though neglectful of his family, soon to include a fourth child, Sawchuk hadn't let his drinking interfere with his career.

"Terry never drank the day of a game, or the night before," Pat recalls. "It was only after a practice or after a game. Never, never before! That doesn't mean he stopped drinking during the season, but he seemed to control it just a bit more!"

In fact Terry headed to the 1959 training camp with an uncharacteristically relaxed attitude. He explained it all to Marshall Dann of the *Detroit Free Press*: "Well, I'm loafing a lot more. I don't mean loafing on the ice, I mean loafing in my attitude and loafing in general off the ice. I always figured I needed hard work to get my timing and to stay sharp. In training camp, exhibitions, and practices, I always played every shot as if a game depended on it. Maybe that was right for me at the time. It does make sense for a young goalie, but this summer I spent a lot of time loafing at Ed Morey's golf club and I found I was relaxed like Perry Como when I got to training camp.

"So I kept on loafing in camp, in the exhibitions, and in practice. I looked at all the shots and studied them, but I didn't try to stop them. All I wanted to do was work up a light sweat. This was the first year I ever gained weight after the season started. I felt a lot fresher on the ice and I wasn't all beat after a game ends."

Terry's new state of well-being certainly didn't sit well with some of his teammates.

"Sometimes, Terry would give you ten, maybe fifteen, minutes of practice and that was it," Alex Delvecchio says. "And if you pissed him off with a high shot, the next time you came down on him, he'd deliberately step out of the net. He'd say 'to hell with ya!' I know it used to really piss some of the younger guys off."

If Terry was Dr. Jekyll in practice, he was certainly still Mr. Hyde in games. After appearing in his eighth All-Star Game in Montreal on October 3, taking a 6–1 beating from the Stanley Cup champion Canadiens, he shut out Chicago, 2–0, on October 14, then blanked the Leafs, 3–0, four nights later. Terry allowed only five goals in his first six games and his play was called spectacular.

Then in a Sunday-night game against the first-place Canadiens, who led the Wings by a single point, Terry was struck on the left knee by the stick of Jean Beliveau in a 2–1 loss.

Three nights later in New York, Terry was cruising along in the third period with a three-goal lead when the leg injury began to bother him. When he missed a thirty-five-foot rising shot off the stick of Camille Henry, he was clearly favouring the leg as he struggled to his feet. The Rangers pounced on

Terry with two more goals in the next five minutes and the Red Wings emerged with a tie and a gimpy-legged goalie.

Terry was back in form two nights later as he and Jacques Plante put on a goaltending clinic at the Forum. "Jake the Snake" emerged with a 1–0 victory. For the next three weeks, Terry and his Pirates played excellent hockey. The Wings stayed hot on the trail of the first-place Canadiens, and Terry had allowed only forty-nine goals after his first twenty-one games for a respectable 2.33 goals-against average. "I read where some guy in Toronto says I'm playing rebounds differently," Terry joked to reporters. "I was glad to read that because it was the first time I knew about it."

But for some reason, the renewed success was not enough for Terry. He continued to drink, which resulted in more problems on the morning of Thursday, November 26, Thanksgiving Day 1959. Pat remembers: "Terry kept on drinking that year and every time he did so, his legs would ache something fierce the next morning. Other people would have hangovers but not Terry — his legs would ache so bad he could hardly stand it. And on the night before Thanksgiving, he really boozed it up, and he really paid for it."

At ten-thirty a.m., Terry was in such agony that an ambulance whisked him to hospital, where it was reported cryptically that he was treated for a "virus."

Terry returned after a three-game absence, and in mid-December the Wings were still in second place behind the Canadiens and their now-masked goaltender, Jacques Plante. Though Plante was the first to wear a mask in a game on November 1, goalies around the league had been donning them in practice since the year before. In fact, Terry had regularly worn a clear plastic faceguard in practice.

The innovation was certainly controversial. Plante allowed thirteen goals in two weekend games at the start of the new year, and coach Toe Blake blamed the mask. "He can't see in that darn thing. He loses sight of the puck at the sides!"

By the end of January, the Wings began to falter, losing three of four games and falling into third place, a point back of Toronto. The Wings were having trouble holding a lead and seemed to have particular trouble in the third period of games. Without their hot start, Detroit would easily have been in fifth place by now.

At home, Pat went into premature labour on December 22, forty-seven days before the baby was due. Pat's doctor's injections were able to stop the labour, but she was admitted to hospital until the birth of the baby.

"For the first two weeks they wouldn't allow me to put my feet on the floor," Pat says. "I was worried about my kids — I missed them! I just wanted to get out of there."

"Red Kelly's wife, Andra, used to bring me food up the back stairs, she was a real sweetheart. Terry came up a couple of times and complained that I was in the hospital, which made me feel real good. 'How long are you going to be in here?' and 'Does that doctor know what he's doing?' Then, the night Carol Ann was born, I think I had three pains and then boom, there she was. I was back in my hospital bed in forty minutes. They said my bed wasn't even cold!"

At 11:55 p.m. on Sunday, January 31, 1960, Carol Ann Sawchuk came screaming into the world at five pounds, twelve ounces. Terry called from New York, where the Wings had blown a 3–1 lead to settle for a 3–3 tie. Once back from his road trip, Terry drove Pat home from the hospital. Just a few days later, Terry's drinking made the pains in his legs flare up. Terry was again taken to the hospital by ambulance and was forced out of the lineup due to the severity of the leg pains.

Terry missed nine games as Dennis Riggin was called up to take his place. Terry was admitted on February 15 to the University of Michigan Medical Center for testing. Finally a diagnosis was made. The star goaltender was suffering from "viral neuritis," an inflammation of the nerves in his legs caused by a virus. Anyone familiar with Terry's bouts of drinking would know, however, that the condition was irritated by alcohol, not a virus.

Terry was quickly put on a balanced diet and vitamin supplements, and the condition began immediately to reverse itself. But he was told that continued heavy drinking would mean a return of the neuritis symptoms, with more permanent effects. He didn't have to be told what that would mean to his hockey career.

During his layoff, Terry agreed to an in-depth, ninety-minute interview with *Detroit News* sports editor Sam Greene and writers John Walter and Jim Higginbottom. He was asked to comment on Red Kelly and Billy McNeill, recently traded to the Rangers and refusing to report.

"They're my friends," Sawchuk said. "What they did is their business. It would be wonderful if you could read people's minds and didn't have to wonder what was behind their actions."

It was a very insightful answer, considering his recent behaviour with the bottle. He was then asked if he would quit hockey should he be traded.

"No!" he answered. "I'd go wherever I was traded. I'd like to play a couple more years. With four kids, I need the money. Hockey has been very good to me, money-wise."

How about coaching after his playing days were over?

"I don't know — coaching really is rough. You've got eighteen personalities [to manage]. Some you have to push, some you have to holler at. Some you say nothing to and others need a pat on the back. What a rough job a football coach must have with a squad of thirty-five."

Would he like to referee?

"No, sir! That's worse! I'd like to be a hockey scout. We had a hockey school last summer in Toledo. I got a lot of enjoyment out of it."

Who was the best goalie around?

"They're all good. Jacques Plante probably ranks as number one. Plante would be just as good or better with another team . . . If Worsley weren't with New York, they'd really get whitewashed. He's down on the ice half the time but few goalies can recover as quickly as he can. Glenn (Hall) has about the best [glove] hand I've ever seen. He's a stand-up goalie and not used to going down. There's such a thing as going to the ice too fast. That's where a good coach comes in. Johnny Bower is playing well for Toronto. Harry Lumley of Boston is an angle player, a stand-up goalie who can beat opposing marksmen more often because he plays the percentages instinctively."

Terry went on to state that Jean Beliveau of Montreal gave him the most trouble with his screening and Vic Stasiuk for interfering with the goalie. He was asked which type of shot was the hardest to stop? To those who played with Terry, his answer did not come as a surprise.

"Flip shots. They're tough to judge as to how they're going to bounce. You may move out and then have the puck take a crazy bounce sideways. You really look like a chump. Sometimes you lose the puck against the crowd background in Chicago and Montreal. They're not as well-lit as the other rinks."

At the end of the session, Terry was asked about the condition of his legs.

"I've been feeling great except when that virus neuritis affected my legs Thanksgiving Day. They gave me a little trouble again at New York (January 31). Dennis Riggin has been doing a fine job in my place, but I'm ready to go again now."

When Terry returned to the team in late February, the Wings were still in the thick of the playoff race. On March 8, he shut out Plante and the Canadiens, 3–0, for his fifth shutout of the season and the eighty-first of his career.

The Wings ended the season in fourth place with sixty-seven points, edging out Boston by three points for the final playoff spot. Terry had played in fifty-eight games, earned five shutouts, and allowed 156 goals for a 2.69 average, his best since his return to Detroit.

The Wings and their semifinal opponents, the second-place Toronto Maple Leafs, were a study in contrasts. The day before the series started, the Leafs were so keyed up that intramural fights prompted coach Punch Imlach to order his team off the ice only twelve minutes into a practice. The Wings, meanwhile, were loose and relaxed. Reporters asked the veterans for their greatest Stanley Cup thrill. Gordie Howe said Leswick's 1954 overtime winner was his favourite. Marcel Pronovost cited his first Cup in 1950, while Delvecchio and Sawchuk recalled the '52 sweep.

The Wings upset the Leafs in the opening game at Maple Leaf Gardens, 2–1. Before the second game, Leaf boss Punch

Imlach dropped 1,250 one-dollar bills on the floor of the dressing room to show his boys what they stood to lose if eliminated. The Leafs responded by tying the series with a 4–2 win.

The third game at the Olympia went into a third overtime period before twenty-two-year-old Leaf Frank Mahovlich took a pass from ex-Wing Red Kelly. Imlach had obtained Kelly after he'd refused the trade to New York, and switched him from defence to centre. The Big M's shot beat Terry to give the Leafs a 5–4 win a and a 2–1 series lead. Kelly had also set up the winning goal in Game Two.

The Wings had some life left in them, as they won Game Four, 2–1, in overtime to send the series back to Toronto tied at two games each. But with memories of the pile of money still fresh in the Leafs' minds, they took the fifth game, 5–4.

With the Leafs ahead in Game Six, 3–2, and the play buzzing around the Wings' net, Toronto's Frank Mahovlich picked up the puck.

"I had the puck in the corner," Mahovlich explained after the game, "and made a run at the net. Sawchuk kicked out my shot and fell down, and I slid alongside the net. Johnny Wilson, now a Leaf, poked the rebound to Red Kelly and the puck trickled into the crease. I was lying down and reached for it with my stick. Just about that time Haley [the Wings' Len "Comet" Haley, who'd scored the Game One winner] came flying in on his knees, hit the puck and my stick, and skidded right into the net. I guess I scored it, but really, who knows?"

The goal by the Big M was the clincher as the Leafs eliminated the Wings with a 4–2 victory. Toronto goalie Johnny Bower was the key to the series as the thirty-five-year-old allowed only sixteen goals on 225 shots, while Terry allowed twenty goals on 186 shots.

Toronto coach/GM Punch Imlach had much praise for the Red Wing netminder. He said after the series, "Every time I looked, Terry Sawchuk was robbing one of our guys on a breakaway. If Bower was great, so was Sawchuk."

But those around Terry began to notice that he was becoming moody. "From the beginning of our marriage, we were strangers trying to get to know each other," Pat says. "He could be so sweet and then turn on a dime!"

Jimmy Peters, though no longer a teammate of Terry's, continued to see him often.

"The change I noticed in Terry was when he began to drop over to my place on Sunday mornings in the summertime and he also began dropping in on neighbours here and having a bit of a drink. That's when I noticed and figured he had a drinking problem."

Given his past brush with the neuritis in his legs, it was baffling that Terry continued to drink at all. Still, Terry must have thought that all was well when, on August 26, he signed his contract for the 1960–61 season. The last time he had had a battle with the bottle and been forced to miss some games, Jack Adams had traded him. One must wonder if Terry's bargaining position was weakened by his failing health. In any event, unbeknownst to Terry, Adams and coach Sid Abel had a contingency plan in place.

"We were in the middle of a team meeting," Jimmy Skinner, by now the director of the Wings' farm system, recalls, "when Hank Bassen walks in and Terry takes one look at him and snarls, 'What the fuck is he doing here?'"

Bassen had been recalled from the Western league, where he'd been the "Most Valuable Player" the year before. Abel and Adams had no intentions of enduring another goaltending crisis. Abel explained to the press that Terry had missed twelve games the previous season, and the Wings intended to keep two goalies on the roster to avoid being caught short again. Terry still fit into the Wings' plans, but on management's terms.

During the 1960–61 season, Terry would find himself sitting in the stands more than he'd play in the net — Bassen was playing the majority of the games.

"To Terry, this was a personal challenge to his ability to handle his job adequately by himself," remarked Pat Sawchuk. "It really rocked his world. If he sat out a game, there are no words to describe his depression. I felt so sorry for him. He took it personally."

In late November, Hank Bassen was forced out of action with a sprained ankle.

On November 27, Terry suited up for a game against the visiting Maple Leafs. The crowd of 14,459 roared its approval. Terry was up to the task, making key saves, and Gordie Howe assisted on Howie Glover's first-period goal to draw him one point shy of Rocket Richard's all-time total point record of 1,091.

Late in the second period, Terry contributed offensively as well as defensively. He rushed behind his net and rifled the puck around the boards to a waiting Gordie Howe, who carried the puck down the right wing into the Leaf zone. Howe fired a pass to a speeding Norm Ullman, whose shot squeezed through Johnny Bower's pads and dribbled over the goal line. Gordie's assist drew him even with the Rocket. Terry's third career assist put him just 1,088 points behind his teammate.

Up 2–0, the Wings attempted to maintain their hold on first place and extend their longest Olympia winning streak in four years to six games. With just under three minutes left in the game, Marcel Pronovost drew a penalty and the Leafs pulled Bower to give them a two-man advantage. Terry was dazzling, making amazing stops. Allan Stanley let go a point-blank backhander that Terry acrobatically knocked down and then dove dramatically to cover up. The ovation was thunderous as Terry got back on his feet. Terry's fine play almost overshadowed Howe's accomplishment. It was Terry's eighty-third career shutout.

This flash of his old brilliance wasn't enough for the Wings' braintrust. When Bassen's ankle healed, he continued to play as much as Terry, even more.

"Terry could not stand to be second fiddle," Marcel Pronovost says. "He couldn't stand not playing at this point in his career and he went upstairs to the management and asked to be traded."

Then, during a television interview in Montreal, Terry said flatly that if he was not going to play on a more regular basis, he wanted to be traded to another team. But only the Bruins were looking for goaltending help, and a trade back to them was definitely not in the cards. Terry would have to stay and make the best of a bad situation, which did have its lighter moments.

"We're in a game at the Olympia," Marcel Pronovost recalls. "And you can hear this fan every once in a while yell out, 'Hey, Saw*buck*! Hey, Saw*buck*!' During one of the breaks, Terry calls me over and says, 'Hey, Marce, can you spot that son of a bitch that is yelling that?' 'Okay, I'll keep an eye out for him.' Sure enough, the guy stands up again and yells, 'Hey, Saw*buck*!' and I get a reading on him. So at the next stoppage of play I goes to Terry, 'Uke, I spotted him.'

"So now, the next game, Terry is not playing and he makes a beeline for the organ loft and spots this same guy, who's quietly watching the game. The guy then feels a tap on the shoulder, turns around, and a seething Terry, nostrils flaring, grabs him by the scruff of the neck and says, 'The name is Saw*chuk*, not Saw*buck*!'"

Before the season ended, Terry had clawed his way back to participate in more than half the games. In the season finale against Montreal, he put the team and the rest of the league on notice that he was back, making thirty-six saves in a 2–0 Canadiens victory.

Even though he thought Bassen had been better over the long haul, Abel knew Terry well enough to know that if he did get hot, anything could happen in the playoffs. The Wings had finished fourth, twelve points ahead of the Rangers, setting up a semifinal match with Toronto for the second year in a row. The Wings' coach named Terry his playoff goaltender.

Johnny Bower, nursing a sore leg, missed the series opener but his Leafs still squeaked out a 3–2 double overtime victory. But over the next four games Terry allowed only five goals as the Wings swept aside a team that boasted the 1961 Vezina winner and the league's second-most potent offence. Terry was one of the three stars in all five games, leading Gordie Howe to comment, "Terry is the Terry of old, playing like he did when we were winning Stanley Cups and he was the greatest." When Chicago goalie Glenn Hall posted back-to-back shutouts in Games Five and Six of the other semifinal series, the Hawks' elimination of the defending Stanley Cup champion Canadiens set up the first all-American Stanley Cup final since 1950.

Going into the finals, Terry was full of confidence but a tender, black-and-blue left shoulder had been bothering him a bit.

Pat remembers Terry always being beat up.

"From the moment the season began, Terry would come home with these great big bruises all over his body. He bruised something awful. But you couldn't keep him out of the net."

Jerry, the eldest of the Sawchuk kids, remembers the effect the sight of his battered father had on his friends.

"Sometimes at home, he would walk around the house with his shirt off, his chest was always black and blue. The neighbourhood kids would see this, plus the scars on his face and were scared to death to come over. They thought he was the Frankenstein monster!"

The 1961 Stanley Cup finals opened in the noisy confines of Chicago Stadium on April 6. As Terry bent down in his crouch to face Glenn Hall, "Mr. Goalie," in the opposite net, he knew more than anybody that goaltending would be the key to the series.

He also knew he would be without the full services of one of his important pirates. Marcel Pronovost recalls: "Before the final series began, I turned from a Norm Ullman slap shot in practice and the puck caused a slight fracture of a small, non-weight-bearing bone, the fibula.

"I wore a removable cast, hobbled to the arena on crutches, got dressed except for that one foot, while the rest of the team went out for warmup. Five minutes prior to the national anthem, the doctors came in with the needles and froze the ankle. I'd lace up the skates, tape the ankle, and out I would go. That's how I began that series against Chicago."

Terry started off well, holding the Hawks off the scoreboard, when he raced from his net to play an errant puck to his left. An oncoming Hawk, Murray Balfour, barrelled into the goalie. The collision left Terry lying on the ice, clutching his sore left arm, in complete agony. The game was held up for several minutes until Terry gamely insisted that he was ready to continue. Chicago pumped three quick goals past him before the first period ended, and Sid Abel decided to put Bassen in to start the second. The Wings battled back with two goals but couldn't get the equalizer past Hall in a 3–2 Chicago victory.

Still in pain, diagnosed with a pinched nerve in his left shoulder, Terry watched Game Two from the sidelines as the Wings' defence tightened up around Bassen. The strategy worked as the Wings evened the series with a 3–1 victory heading back to the Olympia. Still in pain, Terry watched the Hawks take the series' lead by notching their own 3–1 victory in Game Three.

The shoulder felt well enough for Terry to return to action in Game Four. He put in a stalwart performance as Bruce MacGregor's first NHL goal with seven minutes remaining in the game gave the Red Wings a 2–1 victory to again tie the series.

Terry was between the pipes for Game Five and, for two periods, the teams exchanged goals and shots. In the third period, the Wings' defence collapsed as the Hawks slipped three unanswered goals past Terry en route to a 6–3 victory in which the goaltenders faced a combined eighty shots.

Bassen returned to the Wings' cage for the sixth game but the Hawks cruised to a convincing 5–1 victory for their first Stanley Cup title in twenty-three years.

In the off-season, there were rumours that Sawchuk was considering retirement, brought on by his frustration with the two-goalie system. Pat recalls: "There were only two things that rocked Terry's life and career. The first was being traded by Jack Adams to Boston in 1955, and the second was the two-goalie system. He hated sharing his net. In time he adjusted to it, but at first he considered it a personal slap in the face! He sometimes mumbled about quitting, but he couldn't. It was his life. It was the only thing he knew how to do."

It was at this stage in his life when son Jerry began to see changes in his father, changes that were not for the good.

"Dad was turning into a very unpredictable man. He would be real nice one moment and just as mean as could be the next. He would turn so red in the face and a big vein would pop out of his forehead. When that happened, you were scared because you were about to get hit. I seemed to be the target whenever he lost his temper. Needless to say, this happened a lot."

Jerry says that at this point, Terry had lost control of his drinking.

"Dad used to come home at night, all boozed up, and knock down all the mail boxes on Golfside Drive. He'd take them all out. The neighbour right next to us got fed up, so he put his mailbox on a ten-inch steel railway girder. Dad never knocked that one down again."

Terry continued to play Russian roulette with his health by drinking throughout that summer. Jerry remembers an ambulance being summoned one morning when his father couldn't get out of bed. Jerry thought his father had arthritis in his legs, but in reality it must have been the remnants of his neuritis which his incessant drinking threatened to resurrect.

Terry reported to the Wings' camp that September and signed a contract for the 1961–62 season, squelching rumours of his imminent retirement.

Bill Gadsby, a veteran defenceman acquired from the Rangers, recalls his reaction to playing in front of Terry.

"I remember being impressed by Terry when I played against him but I was doubly impressed when I played in front of him. He'd come up with those big saves, man oh man, it was just amazing. I also remember not being in Detroit very long when Terry took me aside and said, 'Bill, if you're going to block shots, keep your legs together. I have a better chance of stopping it when it comes beside you than when it comes through your legs.' As a defenceman, that helped me out a lot. And we worked well together."

On November 12, the Red Wings hosted the first-place Canadiens. Terry drew the starting assignment as Hank Bassen, who was still platooning with Terry this far in the season, was dispatched to the Edmonton Flyers to fill in for the injured Dennis Riggin. At the eleven-minute mark of the opening period, a ten-foot backhand shot by Henri Richard struck Terry on the right side of his face near his nose. Blood was everywhere. Play was halted and Terry was taken to the first-aid room.

"I remember that cut because it was quite nasty really," says Dr. John Finlay, then the Red Wing physician. "[It] involved the corner of his nose and it took some fancy suturing to close it, yet we used only five or six stitches, something to that effect. It was odd."

After a nineteen-minute delay, Terry returned to the game and shut out the Canadiens, 3–0, stopping all twenty-two Canadiens' shots.

"Well, that makes two victories for the Sawchuks today," Terry said proudly. "My son Jerry's team won a pee wee game, 3–1. Jerry did the splits to beat Mark Howe, Gordie's son." But the smiles would be few and far between for the Wings.

"We all had a tough year that year," Marcel Pronovost says. "For the four years prior to this, I had made the All-Star team, but in that '61–62 season I couldn't do anything right. We all heard the boos and we all heard the trade rumours. We all had garbage thrown at us."

Despite Terry's five shutouts this season, he racked up the highest goals-against average of his career, 3.33. A year after playing for the Cup, the Wings finished out of the playoffs in fifth place, four points behind the Rangers.

Soon after the end of the dismal season, the thirty-five-year tenure of Jack Adams came to an abrupt end when Red Wing president Bruce Norris gave him his walking papers. The man who had always had a soft spot for Terry was now gone, replaced by someone who hadn't hesitated to use Hank Bassen — Sid Abel, who assumed the dual role of coach and GM. Now, more than ever, Terry knew he would be skating on thin ice.

He dealt with the potential problem in the only manner he knew how. "At this point in his career, in his life, Terry seemed like someone who was slowly committing suicide," Marcel Pronovost recalls. "He didn't give a damn. He drank if he wanted to, ran around, and did what he wanted to."

As his reckless behaviour spiralled out of control, he was completely oblivious to the consequences.

12

THE MAN IN THE MASK

I N the spring of 1962, Pat Sawchuk informed Terry once again that she wanted a divorce. As great as his shock had been when she made the same announcement four years before, he must have been even more taken aback this time, as he seems to have been oblivious to the behaviour that drove his wife to this point.

There was no doubt that Terry loved Pat and the children, yet his conduct at this stage of his life, for the most part, indicated just the opposite. Terry Sawchuk certainly harboured misguided attitudes about women and family. With the exception of Pat, Terry felt women were on earth either to serve men sexually or to provide for them in a nurturing sense. Having not been close to his mother, Terry found it impossible to develop trust and emotional relationships with women.

His hockey career, his deepening alcoholism, and his forays into extramarital flings — though few but public — were all means of avoiding responsibility and intimacy with his family at home. Terry had a tough, hard side to him, a side that had served him in good stead to become a top NHL goaltender. But 'that' life had its own fair share of pitfalls of which alcoholic habits and the continuing availability of beautiful and sexually willing female "groupies" were all too easy for Terry to fall prey to.

Up to this point in their marriage, Pat had been by far the one working at it the most. Though Terry provided financially for his wife and four children — albeit grudgingly at times — she was the linchpin of the Sawchuk household. Even during the off-season, or on days off, Terry was essentially an absentee husband and father.

When Terry did come home, it was almost always in an impaired, argumentative state. His was certainly a Jekyll-and-Hyde personality. He was an intelligent man, and certainly capable of feeling deep emotion. He just did not know how to let a more loving side show. Unfortunately for his family, Terry's love had to be kick-started, and Pat's renewed desire for divorce achieved its goal of seizing Terry's attention. As in 1958, he was remorseful to the point of tears. He didn't want to lose Pat, the only woman he'd ever loved. He promised, again, to mind his ways, said he'd make good on his promise. To demonstrate his good intentions, they planned a trip together to Daytona Beach, Florida. Even today she recalls that week as the best time she and Terry ever shared together as a couple.

"We went out to dinner, we walked. He knew I liked sweetbreads — they're a delicacy in French restaurants, so he called a whole bunch of French restaurants in the phone book until he found one that had sweetbreads on the menu. It was so close we walked to it. It was a beautiful evening and we had a romantic supper. As we walked afterwards, he reached out and grabbed my hand, which was a first. Terry was not the romantic type.

"We golfed together, swam in the ocean, went sightseeing on a boat. It was far, far better than our honeymoon. If he was trying to get back into my good graces, it worked. I was sucked right in."

As cold and uncaring as Terry could sometimes be, his feelings at this juncture seemed genuine. Pat recalled him being more attentive to the kids. He bought and assembled a small pool for the backyard, played with the kids more, had backyard barbecues. Terry even curtailed his drinking, except for one particular Fourth of July celebration. Pat recalls the moment like it was yesterday.

"We often went to my Dad's golf course for fireworks except this one year, Terry had gotten us our own. Now Terry is half crocked and laughing with little Jerr in the front yard, and he has Jerry light some firecrackers. I'm beside myself with worry. 'Ah, be quiet,' he says. 'You're getting all upset for nothing!' 'Nothing, my foot!' I said. I swear to God that Terry did things sometimes just to aggravate me. Well, they did have an explosion and it burnt a hole in the front grass the size of a garbage can cover and Jerr got burnt, though not badly, thank God! I could have killed Terry!"

Another indication that Terry's overall well-being had improved was the fact that he put on quite a bit of weight this off-season. While he didn't balloon to 219 pounds as he had in his sophomore year of 1951–52, he still did get somewhat chunky.

Pat continues, "Terry would love it when the season was over and he could eat more than he could during the season. I would make his favourite Ukrainian dishes that his Mom made him — jellied pigs' feet, or head cheese, which was his absolute favourite. I also made him kasha baked with onion and bacon. Yes, that summer of '62 I would say he put on a little bit of weight."

Later that summer, a cherubic Terry joined teammates Marcel Pronovost, Bill Gadsby, Gordie Howe, and coach Sid Abel on a fishing trip to the Florida Keys. Marcel Pronovost recalls this particular trip.

"It was rough, let me tell you. The seas were twenty-five to thirty feet high. The captain was very hesitant to go out. We weren't out very long when Terry hooked onto a big black fin Benito Tuna. It took about forty-five to fifty minutes for him to bring it in. After he caught his fish, he had to sit around and wait as we rotated the two seats until everyone had caught a fish. Howe caught a sailfish."

Bill Gadsby picks up the story, revealing that Terry, coming as he did from land-locked Winnipeg, wasn't cut out to be a mariner.

"We're having a great time, having a lot of laughs and a few beers. I caught a few barracudas and they called me 'Barracuda Bill.' And we're in these seas, I mean the boat is really going up and down, up and down. Lo and behold if the Uke doesn't get seasick, I mean *really* seasick. I'd say he threw up maybe eight or ten times. He's sitting down there in the galley, turning green, and we leave him down there. The captain keeps asking us if we want to go in to port and we all say, 'Ah naw, we're fine, having a great time.'

"Now it's lunch time and Terry is just suffering. I'm in charge of lunch and the Uke's sitting by the table in the galley, his head down, and I bring out these sandwiches and stuff. Then I open up this jar of garlic pickles. I didn't even think of it; I put the open jar of these pickles right in front of him and he gets one whiff of them and he throws up again. He said, 'You son of a bitch, you did that on purpose.' He went up to the side of the boat and whoa, he was really cheering for Notre Dame after that!

"Till the day he died, whenever he saw me, he'd get cranked up. He never let me forget it! But whoa, was he sick."

Terry didn't go on the fishing trip merely to socialize. He also hoped to get a feel for Sid Abel's plans for "his" Red Wings in the upcoming season. "With Sid in charge, we all felt a little uncertain about the future," says Marcel Pronovost.

It is not known if Terry had a heart-to-heart talk with Abel during their fishing trip, but just before training camp Abel announced he was going with only one goaltender for the duration of the season and challenged Terry, Hank Bassen, and Dennis Riggin to be that goalie.

This truly pleased Terry, as did the arrival on October 4 of another little Sawchuk girl, Debbie Lynn, born while Terry was at training camp.

"Terry wasn't around so a neighbour, Rose Jollie, took me in with Grandma Sawchuk," Pat recalls. "Debbie was a normal delivery, thank God! She was small — all my babies were small. I was out in two or three days. And again Grandma was there to help me, as always."

The first thing Terry did on his arrival at training camp was to inquire with Lefty as to the whereabouts of that fibreglass mask the trainer had fashioned for him two years before. Together they revamped the mask, making the eye holes much bigger to improve Terry's vision, and designing and cutting larger holes in it so the mask would be cooler and better ventilated. Terry would give the mask a serious trial in training camp.

Dr. John Finlay, the Red Wings' team doctor, recalls Terry's experiments with the mask in that training camp.

"I remember that Terry had been hospitalized prior to the 1962–63 season and had to see Dr. Wapotano, the team's general internist. Terry admitted to Dr. Wapotano that he was becoming more frightened of getting hit in the face.

"As a physician, I always found it amazing that these goaltenders of that era could do what they did — especially Terry, because his deep crouch put his face much closer and in line with the path of the puck. It took amazing courage to go into the net barefaced.

"I sutured Terry's face countless times. I remember one time, the lower section of his nose had separated from his face. We stitched it back on and he returned to the game. In any other line of work, you or I would have been immobilized for at least a week with this kind of injury. Terry returned immediately to the game. Really he shouldn't have, but he was such a competitor.

"The maskless goaltenders were under extreme stress. When Terry finally decided to don the mask, I had even more respect for him, and there is no doubt it lengthened his career."

After fifteen professional seasons, Terry donned the mask on a day-to-day basis for the first time in his career. Even though the transition was clearly necessary, it still did not come easy.

"Terry hated the mask at first," Pat says. "Every day after practice at training camp, he'd come home, look in the mirror, and say, 'That goddamn mask is making my face red and leaving chafe marks!' He'd get the cold cream out and put it on. He'd complain he couldn't see, that the sweat in the mask bothered him. He had a real problem adjusting to it after all those years without it. He fought it, didn't like it, but then in time he got slowly used to it. Then it got that it gave him renewed confidence and he'd dive for shots that he never would have before."

Through training camp and on into the preseason exhibition games, Terry wore the mask with renewed vigour and confidence. He easily regained his "rightful" job as the Red Wings' number-one goalie. Bassen and Riggin could only look on in amazement and await their assignments to the minors. Recalling the resistance Jacques Plante had encountered from his coach, Toe Blake, Terry approached Sid Abel. "What would you think if I wore the mask in regular games?"

"It's fine with me," Abel replied without hesitation. Abel later remarked to the press, "Maybe it does something for him mentally . . . for his confidence."

It certainly did. Terry donned his mask for the first regular-season game in New York against the Rangers. Terry confessed to being more jittery than normal, unsure how he'd perform with it on for the first time in a regular-season game.

His first big challenge came early in the second period, when Rod Gilbert and Dave Balon skated over the Detroit blue line with only one defenceman back. Balon wound up with the puck and he shot it into the far corner to put the Rangers ahead, 1–0. Terry realized that Balon would have beaten him with or without the mask, and as the game continued, his confidence grew.

The Wings took a 2–1 lead with minutes to go in the game and Terry held the lead the rest of the way, even stopping Jean Ratelle on a breakaway. Terry called this season opener his toughest game mentally, but one of the most thrilling accomplishments of his career to that point.

"Winning the game wasn't as important to me as proving to myself that the mask was here to stay — at least as far as I was concerned," Terry said later.

Terry appeared in his 725th regular-season game on October 18. Five days before, the dean of NHL goalies had faced the Iron Man, Chicago's Glenn Hall — who hadn't missed a game since the 1955–56 season — and battled to a scoreless draw — the third such result between the two in their careers.

"Terry and I had a lot of shutouts against each other over the years and those scoreless games were dandies," Glenn Hall says today. "When he was in the other net, he brought my level of play up significantly. I knew I had to be at my best if we were going to beat Terry. I guess you could say we were both at our best during those 0–0 games."

On October 28, Terry blanked the visiting Maple Leafs 2–0 for the ninetieth shutout of his career. Terry had allowed just nine goals in his first seven games. Hall, his nearest rival, had allowed twenty-one goals in nine games.

"Terry's been terrific," boasted Sid Abel. "Sawchuk has been making the big saves, the game-winning saves, beating the opposition on breakaways in every game up to the Toronto game Sunday."

Marcel Pronovost recalls the masked "Phantom of the Olympia." "The sticks were getting better and the shooters were getting better. In the fifties each team had maybe four or five guys who could really shoot the puck. In the sixties, with the use of slap shots and better-quality hockey sticks, the curve and all that, everybody on a hockey club could fire the puck. Terry's confidence got a great boost with the mask. He was fearless again."

"I've been lucky," explained Terry, "and getting lots of help." He held out praise for his defencemen: Bill Gadsby, Doug Barkley, Pete Goegan, Howie Young, and especially his old pal Marcel Pronovost, who, it was noted, was also playing with his old puck-rushing zest. He even admitted the mask may have had something to do with his improved play. "I think the mask keeps you more alert. That may sound funny, but I think the fact that you know you're losing a little (sight) keeps you that way." One of the mask's harshest critics was now a convert. The buzz around the league was that, with Sawchuk using the face guard, Toe Blake's criticism of Plante's wearing a mask subsided. "It wasn't until Sawchuk put on the mask that the Canadiens really accepted it," Plante bitterly confessed later. "He was one of the game's superstars and if he wore one, it had to be all right."

On November 1, Terry had registered his third shutout of the season, a 4–0 pasting at the expense of Gump Worsley and the Rangers, as the Wings stretched their undefeated streak to eight games. They would go without a loss in their first ten games, their best start since 1956–57. On December 5, Terry suffered a severe bruise on his right shoulder after being hit by a deflected puck. Dennis Riggin filled in for three games.

Observers noticed Terry was more agile than ever. Oddly, he attributed it to added bulk.

"Well, I'm up to 182 pounds," he said. "I quit smoking before the season started. I used to smoke a pack of cigarettes a day. I've got a better appetite now. I've put on weight."

But later in December, stomach cramps threatened to put him out of action again.

"I thought I had ulcers," Terry later related. Tests at Detroit's Osteopathic Hospital indicated a blocked intestine, but it was not serious in nature. It was reported that he had to go to the hospital for treatment at the end of December. Terry missed only a few games through all of this, and surgery was not performed.

On January 10, an ankle injury forced Terry from the second period of a game at the Forum. He was expected to miss the next game against the Leafs two nights later, but ever the warrior, Terry recovered and suited up. With the league standings unbelievably tight and the now fourth-place Wings hoping to move up, Terry was putting in another stellar performance. At the three-minute mark, he kicked aside a point-blank Dave Keon backhander but the rebound hit Bill Gadsby's foot and went into the net.

With sixty-three seconds left in the opening period, Terry dove to make his ninth save of the game and had Leaf Bob Pulford fall over his outstretched body. Terry put his catching hand down on the ice in an attempt to keep his balance. At that exact moment, Pulford, trying to get back on his own feet, accidentally stepped on the back of Terry's hand. The pain shot up Terry's left arm. Throwing off his glove, he looked at the back of his hand.

"It looked like a little cut at first," he said later, "then it opened up and I could see the knuckle bones. I tried to open my hand as I was going off the ice but the fingers snapped right under. Funny thing, it hurt very little."

Terry was rushed to Toronto East General Hospital, where he was diagnosed as having three severed tendons above the knuckle. The one-hour surgery included gouging the hand to refind the severed retracted tendons, multi-stitching to reconnect the tendons, and then closing the wound.

"I asked the doctor how many stitches he took, but he said he stopped counting after fifty," Terry quipped later. Terry's hand was placed in a cast and he was kept overnight before flying back to Detroit the next day. Doctors told him he'd miss six to eight weeks of hockey.

Terry's oldest son Jerry, who was eight at the time, remembers his Dad's convalescence. "When Dad was home with the cast on his hand, I remember having to help him with a lot of things, especially tying his shoes. I was always tying his shoes."

Despite the layoff, Terry maintained the routine he'd follow if he were playing: up early in the morning, have his coffee, do the crossword puzzle, see eight-year-old Jerry and six-year-old JoAnne off to school, then read the paper and go down to the VFW for a few beers. When he opened the paper on Tuesday morning, January 22, 1963, he learned that he'd been voted the league's most valuable player at the season's halfway point, edging out Chicago's Stan Mikita. He had also tied Chicago goalie Glenn Hall for a berth on the First All-Star Team. The $500 bonus he received from the league no doubt eased the pain of his hand briefly.

Terry's injury led to an innovation. Wings' trainer Lefty Wilson designed and attached a hard protective covering over the exposed knuckle area of Terry's catching glove. The feature was quickly adopted by all goalies in the NHL.

Terry reported to Toronto East General on February 12 to have his cast removed, and manager Sid Abel said he hoped Terry would be able to return to the lineup for a game in Chicago on the 23rd, which he did. But after missing seventeen games, Sawchuk was clearly not in game shape, as fatigue got the better of him and he was pulled after two periods. But the next night, he was the Terry of old in a 3–2 decision over the Rangers. He went on to finish the season in grand style as the Wings were the thick of the closest four-way race for first place in league history. When the dust finally settled, the Wings were in fourth place, just two points back of third-place Montreal, four back of Chicago, and only five behind the league-leading Toronto Maple Leafs.

Prior to this season, the maskless Sawchuk's expressive face — his steely gaze of concentration and the utter pain he displayed when scored upon — had been a memorable part of watching a Red Wing game. But Terry's mind was made up as early as December that he would no longer play barefaced.

"I'm heartily in favour of the mask," he said. "Your peripheral vision is affected and there are more screen shots in these days of gang attacks than ever before. Sure, it is a little tougher to see a puck lying down around your feet, but you'll go after shots with a mask on that you didn't before — that you instinctively ducked. So, in the long run, it evens up."

On another occasion he concluded, "I don't care how long you play this game, you still flinch when someone lets one go at your head. Now that I've tried a mask, I can't figure why anyone plays goal without one."

By this time Terry's older children were becoming aware of and understanding what their father did for a living. As eldest son Jerry recalls, sometimes the Sawchuk notoriety rubbed off on them.

"At this point, I started to realize my father was a superstar. I played on a pee wee team with Mark and Marty Howe and Kenny Delvecchio. If we ever played a game in Canada, across the border, parents would ask for *my* autograph, almost before I could even write.

"Going into the Red Wings' locker room after practice was fun. Gordie Howe would tease the hell out of us kids. He was the best. He nicknamed me 'Mary.' I hated that name!

"At one game, I snuck down behind Dad's net at ice level to watch him. He saw me there and gave me a nasty look. After the game he really gave it to me. I think I had broken his concentration.

"I also recall Dad screaming at night in his sleep. He was yelling really loud. Mom told me he was dreaming about the game, yelling Marcel's and his other defencemen's names. The game that he loved was killing him mentally."

Earlier in the season, Terry had publicly stated that he found Chicago's Bobby Hull, the "Golden Jet," tough to stop because "he makes all kinds of moves and has an awful good shot."

Hull proved to be a pain in the butt as the Wings and Hawks met in the 1963 semifinals. Despite a bad right shoulder, he scored two first-period goals en route to a 5–4 Chicago victory in Game One. Four power play goals paced the Hawks past the Wings, 5–2, in Game Two.

But Hull broke his nose in Game Two, and with Gordie Howe leading the way, the Wings won the third game back at the Olympia, 4–2. The Golden Jet, eyes blackened and almost shut, managed to score the lone Chicago goal on Terry in a series-tying 4–1 Detroit win.

In the fifth game, in Chicago, Glenn Hall faced forty Wing shots as the Hawks' defence collapsed and Detroit prevailed, 4–2. In fact, Hall had faced 130 shots in the Wings' three victories. The sixth game, back in Detroit, was a blowout. The home team sailed to a 7–4 victory and eliminated the Hawks. Despite his injuries and lack of support, Hull scored three of the Hawks' four goals in Game Six, giving him a remarkable eight goals in the series. As Terry said, Hull had an "awful good shot."

In the other semifinal, the defending Stanley Cup champion Leafs breezed past the Canadiens in five games, driven by the excellent goaltending of the ageless Johnny Bower, who racked up two shutouts against the Habs. Bower and Sawchuk would face each other as they had done in the Calder Cup final of 1950. Terry had shone and won that time. Could it happen again?

It didn't look good in Game One as left wing Dick Duff beat Terry twice in the first sixty-eight seconds, setting an NHL record for fastest two goals from the start of a game. The Wings never recovered and eventually lost, 4–2. The second game saw the Leafs notch three goals before the Wings retaliated, and the Toronto squad won by an identical 4–2 score.

Back in friendlier surroundings at the Olympia, Vic Stasiuk scored in the first minute and Terry stopped thirty of thirty-two Leaf shots to pace the Wings to a 3–2 win, putting Detroit back in the series.

In Game Four, Red Kelly proved to be a thorn in Terry's side by scoring two goals in another 4–2 Toronto victory.

"As a Wing, I had been taught to shoot low, about a foot off the ice, and just off the post of the net," Kelly says, "and see, Terry knew this. So I remember having a close-in chance on

Terry and thinking two things: one, 'What would Rocket Richard do on Terry?' and two, 'What would Terry expect *me* to do?' So when my chances came, I put my shots upstairs and I was able to beat Terry. Of course, he beat me a lot more often than I scored on him.

"Personally, I would have gone through a cement wall to score on Detroit. They had traded me away, so I always wanted to beat them bad."

Back at Maple Leaf Gardens for Game Five, Stanley Cup fever was in the air. The temperature in the arena rose after Dave Keon notched a short-handed goal late in the opening frame. Alex Delvecchio evened things early in the second and the defensive duel between the Uke and the China Wall stretched late into the third period before Eddie Shack beat Terry with just under seven minutes remaining in the game. Still, Terry refused to yield another inch as amazing stops on Shack and Dick Duff kept the game close.

With two minutes remaining, the Wings got the break they were looking for when the Leafs' Bob Pulford took a holding penalty. With time winding down, Terry was pulled for an extra attacker. Johnny Bower held fast until the pesky Dave Keon grabbed the loose puck and fired it into the vacant Wing net to seal a 3–1 victory.

The Stanley Cup was presented to Leaf captain George Armstrong for the second time in as many years. As Terry sat in the Wings' dressing room, listening to the celebrations on the Gardens ice, he was bitterly disappointed. Still, 1962–63 had been a year in which Terry had regained many things he might have given up for lost: his marriage and family, his job as a regular NHL goalie, and, as the midseason MVP award attested, his place among the league's elite players.

13

THE RECORD BREAKER

AN announcement from the NHL office in the spring of 1963 no doubt helped ease Terry's disappointment over the Stanley Cup loss: his brilliant play in an injury-shortened season had earned him a berth on the Second All-Star team. As Pat notes, however, it's anybody's guess what Terry did with the cash bonuses such accolades provided.

"Terry had this paranoia about money. Whenever he won money, winning the Stanley Cup or a bonus or All-Star team or something, I or the children never saw any of it. I used to be embarrassed about how our kids looked as compared to the Howe or Delvecchio kids. Terry didn't care about that kind of thing. I remember having to get a prescription for one of the kids and he had a fit over the cost of the medicine. This was for his children, for gosh sakes! I remember his mother lecturing him about money for the kids! They really got into it over that!"

It is perhaps an ironic twist that Anne Sawchuk, so distant and quick to conflict with her son, grew so very close to Pat and the children.

"Grandma Sawchuk was a real grandma! She loved to take care of the kids. She and I were inseparable. We would pack up the kids, go to the zoo or whatever. She'd walk with all her stuff, pots and pans, to our house to make perogies. Or on

Sundays we'd go to church and then over to Grandma's for breakfast, and she'd have the toast piled a mile high and the kielbasa ready in the oven. Terry's mom was my best friend. [She and Terry] certainly loved each other, but were incapable somehow of showing it.

"Grandma happened to be home this one night when Terry came home drunk out of his mind. We watched him go into the en suite bathroom and make motions on the wall like he was changing the stations on the T.V. I felt so sorry for her to be seeing her son acting in such a bizarre way. She certainly knew what he could be like, but this incident was an eye opener for both of us. The next day he acted as if nothing had happened."

By this time in their young lives, the Sawchuk kids by virtue of their numbers alone were beginning to take over the neighbourhood. In the spring of 1963, Pat was expecting their sixth child. On those occasions when Terry was able to be a father, the kids basked in their father's love. Pat continues: "We had birthday parties behind the house on the picnic table and we'd have fun. We'd have the old coffee can with all the pennies in it and play poker. Our kids knew how to play poker real young, but it was fun. Terry and I used to play for hours with the kids. And Sunday mornings he would make breakfast. The kids loved that. It was attention from their father. That's all they ever wanted."

After yet another training camp, Terry headed to Toronto to participate in yet another All-Star Game, his ninth, which ended in a 3–3 tie.

Four days later, Terry was home with Pat when she suddenly began to go into an intense labour. Without warning, the pains began quickly and strongly. They rushed to the car and made another mad dash to the hospital. Terry was white as a ghost. Pat recalls, "I'm clawing the top of the car. It's after four o'clock in the afternoon and we get caught in rush-hour traffic. We get stuck, dead stop, on this ramp; I mean, we can see the hospital, but we aren't moving. Terry is honking the horn like crazy but we aren't moving. My water is ready to break and I am scared. I think, 'My God, this is it.' Well, we finally get to the hospital and Terry is just shaking. I have him drop me off at the door. I take the elevator up to obstetrics while he parks the car. By the time he comes in, he is already a father again!

"We named this boy Terrance Michael because I wanted another Terry Sawchuk around — not so much a Terry, Jr., but another Terry. What a memory his delivery was, let me tell you. I know Terry never forgot it!"

As the season opened, Detroit's two greatest hockey stars, Gordie Howe and Terry Sawchuk, both entered the regular season closing in on lifetime records. Gordie's two goals in the season's first game, a 5–3 win against Glenn Hall and the Black Hawks, put him only two short of Rocket Richard's mark of 544. A phalanx of reporters began following his every move and shot. The attention increased when he scored once in the Red Wings' next win, a 3–0 Sawchuk shutout of the Bruins. On October 27, Howe tied the Rocket on home ice. The pressure on Howe to break Richard's record would prove a distraction for the Wings, as they diverted their efforts from winning games to feeding Howe the puck at every opportunity. But Howe had hit a dry spell, going scoreless over the next five games.

On November 7, Terry turned aside all twenty-five shots he faced against the New York Rangers in a 1–0 win. Suddenly the spotlight was on the Wings goalie, who was one shutout shy of tying George Hainsworth's career mark of ninety-four. Despite the win, the crowd of 11,546 came away disappointed as Howe hit the post of the empty Ranger net in the last minute of play.

Three nights later, against the visiting Canadiens, the Wing offence was again listless while Terry remained larcenous. He put in a stellar first period, stopping all twelve Montreal shots. Gordie, however, continued to come up dry until, with just under five minutes left in the second period, he converted a Bill Gadsby pass for goal number 545. Although Howe could now relax, Terry could not. The game was delayed ten minutes while the Olympia's ice was cleared of debris. As play resumed, the Canadiens continued to pepper Sawchuk, sending thirty-nine shots his way in all. But Terry couldn't be beaten. Tonight Terry would tie his idol's shutout record.

Finally the buzzer sounded, bringing to a close a magical

night. As a throng of well-wishers, cameramen, and writers jammed the Detroit dressing room, Terry threw his arm around Gordie to offer his congratulations. The night clearly belonged to Number Nine.

Finding it almost impossible to work in the crowded dressing room, trainer Lefty Wilson astutely pointed out, "Never mind Gordie, now they can start following Terry!" Terry himself couldn't have cared less. He had always said that Gordie was the greatest player he had ever seen and he relished Gordie taking the spotlight away from his feat. The less attention, the better.

Oddly, although the pressure was off Howe, his goal production did not return to normal. The offensive collapse coincided with injuries that weakened the blueline corps, and the Wings slumped through the end of November when Terry experienced a wrenched back. The injury was especially debilitating to a goalie who crouched the way Terry did.

"Terry used to bend down so low when he played that his back was perfectly flat," Pat recalls. "I often told him that I could set a table on it and not a dish would fall off. How he had never gotten a sore back until this point in his career was beyond me. But then he got it good."

On November 30, Roger Crozier, a small twenty-one-year-old goaltender from Bracebridge, Ontario, was called up from the Wings' American league affiliate in Pittsburgh. That night the Wings turned up their level of play dramatically to protect their young rookie. Crozier suffered a shattered cheekbone from a Frank Mahovlich slap shot, but he still finished the 1–1 tie game. Abel was overjoyed at the rookie's performance. The general manager declared Crozier to be the goaltender of the Wings' future, despite the fact that the injury would sideline him for two weeks.

Terry came back, trying gamely to play through the sore back, but his fate was out of his hands. Sid Abel had decided that Crozier was his number-one goalie. When Crozier went undefeated in his first five games back, Abel commented, "We're delighted with Crozier. You'll see a lot of him before the season's over."

The pundits began writing the obituary on Terry's career. On the other side of the equation was Jacques Plante, now tending goal for the Rangers.

"No matter how good he plays," Plante said of the acrobatic Crozier, "he won't be as good as Sawchuk."

Yet Abel had made up his mind: "Terry is still a fine NHL goaltender, but he's getting older and needs more rest. I think I'll probably play Roger in stretches of eight to ten games and if it appears he's wearing down because of his size [five foot seven, 145 pounds], Terry will go in for five or six games."

Christmas of 1963 approached, and the Red Wings families gathered at the Olympia for the annual Christmas party and skate.

"We would have Christmas parties at the Olympia and Santa would come down from the roof and give presents away," says Kathy Sawchuk, six years old in 1963. "Then we would sit on a wooden chair on the ice and Dad would skate behind us and push us everywhere."

"Sonny Elliott would play Santa," Pat remembers with a laugh, "and he used to be so funny. He'd say some really under-the-table comments that the kids wouldn't catch but that would just break up the adults."

By mid-January, Abel had abandoned his earlier plan and he began alternating Crozier and Terry with each game. With Sawchuk back in the picture, attention began to be paid to his run at Hainsworth's shutout record.

"It had been expected that the Rocket's goal record would be passed," Marcel Pronovost says. "It was only a matter of time. However, the shutout record of Hainsworth, now that's another story. Nobody ever thought it would be touched, but Terry was on the verge of doing it. We couldn't believe it."

Now it was Terry's turn to be hounded by the press, as each game he played could be the record breaker, even though it had been over two months since his last shutout. It seemed unlikely he would turn the trick on Saturday, January 18, 1964, as the Wings travelled to the Forum for a game against the Canadiens. Terry had not gotten a shutout in this rink in over eight seasons, and besides, the Habs hadn't lost a game in their own rink since November 16.

The teams exchanged thirteen shots apiece in the first period but the Wings came out stronger and took a 1–0 lead. Early in the second period, Terry made brilliant stops on Ralph Backstrom and J. C. Tremblay, and the play got chippy. Frustrated by Terry's performance, Montreal's John Ferguson took matters into his own hands halfway through the game when he butt-ended Terry in the stomach during a mad scramble in the crease. Dazed and breathless, Terry hit the ice, as the play was whistled dead. Trainer Lefty Wilson ran out to provide first aid but found that Terry was just winded. After catching his breath, an angry Uke got to his feet. The game took on an even more serious, deadly tone. Terry finished even stronger and ended the period with his shutout still firmly intact.

As the third period started, the two teams and the assembled press were keenly aware what was at stake. The third period was wide open. Pulses quickened as the minutes ticked by and Terry turned back the waves of Canadiens. With Detroit up 2–0, Montreal coach Toe Blake called goalie Charlie Hodge to the bench in the last minute in favour of an extra attacker. The Habs did not want to be the victims of a second record being set by a Red Wing. Marcel Pronovost remembers the Habs' manoeuvre.

"I played the last two minutes of that game and when they pulled Hodge, we thought, 'You sons of bitches, you won't give Terry his record, eh? We'll show you!' It only made us all madder and we dug down even deeper."

So focused on the shutout in that final minute were the Wings that, when Howe and Delvecchio both broke in on the empty Habs' net, instead of shooting, they passed the puck around to kill the clock and prevent Montreal from scoring. At the final buzzer, Terry was mobbed by his teammates. He was the new shutout king of the NHL with this, his ninety-fifth shutout in 798 games, surpassing Hainsworth's mark set in 1936.

Although disappointed that his record-breaking shutout hadn't occurred at home, Terry didn't mind being the centre of attention as euphoria reigned in the Wings' dressing room afterwards.

"What now? I guess I'll just have to start on the next ninety-five!" beamed the Uke to the assembled horde of newspapermen

1. Terry with daughters Kathy and Carol, about 1964.
— Courtesy Sawchuk family

2. Terry enjoyed being in bars, and occasionally worked behind the counter, as this 1964 photo shows. Note the tribute to his shutout talents in the mirror.
— Courtesy Sawchuk family

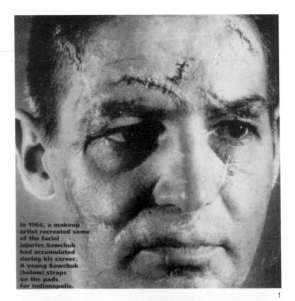

1. In 1966, a make-up artist enhanced stitches in Terry's face to demonstrate the hazards of goaltending. The photo shocked millions of *Look* magazine readers.
— *Look* magazine

2. Leading the Leafs onto the ice, February 7, 1966.
—Bob Peterson/*Time/Life*

In 1966, a makeup artist recreated some of the facial injuries Sawchuk had accumulated during his career. A young Sawchuk (below) straps on the pads for Indianapolis.

1

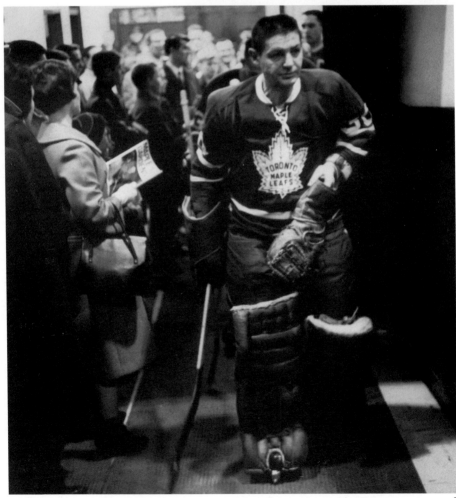

2

1. Stan Mikita breaks in on Terry.
— Frank Prazak/Hockey Hall of Fame

2. Terry's goaltending style was innovative, but his fundamentals were always sound. Here, he makes a great skate save as a Maple Leaf in 1967.
— Courtesy Sawchuk family

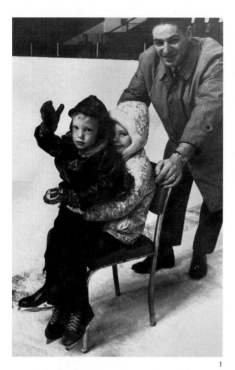

1. Despite a bad back, Terry pushes little Terry and Debbie at the Leafs' Christmas party in 1966.
— Leo Harrison

2. Terry receiving the King of the Year award from Jiggs McDonald at the Kings' Fan Club dinner, Christmas 1967. The gift had seven little cherubs on it, with an open spot if the Sawchuks decided to have an eighth child.
— Courtesy Jiggs McDonald

3. Terry jogging on the spot in front of his family, for the press, at their home at Hermosa Beach, California, in September 1968. His days as a King and a married man were numbered.
— Los Angeles *South Bay Daily Breeze*

4. The happiness that Terry and Jerry Sawchuk show in this picture is deceiving. Their relationship was often tense, sometimes violent. Soon, Terry would return a last time to the Red Wings, then move on for a brief stint with the New York Rangers. In 1970, Terry died in an off-ice incident.
— Los Angeles *South Bay Daily Breeze*

who now crowded in front of him. Gordie Howe sat proudly beside him, tousling his brush cut while Sid Abel patted him on the back. But he added, "In our position, the win's the important thing. I didn't have too much time to worry about pressure from the record. We need the wins."

Howe was more enthusiastic.

"He was wonderful, wonderful. He's an old pro all the way. Nah, I don't think he felt any pressure, he's too much of a pro. He plays them all great."

"I had luck going with me tonight," Terry said. "You have to have that. One (shot) hit the top end of the stick. I never did see it. Still, for one like this, you have to play sixty minutes."

"I felt, and I still do, that Terry's record really was much harder to get than Gordie's," Pronovost says today. "To get a shutout you're not allowed one mistake."

The ensuing accolades that Terry received in the following days gave him a boost, as did the improvement of his aching back. His game began to quickly improve and, despite breaking the little finger of his catching hand in late January, he didn't lose another game to injury. When goalie Hank Bassen on the Pittsburgh farm team came down with a leg injury, Crozier was the logical choice to send down.

On February 5, in a game at Chicago Stadium, Terry noticed he had been falling to the ice too much, which had cost his team the game. He decided to change his style and concentrate on standing up more on the first shots. The results were tangible and timely.

The next night in Detroit, he shut out the Hawks, 4–0, for the ninety-sixth shutout of his career, widening his lead on Hainsworth. Not one to rest on his laurels, Terry set another new NHL record when he stepped onto the Boston Garden ice on Saturday, February 8, to play in his 805th regular-season game, eclipsing Harry Lumley's mark set four years before.

These were certainly heady times for the Uke, but they got even headier. After a three-game winning streak vaulted Detroit past New York into fourth place, the Wings never looked back. As February ended, they had won eight of twelve games. Terry's play was described as brilliant.

The Wings' schedule in March was brutal: a gruelling stretch of seven games in eleven nights, during which the Red Wings would play in all six NHL cities. They withstood the test with a record of 3–3–1. Even in the three defeats, the Detroit goaltender was fabulous, although weary without Crozier around to spell him. On March 10, *Detroit Free Press* columnist Jack Berry implied that Sawchuk should be the logical choice for Wing MVP, even over Gordie Howe, who had won the award ten times in the past twelve years.

The Wings finished the regular season seventeen points ahead of the fifth-place Rangers. They entered their semifinal playoff series with second-place Chicago as the hottest team in the league down the stretch. Still, the Hawks had finished thirteen points ahead of the Wings and had openly boasted they would dispense with Detroit in four straight. The Hawks' bragging was like music to the ears of the hyper-competitive Sawchuk, but Hull, Mikita, and company backed it up with a 4–1 win on Chicago Stadium ice in Game One.

In the first five minutes of the second game, Terry jumped on a loose puck near his net and, as his glove hand hit the ice, he jarred his left shoulder, just as he had done two years before against these same Hawks. Pain shot through his shoulder like a bullet. It wouldn't go away and he was forced to leave the game. Undaunted, the Wings tightened up their defence and squeezed out a 5–4 victory in front of back-up goalie Bob Champoux, who was on hand because Roger Crozier was in Pittsburgh, aiding their cause in the American league playoffs.

Terry was admitted to Detroit Osteopathic Hospital where he was diagnosed with a pinched nerve, for which he was placed in traction. In one of the classic tales of Stanley Cup folklore, Terry, his shoulder still painful but significantly better, temporarily left his hospital bed and headed to the Olympia for Game Three. In one of the bravest performances of his career, Terry stopped twenty-six shots to record a 3–0 shutout and give the Wings the series' lead, two games to one. Then he returned to hospital for more treatment, where weights attempted to keep his arm flexed and open to allow the nerve to slip back into its place in the shoulder socket.

Terry was still in pain as he suited up for the fourth game. He tried to ignore it but each time he moved his arm a certain way, the pain shot through his shoulder. Still, his concentration didn't waver even as he caught a glimpse of Pat sitting near the glass, and not in her usual seat. Just out of hospital herself after having her appendix removed, her attendance at the game was a surprise for Terry. "Still," she related to the press after the playoffs, "he didn't give me a second look until the next face-off!"

Terry got through the first period but during the intermission, the shoulder continued to bother him. Finally, two minutes into the second period, he couldn't go on. Clutching his shoulder, he watched Crozier come out to take his place. The Wings lost the game, 3–2, and dropped the fifth game by the same score in front of Crozier as the Hawks took the lead in the series.

With Terry gamely back in the net at Olympia for Game Six, the Red Wings seemed inspired, limiting the Hawks to twenty-six shots in a lopsided 7–2 victory. The next day, Sid Abel let it be known to reporters on whose shoulders the fate of the series rested.

"I don't know what it is Terry has against Chicago, but it looks like he's hot right now. I want him in the nets tomorrow night. That's the big one; the only one right now."

Terry held off the Hawks with the Red Wings cruising to a 3–1 lead. The Hawks struggled into the second period when left wing Reggie Fleming noticed Sawchuk was out of his crease after playing the puck beside the net. Fleming slammed Terry into the end boards, leaving the goalie in a dazed, semiconscious heap. Ever the warrior, Terry was back on his feet within a few minutes. He continued to play despite feeling dizzy and shaken up, but Bobby Hull scored and, as the period ended with the Wings ahead, 3–2, Terry still was not himself. After a talk with Lefty Wilson and Sid Abel, it was decided to put Crozier in for the third period. This time Crozier held off the Hawks, while in front of him Parker MacDonald scored an insurance marker for a 4–2 win that put Detroit into the finals against the Leafs, who needed the full seven games to get past Montreal, setting up a rematch of the 1963 finals.

As the Wings prepared for their third Stanley Cup final in four years, bettors had them as 3–1 underdogs to the two-time champion Maple Leafs who had taken nineteen of a possible twenty-eight points from Detroit in the regular season. Still, veteran centre Alex Delvecchio cautioned the naysayers on the eve of the series.

"We've got some rampaging younger players, some good veterans, and Gordie Howe," he said, adding, "And Terry Sawchuk knows a thing or two about what it's like to play in a Stanley Cup final."

What the Wings did not have going into this year's finals was a healthy Terry Sawchuk.

The letdown that Detroit coach Sid Abel feared might happen after the tough, exciting Chicago series, materialized in Game One. The Red Wings were up 2–1 when, with Toronto on a power play, Wings defenceman Bill Gadsby gave the puck away to George Armstrong, who beat Terry for the tying goal. With overtime imminent, Norm Ullman fired a dangerous cross-ice pass that Bob Pulford intercepted and then broke in alone on Terry. With two seconds left on the clock, Pulford rifled a shot past Sawchuk to give the Leafs a 3–2 victory.

From his ringside seat in the Gardens that night, former goaltending great Turk Broda gave a bitterly scathing, albeit self-contradictory, assessment of Terry's play.

"Sawchuk's a bad goalie. He's two years over the hill. He should have been done in 1962 and you know what saved him? The mask. He goes down too much now. He doesn't stand in and play the puck. But with the mask, he's taken a strain off his mind about getting hit in the face and he's added years to his career."

Detroit played a strong second game, taking a 3–1 lead into the third period, when Red Kelly brought the Leafs closer with a tally at the twelve-minute mark. The Leafs again tied it up, this time with just under a minute remaining, to send the game into overtime. The Leafs had been outshot, 41–28, and in the overtime session play remained mostly in Leaf territory. A nifty passing play from Ullman to Howe to Larry Jeffrey gave the Wings the series-tying goal.

The third game, two nights later in the Olympia, had the Wings building up a 3–0 first-period lead. But the Leafs fought back to tie the game with a minute and thirteen seconds left on the clock. Not to be outdone, Alex Delvecchio notched the winner with seventeen seconds left by neatly tucking a Gordie Howe pass from across the goalmouth through the China Wall.

Stanley Cup fever boiled over in Detroit for the series' fourth game. Fifteen thousand and thirty-five fans packed into the Olympia while an additional 4,739 packed into the nearby Palms and Woods movie theatres to watch the game via closed-circuit television. This time, the Leafs came out flying, outshooting the Wings, with Dave Keon giving Toronto a 1–0 lead.

The Wings turned on the heat in the second period, notching two goals. Then, with four minutes in the period and two Wings in the penalty box, Keon got his second goal of the game, tying things up heading into the second intermission.

The Leafs appeared to be sagging in the third, until a long bullet off the stick of Andy Bathgate sailed over Terry's right shoulder, finding the top corner of the net to give the Leafs the lead. Sid Abel threw caution to the wind in the game's final two minutes, putting five forwards and no defencemen on the ice. The strategy seemed to work as the Wings applied pressure on Johnny Bower. Then Bob Pulford stole the puck and broke away. Terry made a fabulous save on Pulford, but was in no position to react to Frank Mahovlich, who backhanded the rebound past the sprawling goalie for the insurance goal that tied the series.

The pinched nerve continued to bother Terry as he took morning injections to help with the pain prior to Game Five at Maple Leaf Gardens. He was able to sleep for only a couple of hours at a time until the pain reawakened him. However, he was determined to continue.

Dave Keon again appeared to have Terry at his mercy in the opening minutes of the fifth game. Nevertheless the Uke had the crowd of 14,311 screaming in frustration as he kicked out his left leg to steal a sure goal. The Leafs kept up the pressure, forcing Terry to make another fabulous stop on George

Armstrong before Gordie Howe put the Wings up 1–0 halfway through the period.

At the start of the second Keon got another breakaway. This time, with the Leafs short-handed, Terry again prevailed, turning away the Leaf centre's backhand shot.

Only with two Wings in the penalty box at the three-quarter mark of the third period did the Leafs beat Terry at all. Still, Sawchuk was able to stop Andy Bathgate's point shot, and took George Armstrong's rebound on the mask before he was finally beaten to make the score 2–1 Detroit. Terry closed the door the rest of the way, despite being bowled over into his own net at one point by a sliding Parker MacDonald. At the final buzzer, he was mobbed by his teammates, as they knew who had won this game for them and put them one win away from their first Stanley Cup in nine years.

"I think Toronto figured they'd sweep us right out in four straight games," commented Sid Abel. "Well, the Uke has taken care of that. Sawchuk was as good as he has ever been in any game. They wouldn't have beaten him even once without that double penalty."

Toronto coach Punch Imlach had grudging praise for Terry's performance.

"He played as well as I have ever seen him play. We had good chances but didn't score. Keon should have had three goals. Armstrong, Pulford, Mahovlich . . . all should have had goals."

"He's as good as I've ever seen him right now," added Marcel Pronovost, who also put in a strong performance, despite a bad ankle. "Uke has the old desire, the old drive he used to have."

Before the series shifted to Detroit for Game Six, the Maple Leafs indulged in a bit of brinksmanship, placing the Stanley Cup, packed neatly in its case, in the Wings' dressing room, among the Wings' baggage. Coach/GM Sid Abel would have none of it.

"It belongs to them right now, let them carry it as long as they're supposed to. We'll be happy to take care of it after we win it."

As the sixth game began, Toronto showed no intention of

handing over the Cup for keeps. Bob Pulford scored a short-handed goal with just under three minutes left in the first period to put Toronto up by one. The second period was wide open: five goals were scored as the teams emerged tied at three.

In the middle of the third period, Leaf defenceman Bob Baun stopped a Red Wing slap shot with his ankle, sustaining what would become the most celebrated injury in hockey history. Minutes later, his ankle buckled under him and he was carried from the ice on a stretcher at 13:13 of the third period. The Wings, who had been coming on strong up to the point, were cooled off in the final frame by the delay in the game. The score remained 3–3 as regulation time ended.

Baun was suspected of having a cracked or fractured fibula. The Leaf doctor froze the ankle and taped it up tightly, and Baun returned to participate in the overtime period. Marcel Pronovost clearly recalls the next sequence of events.

"Baun ends up with the puck at our blue line and he takes a shot at our net. Baun's shot could not have broken a pane of glass, but it hits Bill Gadsby in the ass and deflects into the net behind Terry, and the Leafs win it. And the big story is 'Baun wins it on a broken ankle!' He's the hero!"

Before Game Seven, Sid Abel accused the Leafs of more trickery. He didn't believe Baun's leg was broken.

"I'm convinced it was a gimmick to delay the game," Sid Abel lamented. "Baun came back too soon for what was supposed to be a sprained or broken ankle. And where did the stretcher come from in such a hurry? Usually we have to send fifteen ushers hunting for one. I found out that Toronto brought their own stretcher. Now isn't that a strange piece of equipment for a team in the Stanley Cup finals to be lugging around?"

Alex Delvecchio swore the shot hit Baun in the knee and not the ankle. "I know because it was my shot that hit him. It was nothing more than a big stall."

Broken leg or not, Baun was in the Toronto lineup for the deciding game at Maple Leaf Gardens, in which the Leafs had all the momentum on their side.

In the fourth minute of play, Andy Bathgate broke in alone on Terry, who moved out to cut down the angle. "I thought

Andy would go for the far side," Terry later remembered. "I gave him about eight inches on the short side and he picked that top corner clean as a whistle."

The second period was scoreless as both teams checked tightly. The 1–0 Toronto lead carried to the four-minute mark of the third when Dave Keon let go a blast at the Wing net.

"The puck dropped on me," said Terry, "just when I thought I had it. Instead, I only got a piece of my glove on it." The arena erupted and the goal took the life out of the Wings. On a roll, the Leafs tallied twice more and won their third Stanley Cup in a row.

"We should have won that series," bristles Marcel Pronovost today. "We had 'em coming home. We should have won!"

Terry did not have much time to contemplate the disappointing loss as he and Pat flew into Winnipeg, where he was to be the keynote speaker at the Winakwa Community Club's first annual Sportsmen's Dinner. Caught by reporters while visiting with his aunts and uncles — Mr. and Mrs. John Tatarnic and Mr. and Mrs. Michael Zuk — he said that, much as he admired Gordie Howe, he considered his chum Marcel Pronovost the most underrated hockey player on the Detroit club.

"Pronovost was our key man all season and particularly in the playoffs. I know that any time we were in trouble, I always looked for that No. 3. They talk about the time Howe spends on the ice, but game in and game out, Marcel was in action close to forty minutes and sometimes more."

At the Sportsmen's Dinner, more than 500 guests saw Terry and former Chicago Bear football star Curly Morrison made honorary citizens of St. Boniface, Manitoba. In his talk, Terry praised the Stanley Cup champion Leafs. "They were as good or better than we were," Terry stated, adding that the Rangers actually helped the Leafs win the Cup by trading Andy Bathgate and Don McKenney to them. "I don't know what the Rangers were doing!"

As Terry returned to Detroit, he could not help but feel optimistic. In a season that echoed the one before, he had surmounted many obstacles thrown at him – the injuries to his back, finger, and shoulder, as well as the challenge to his job posed by young Roger Crozier. And when Detroit's hockey writers named Sawchuk the Red Wings' most valuable player of 1963–64, his future with the club seemed secure.

And what a club he played for! A core of veterans such as Howe, Delvecchio, Ullman, Gadsby, and Pronovost had been supplemented by promising newcomers Floyd Smith, Paul Henderson, and Eddie Joyal. More Stanley Cups seemed imminent.

No one could have imagined in April and May of 1964 that, while another Cup win was in the cards for Terry, it would not be with his beloved Red Wings.

14

SHARING THE LIMELIGHT

"*T*ERRY was certainly getting older," Marcel Pronovost says, "and the consensus seemed to be that with Crozier coming up, well, something had to give."

On June 9, 1964, the eve of the intraleague waiver draft, Detroit general manager and coach Sid Abel spent a sleepless night trying to decide what to do about Sawchuk. He could not deny that Terry had earned the team's MVP award with his fine play, but Roger Crozier's star was rising. And Terry would never share the chores in net, let alone accept a backup role. Terry's drinking and his advancing age were also at the back of Abel's mind.

Toronto's coach/GM, George (Punch) Imlach, found himself in a similar bind. His star goalie, Johnny Bower, had played in fifty of the team's seventy games, but, at age thirty-nine, he was no doubt going to need more rest. Imlach entered the draft hopeful of claiming the Canadiens' Gump Worsley, who had been supplanted by Charlie Hodge and was sure to be left unprotected by the Habs. The first two rounds went by uneventfully as the league shuffled its spare parts. The Wings picked up defencemen Gary Bergman and Murray Hall. The Leafs picked up retired winger Dickie Moore from Montreal and dropped Gerry Ehman, whom they expected the Rangers would grab for the waiver fee of $20,000, money the Leafs would then use to grab Worsley. But the Rangers passed on their second pick, leaving the Leafs without the funds to claim the Gumper.

Imlach conferred with Leaf president Stafford Smythe, who said, "Wait and see what happens this round." The Leafs let the second round go by without putting in a claim.

Then, in the third round, Sid Abel made a couple of moves that stunned all in attendance. Detroit claimed George Gardner, a little-known goalie coming off his second year in Boston's farm system. Allowed to protect only two goalies, the Wings left Terry Sawchuk exposed. The Leafs, who picked next, could barely believe their luck or contain their enthusiasm. When Clarence Campbell announced it was the Leafs' turn, Imlach practically interrupted him by shouting "Sawchuk!"

If Imlach's glee at obtaining Sawchuk had Sid Abel second-guessing himself afterwards, it didn't show.

"We feel we can go all the way with Roger," he told reporters. "It might have turned out that we would have asked Terry to go to the minors. Instead we decided to get another young goalkeeper. Our scouting reports speak highly of Gardner. We're parting with [Terry] reluctantly. Sawchuk's been great for us. Three times an All-Star and he's got a ton of shutouts . . ."

Observers around the league were at a loss to understand Abel's decision. Their bewilderment was best summed up by Chicago coach Billy Reay.

"If they wanted to go with Crozier, why didn't they try to trade Sawchuk? They would have to have gotten something better [in return] than $20,000."

Even Abel's fifteen-year-old daughter Linda couldn't fathom her father's actions. Placing a long distance call to him the moment the draft ended, she asked him, "Dad, what are you doing?"

"I think she thought somebody had hit me on the head with a hammer because I let Terry go," Abel joked. But it was Punch Imlach and the Toronto Maple Leafs who were really laughing.

Now that he had both star goalies from the 1964 finals on his team, Imlach wasn't tipping his hand as to which would be the Leafs' number one goalie the next season. Training camp would decide that, he said. "If it's Bower and Sawchuk, they could play thirty-five games apiece."

Terry was in his backyard fixing part of a fence when a reporter phoned to inform him of his selection by the Leafs.

"I'm shocked, stunned, yes, even disappointed," he said. "I had no idea that being left unprotected was even being considered. I want to play hockey — in the major league. I wouldn't listen to anything involving the minors. And no, I wouldn't object to rotating with another goaltender. I don't think Bower or myself can be at our best for seventy games anymore. I know those rests did me the world of good the last three or four seasons."

Terry refused further comment until he heard from Imlach, which occurred that night.

"He seems satisfied to play for us," Punch told the press the next day. "We don't expect any problems to arise."

Red Kelly says, "I think Terry knew immediately he would be teamed with Bower. Johnny was a great goalie, too, and he wasn't going anywhere. Terry knew coming in that there would be two number-one goalies and that they'd be sharing the net."

Of course, another off-season meant more visits to the VFW for Terry. However, daughters Debbie and JoAnne have fond memories of their dad that summer.

"I remember one time Dad took us to the VFW," Debbie says. "He would only take us there once in a while and usually we would have to wait and wait until he got done drinking. Well, this one time, Dad left early. I couldn't believe it. And when we got home he taught me how to ride my first bike."

"Another fine moment was when we went fishing," JoAnne says. "We were up at four-thirty, five in the morning. Dad and I went to the lake, borrowed a rowboat, and off we went. Dad rowed and my friends couldn't believe 'Mr. Sawchuk' was fishing with JoAnne. Little did they know that we had all the good fishing spots. We fished all day until we had a stringer full of bass and bluegills. We caught tons of fish, called it a day, and had a huge fish fry that night.

"It's funny. I sit back and listen to my sister talk about that time, 'Remember when Dad had that big fish fry in the back-yard?' and I answer, 'I sure do!'"

That September, Terry headed to the Leafs' training camp in Peterborough, Ontario, with mixed emotions.

"Terry didn't want to go to Toronto," Pat recollects. "I mean, it was only natural. His home, family, and friends were all in Detroit, but he went and, as always, was prepared to give his all."

Not lost on Terry was Abel's comment that he might have sent Sawchuk to the minors if the Wings had kept him. And although Punch Imlach seemed happy to have him, Terry knew Imlach's reputation as a drill sergeant. For these reasons, Terry knew his loafing days were over. He was also aware there was stiff competition for Toronto's second goaltending slot. Bower was a shoo-in to make the big team, having led the NHL with a 2.11 goals-against average. Sawchuk would have to beat out Don Simmons, who had played in twenty-one games as Bower's backup the year before, and Gerry Cheevers had raised eye-brows with his play for the Leafs' Rochester farm club.

After five days of Imlach practices, Terry was not so sure he wanted to be a Maple Leaf. "I skated more here in the first five days than I did in Detroit in five years," Terry complained.

In his autobiography, *Hockey Is a Battle*, Imlach wrote, "I figured the same as those track coaches who say that, if you're going to run a mile, you practise for it not by running one mile, but by running ten miles. If you're going to play a hockey game in an hour, you should be able to practise two hours. That's the way you build endurance. You can't build it in half-hour practices."

The Leafs' success under Punch couldn't be denied — the Leafs had just won their third Cup in as many years. His repu-tation for getting extra mileage from aging players also spoke for itself. And after a gruelling training camp and a schedule of *eighteen* exhibition games, it was the two "old" goalies, whose combined age was seventy-four, who made the team — to no one's surprise.

On October 10, 1964, Terry participated in his tenth All-Star Game. For the first time since 1954, Terry was a member of the "home" team — the Cup champion Leafs. Toronto lost, 3–2, to the All-Stars before 14,200 at the Gardens. The highlight was a second-period goal on Terry by Jean Beliveau, who was assisted by Gordie Howe and Bobby Hull.

Bower played strongly in the season opener, a 5–3 Leaf victory in Detroit. Terry saw his first action as a Leaf four nights later, in a 3–3 tie with the Rangers at Madison Square Garden. If the sight of Terry in Toronto colours was jarring, it was also odd not to see him in sweater number 1 for the first time in his professional career. As Bower already wore number 1, Sawchuk shuttled among other available numbers. Terry began the season in jersey number 25, but also wore numbers 24 and 30. When the press asked him about being without his familiar number 1, Terry snarled, "You don't stop pucks with numbers!"

After eleven games, the Leafs were tied for second place alongside the Canadiens. Cruising along in first place were the reborn Red Wings, led by thirty-nine-year-old Ted Lindsay, who'd come out of retirement, and the league's hottest goaltender, Roger Crozier. Crozier's 1.72 goals-against average was better by far than Bower and Sawchuk's composite average of 2.36.

Terry would suit up against his old team in a home game on Wednesday, November 11. In the first period he was caught badly out of position by the Wings' Bruce MacGregor, but blocked thirty other shots en route to a 3–1 win. Terry later told the press, "I had a soft night's work with Brewer, Baun, Stanley, and Horton playing so well on defence. Man, did they belt those Wings."

Ten days later, on November 21, Terry recorded his lone shutout of the season, outduelling Glenn Hall and the Hawks, 1–0, at the Gardens. Two weeks later, Terry and the Leafs had a rematch against Crozier and the Red Wings. The Leafs crushed Detroit, 10–2. Afterwards Terry, ever mindful of another goalie's pain, put his arm around Crozier as they walked down the common corridor towards their dressing rooms. Sawchuk whispered a few words to his successor, then turned back to be introduced to the crowd of 14,135 as one of the game's three stars. Later he sheepishly told the press who questioned him about his actions towards the young man who replaced him in the Wings' net.

"I told him to forget it, start over Sunday against Montreal. He got bombed once last year, too (by the Canadiens, 9–3), and he came back. He's a good kid, a real good kid. That can happen to any of us and I just thought he could use a pat on the back."

Wise words coming from a man who was giving the Leafs superlative goaltending, having lost only two of his first thirteen games. As the Leafs hosted their families at Maple Leaf Gardens on December 22, Pat arrived with the six kids to spend Christmas with Terry. *A Toronto Star* picture showed Terry huddled in the net with his family, all eight of them holding goalie sticks. The picture conjured up the image of Terry as a good family man. Pat laughs cynically at the thought.

"That first year," she explains, "Terry shared a two-storey house with [Leaf forward] Ron Stewart. The kids and I stayed back in Detroit but once in a while we visited him, you know, like at Christmas. Well, there was one time that I came unannounced, to surprise him. The door was locked so I knocked."

"Who is it?" Terry yelled.

"It's me, Pat," she answered.

"Holy shit, it's my wife! You'd better get out of here," Pat could hear Terry whisper to an unknown guest.

"I'll be right there, dear!" Terry yelled out through the locked door to Pat. She could hear the pitter-patter of feet and the opening and closing of a back door somewhere. After a minute or two, Terry finally opened the door.

"Hi, I was in the washroom," he said, trying to look calm. Pat nodded and walked into the house. All looked normal until she walked into the washroom and found a diaphragm by the sink. She picked it up and carried it out to Terry with a smile.

"Terry, what's this? Are you going weird on me and using these kinds of things now or something?"

"Oh that!" he deadpanned. "Ron and I have been putting that under the refrigerator so that it slides easier!"

Today Pat still laughs at that incident. "Only Terry could come up with such an excuse!"

Two late-December losses to the surging Chicago Black Hawks dropped the Leafs to fourth place but Sawchuk and Bower had taken the lead for the Vezina Trophy by January.

The two veterans had formed a close bond over the season, even making a pact that if either of them won the prestigious award, they would split the $1,000 bonus. Furthermore, they told their teammates, they both would pay for a season-ending team party, should one of them win. Almost overnight the Leafs' defensive game improved.

Terry was out of commission for much of January 1965 after a practice shot by Eddie Shack broke a finger on his catching hand. When he returned, he found Bower had kept them in the thick of things.

Going into the final weekend of the season, Toronto had allowed 169 goals to Detroit's 170, and as luck would have it the two teams were slated to play a home-and-home set. Terry had played in thirty-six games as a Leaf, while Bower had received the nod thirty-two times. Punch Imlach stayed with whichever goalie seemed hot, and at the moment that meant Bower. Under league rules the Vezina went to the goalie who had played the most games for the team that had allowed the fewest goals, so ironically it was up to Bower to protect "Terry's" Vezina lead. (The Wings had no such problem. Detroit was the only team not to employ a two-goalie system, as Crozier would become the last goalie ever to play in all his team's games.)

As the Wings came into Toronto for the Saturday-night game, Terry announced that he would refuse to accept the Vezina unless Bower's name was inscribed alongside his own as an official co-winner. The chances of that happening seemed less likely when the powerful Wings trounced Bower and the Leafs, 4–1, to put Crozier two goals in front of the Toronto tandem.

The next night in Detroit, Terry, too nervous to watch, sat in the dressing room rather than on the bench. Don McKenney opened the scoring in the first period and then Tim Horton's slap shot made it 2–0 for Toronto in the second.

The race deadlocked with one period to go, Terry, unable to take the suspense any longer, made his way to the end of the Leaf bench to watch the climactic final twenty minutes. Leaf rookie centre Pete Stemkowski put the Leafs ahead, 3–0, before, with a minute left to play, the Wings pulled Crozier for an extra attacker in a bid to tie the Vezina race for the first time in its history. Terry stood on the bench as the seconds ticked away. Leaf centre Dave Keon slid another goal into the empty Detroit net with three seconds left on the clock, and Terry raised his arms in jubilation. On the ice, Bower threw his stick up in the air and, when the buzzer sounded, Terry and Bower embraced warmly and were mobbed by their teammates.

"I was too nervous to watch for two periods but I was rooting and making every move with him (Bower) in the last twenty minutes," Terry said afterwards. "What reflexes! He was like a teenager. I never saw anything like him. He eats that puck." Bower had stopped thirty-seven shots en route to this historic shutout.

Terry was asked if winning the award in the Olympia at the expense of his former team made it more satisfying.

"You're darn right I'm happy the way it happened! Yeah, there was a little more satisfaction doing it against them. But there's the guy who won it," Terry said, pointing to his partner. "They can put Bower's name on the thing." In fact Bower's goals-against average of 2.38 was the lowest in the league and better than Terry's 2.56.

Leaf player representative Bob Pulford said he would ask the league's board of governors to amend the Vezina rules to honour Terry's request that Bower be recognized as an official co-winner. "The league is now forcing all teams to carry two goalkeepers, so it is only sensible that the Vezina should be a joint award," Pulford pointed out. "It is ridiculous that a man playing thirty-six games should get everything and the guy playing thirty-four games gets nothing."

First there was the matter of the Stanley Cup playoffs, in which the Leafs would face the Montreal Canadiens. Bower had the hot hand going into the playoffs. The prospect of watching from the bench combined with his always-sore elbow and back had Terry in the foulest of moods. Terry's frustration showed in comments made in the press.

"Next year, I won't have these problems anymore. I don't think they'll even protect me in the summer draft. They still have Johnny, who is good for another ten years, and Gerry Cheevers in Rochester."

Adding to Terry's discomfort was a new league rule —
which, coincidentally, had been brought on by Terry's incessant shoulder injuries that had delayed games the year before.
Now all backup goalies had to be in full equipment and uniform
for each playoff game. For the first time in his NHL career,
Terry's place for a playoff game would be at the end of the
players' bench. He watched the Canadiens squeak out a series-
opening 3–2 win.

Fate intervened prior to Game Two. Bower accidentally
touched his face and eyes immediately after applying oil of
wintergreen to the rest of his body in a pregame ritual. His face
began to burn and his eyes watered badly and turned red.
There was no way he could play.

On short notice, Terry had to come up with a solid performance as the Habs bombarded him with thirty-one shots over
the first two periods. His excellent play had the Leafs trailing
only 2–1 heading into the third.

Terry kept the Leafs in it until Henri Richard lofted a high
bouncer from the Montreal side of centre ice towards Terry.
Sawchuk slid out towards the puck, but it hit the ice before he
could reach it. It bounced over him and into the net, sealing
a 3–1 Canadiens' victory and leaving a flabbergasted Terry to
lament, "That puck was on its edge, otherwise he couldn't
have lifted it past me from that distance. I just don't live right,
I guess."

Toronto evened the series when it shifted to Maple Leaf
Gardens, backed by strong Bower performances in 3–2 and 4–2
wins. Punch was a true believer again.

"From now on, I don't believe in miracles or ghosts,"
declared Imlach. "Now I only believe in Santa Claus and I pronounce his name Johnny Bower."

Terry seemed despondent during these playoffs. Besides the
benching, Imlach's two-a-day practices were getting to him.

"I guess I'm just too old," he moaned. "These practices are
getting me down!"

When the Canadiens eliminated Bower and the Leafs' season
with wins of 3–1 and 4–3 in overtime, Terry became insecure
about his future. Still, as promised, he shared the Vezina prize

money with Bower and the two men hosted a team party at a local hotel.

At the end of April, Terry returned to Toronto for a television appearance. Still convinced he'd be up for grabs again in the waiver draft, he stated he would report to any team that claimed him.

On June 9, after much public pressure, the league governors ruled that the Vezina would thereafter be awarded to all goalie(s) playing twenty-five games or more for the team allowing the fewest goals. The ruling was made retroactive to include Johnny Bower, who officially became the co-winner of the Vezina alongside Terry.

Going into the June waiver draft, Punch Imlach was in the same predicament Sid Abel had been in the year before. In his eyes Gerry Cheevers was the Leafs' goalie of the future. But it would be dangerous to leave either member of his Vezina-winning tandem unprotected. His autobiography reveals that he even tried to list Cheevers as a skater — among the forwards and defencemen — but the league overruled him.

In the end, Imlach was loyal to his veterans and Boston claimed Cheevers in the draft.

As word reached Terry in Union Lake, he was mildly surprised to learn Punch had kept him. That summer, the Leafs also traded for Terry's buddy, Marcel Pronovost, and dealt his housemate, Ron Stewart, to Boston.

During the off-season, Pat noticed Terry was distancing himself from old friends like the Hanlans and Father Gordon. Perhaps being isolated in Toronto had done that. He just simply stopped calling them.

Randy Wilson, a childhood friend of JoAnne's and twelve years old at the time, remembers a highlight of that off-season.

Having entered the house with JoAnne, Randy was suddenly awestruck by the sight of his idol, Terry Sawchuk, sitting in the living room in his boxer shorts, watching TV.

"Do you know who I am?" Terry said.

"Ya," was the only answer the boy, shaking visibly, could muster.

"Who are you?"

"I'm Randy Wilson," he answered shyly.

"Oh, you're JoAnne's friend. Are you a goalie?"

"Ya," Randy Wilson answered, bright-eyed.

"Do you want my autograph?"

"Ya. I'd love it!"

Terry butted out his cigarette, put aside his crossword puzzle, and went to a nearby drawer. He pulled out a picture postcard of himself in a Toronto uniform, signed it, and handed it to the wide-eyed boy. Suddenly the twelve-year-old's gaze went to the fireplace mantle, upon which sat the newly acquired Vezina Trophy, surrounded by a few pucks. Suddenly, without warning, Terry turned, went to the mantle and grabbed one of the pucks.

"This is a shutout puck, from one of my shutouts. Do you want it?"

"Ya," the boy answered. Terry handed him the puck with a wry smile then returned to his familiar chair by the front window of the living room. He crossed his right leg over his left, looked at the boy, and snarled, "Now, stop staring at me!"

Turmoil was in the air at the Leafs' 1965 training camp. Bob Baun and four other players were contract holdouts, while Carl Brewer had quit after a verbal tussle with Bower and Imlach. Red Kelly recalls Marcel Pronovost's contribution in joining a thin Leaf defence corps.

"Marcel was a strong addition to that team in Terry's second season with the Leafs. He was an extremely powerful skater and a strong defenceman. He fit in nicely on a team that had a lot of veterans."

That autumn, Pat moved to Toronto with the three youngest Sawchuk children to be with Terry for the season. The house he rented was full of fleas and they had to spend a couple of nights with the Bowers while it was fumigated.

The Maple Leafs spent the first half of the season in the lower half of the standings. The Leaf offence sputtered, and Terry's goals-against average was an ugly 3.47 after his first seventeen games, including a 9–0 shellacking in Chicago.

To top things off, in late January, Terry began to be hampered by a pulled groin and a sore back, both tough maladies for a goaltender to get through. In fact, more and more the sore back was compromising his effectiveness, as he unwittingly began to stand more erect when he played, abandoning his deep crouch. Marcel Pronovost brought it to Terry's attention.

"Terry, you invented the crouch for goalies and did your best goaltending out of that position. Now you're standing upright. Why?"

He returned, despite great pain in his back and legs, to his famous gorilla crouch and, on February 9, he registered his ninety-eighth shutout by blanking Ed Giacomin and the Rangers, 3–0, at Maple Leaf Gardens.

Goaltender injuries were a recurring theme in the Leafs' 1965–66 season. In fact, five goalies would play in the Toronto nets that season, and all would succumb to injuries. At one point, both Bower and Sawchuk were out with a pulled groin and a torn hamstring. Bruce Gamble played so well in relief, recording four shutouts in seven games, that it was rumoured Terry would be shipped to the minors once he returned from the injured list. When Gamble pulled a hamstring, the rumours were effectively quashed, but his performance elevated the Leafs briefly into second place.

Terry saw only spot duty down the stretch, not playing a full sixty-minute game after February 16, though his play was good enough to lower his season average to 3.16 goals against. The Leaf nets were in such disarray that in the last game of the season in Detroit, Bower started the game, Sawchuk played the second period, and Bruce Gamble was summoned from the press box to play the third.

The flu bug ravaged the Leaf ranks, Johnny Bower included, which forced a rusty Terry to play the first two games of their semifinal playoff series against the first-place Canadiens. Despite his sore back, tender hamstring, and flu-ridden teammates, Terry played well. Still the Leafs lost, 4–3 and 2–0, and although Bower returned for the next two, the Habs swept the Leafs aside, 5–2 and 4–1, to put a welcome end to the season.

Terry tried to put it all behind him as he headed to the Morey golf course to play nine holes with his oldest son, Jerry. It was a beautiful sunny afternoon in late June, the sun was strong, the sky deep blue. For six holes, the game was going great and, in fact, Terry was proud of how well his son was playing.

Lining up his ball, Terry took a hard swing, and halfway through it, he felt something snap in his back and he went crashing down to the ground.

"Dad was lying on the ground in immense pain and he couldn't get up. I had never seen him in so much pain. I didn't know what to do. Slowly, he got to his feet. Hunched over, he pulled out my score card, looked at it, and said, 'Son, you're shooting a great game. You have a chance to score in the forties. You keep playing!'

"He put his golf bag over his shoulder and walked. He cheered me on at each hole and wouldn't let me quit. I did score in the forties, then I helped him to the car. He was in unbelievable pain. I took his shoes off, then rushed into the club house for help and to call home. I was scared!"

An ambulance rushed Terry to Detroit Osteopathic Hospital as the left side of his body went numb. Over the course of the next few days, extensive tests were done and Terry and Pat were told the stunning diagnosis: at least one ruptured spinal disk, possibly two. Immediate surgery was necessary. If all went well, he would be able to walk again.

What about his hockey career, Terry asked.

The doctor did not give him an answer, except to say time would tell. The doctor did note that there was exceptional disk deterioration and that Terry should have had the operation "at least seven years ago. How you have been able to keep on playing hockey, Mr. Sawchuk, is a medical mystery."

As he lay in a hospital bed, partially paralyzed, in immense pain, awaiting surgery, it seemed his career might be over. Terry Sawchuk silently prayed for another miracle.

15

THE LAST HURRAH

*T*HE human spine is composed of twenty-four separate vertebrae and between each is a disk of cartilage that acts as a cushion for each vertebrae during movement. In a hockey goaltender's back, these disks are under constant stress as he is almost always bent over. It is said that the lower spine, or lumbar region, of a goaltender's spine is under four times as much stress as those of athletes in any other sport. Terry's pronounced crouch put his back under even more stress. Once damaged or ruptured, these disks of cartilage are difficult to repair.

In hospital, Terry was told that if the damage was bad enough, and they suspected it was, the ruptured disk or disks would have to be removed and the vertebrae would have to be fused. He was also told that fusion would limit his bending over. But Terry insisted he wanted to be able to play hockey again.

On June 27, doctors at Detroit's Osteopathic Hospital operated on Terry's back. One disk was removed completely, and the vertebrae it separated were fused. Bits of a second damaged — but not ruptured — disk were cleared away as well. Terry's prognosis as the operation ended was guarded.

In keeping with his character, Terry told no one. In fact, it was only when Pat phoned Harry Watson, manager of the Tam

O'Shanter Summer Hockey School, to inform him that Terry would be unable to join their instructional staff that year, that word of the injury leaked out. Reached at home by the press, Pat refused to give any details as to Terry's condition and neither did the hospital, except to say that "Mr. Sawchuk's condition is satisfactory."

News of the operation caught the Maple Leaf front office by surprise. Stafford Smythe, Punch Imlach, and Harold Ballard were all out of town, so the Leafs' only public comment was made by trainer Bobby Haggert, who said, "It's the first I hear that he was even considering surgery."

Before his release from hospital, the doctors told Terry it was impossible to predict how his back would hold up under the strain of playing hockey. It was entirely possible a further operation, including removal of the second defective disk, might be required. Removal of the second disk would most definitely end his career.

"When the doctors told him that his career was finished, his mind was made up to come back with a vengeance," son Jerry recalls. "That amazing rage or determination that took him to a different level was now with him. He was determined to prove the doctors wrong."

Within weeks of the operation, Terry noticed a significant improvement in his back. With the doctor's permission, he began walking. Never one to do things halfway, Terry walked nearly ten miles the first day.

"I've had this trouble with the lower part of my back and my legs for some time and I just felt it was about time to do something about it," Terry said. "I am feeling like a rookie. I know one thing, I'll be in good shape when I report [to Leaf training camp]."

Terry and his son continued to walk for the duration of that summer. "We walked so much," Jerry concludes, "that it wore holes in my new shoes."

"The surgeon who operated on Terry's back had really done a great job," Pat says. "In no time really, Terry was feeling better than ever. He even stood straighter and seemed taller."

It appeared Terry's summer road on the way to recovery was

straight and clear, but another off-season event was totally unexpected. Pat recalls: "Grandma Sawchuk, Terry's mother, used to phone me every morning. We'd talk every morning, except this one morning she didn't call. Then the phone rings and it's Terry's father, saying she wasn't feeling good, that she had fallen, that there was something wrong."

Terry and Pat rushed to Louis and Anne's, finding Terry's mother next to her bed. She apparently had been sick in the bathroom and tried to get back into bed but had collapsed beside it. Pat continues: "When we saw her, she was still breathing but I could tell she was gone. Her eyes had no life, like they were vacant. She had suffered a brain aneurysm, and at the hospital she was put on life support but she was gone. My best friend was gone."

With this tragedy behind him, Terry looked ahead to training camp. He was feeling better than he had in years, and by the time he was ready to report, he was golfing thirty-six holes again.

"I'm pretty thankful I can walk, let alone skate," Terry said a few days after training camp opened. "You know, my back was so bad (before the operation) I'd been walking hunched over for years. When I arrived in camp, everyone looked at me and said, 'Terry, have you grown or something?' Truth was I was just standing up, so I suddenly looked two inches taller. You wouldn't believe the change it made in me. My temperament is much better now."

Press reports at the time predicted Bower would easily remain the Leafs' number-one goalie and Terry would get stiff competition from Bruce Gamble for the backup spot. But Punch Imlach put that situation in its proper context.

"On the basis of what he [Gamble] did for us last season with four shutouts in seven games, we have to give him serious consideration. But a seven-game emergency role is not necessarily an indication of how well he'll do over a seventy-game schedule."

Terry's optimism about his health was short-lived after a couple of full practices. His back stiffened up from the vigorous skating and the sudden crouching. For the first time, the other disks and back muscles had to compensate for the spinal fusion and they rebelled. Before too long, Terry worried his career was over, especially when he allowed seventeen goals in one scrimmage session. He was stiff and could barely move as he went to see Imlach at his hotel room. He told Punch that he was tired and discouraged, that there seemed no point in sticking around any longer. Easy shots were being scored on him. "I'm through," he said, but Punch wouldn't hear of it.

"Terry," he said, "if the season were opening tomorrow, you'd be our goalie. Why quit? Nobody's asking you to." Punch told him to think of his family, and suggested Terry only practise once a day instead of twice — maybe even take the occasional day off. Terry agreed to think it over. Assistant general manager King Clancy talked to Terry as well and told him the same thing.

"We talked off and on for a couple of days before I got him to agree to stay and give it one more shot," Imlach would later write in his book *Hockey Is a Battle*.

· Gradually, as everybody had predicted, his stamina and timing returned, though the back was still stiff. A Wayne Carleton shot that slashed him for eleven stitches didn't help his mood, but he slowly came around.

On the opening weekend of the regular season, the Leafs played a home-and-home series against the Rangers. New York coach/GM Emile "the Cat" Francis had contributed to the security of Terry's job. In goalie Eddie Giacomin, Francis knew he had a goaltending find, but one that needed some tutoring, and he saw in Terry Sawchuk the perfect teacher.

"We had had some meetings prior to the '66–67 season," Francis recalls. "Expansion was coming and I'm sitting across from Punch Imlach and he looks at me and says, 'Are you looking for a goalkeeper? I have Bower, Sawchuk, and Gamble.' And I say, 'Ya.' So he says, 'Who do you want?' I say, 'Sawchuk.' Punch looks at me with a smile and says, 'Thanks! Who better than an old goalkeeper to know about goalkeepers! Sawchuk's the one you can't have.'"

Bower played two games against the Rangers, tying one and losing the second, 1–0, in Giacomin's first NHL shutout. The next day, Francis was on the phone to Imlach; he still wanted Sawchuk. Punch wouldn't budge. It seemed the more Francis bugged Punch about Terry, the more resolved Imlach was about keeping him. Still, Punch must have wondered about Terry's back when he rushed from the ice at the end of practice on October 25 and slumped on his seat in the dressing room.

"I have days like this, days when I'm so bushed I can hardly move," Terry sighed. The next night, though, Terry started in place of an injured Bower and played strongly in a 3–2 win over Detroit. Outshot 37–31, Sawchuk was named the game's first star.

A week later, Terry got the call to face the Canadiens. Twelve minutes in, the Leafs were up by two, but a second-period Yvan Cournoyer goal brought them to within one. In the first minute of the third, Terry faced a high lob by J. C. Tremblay. Unable to reach the bouncing puck, Terry stooped to play it like a baseball catcher on one knee, but helplessly watched it bounce over his shoulder into the net to tie the game. His seventeenth year in the league and he still couldn't play those bouncing pucks!

The next night, November 3, Terry's back tightened up during a pre-game warmup in Detroit and he was unable to play. Bruce Gamble took his place. Terry rebounded to play a strong game on Saturday the 5th against the visiting Rangers, in a 3–1 victory. He lost his shutout bid when Bob Nevin scored on a penalty shot.

"Terry Sawchuk's greatest strength as a goaltender was stopping breakaways, one on one," Emile Francis says. "He'd stare the other guy down, wouldn't make a move. He always forced the other guy to make the first move. Not too many got by him on breakaways."

Terry put in another strong performance the following Wednesday against Montreal, earning a 3–2 victory. *Toronto Star* sports columnist Red Burnett likened Sawchuk to baseball's great pitcher, Sandy Koufax: when either man smelled victory late in a game, they knew how to close it.

Terry's back was feeling great, and that improved his demeanour substantially. It has been written that Terry's only friend during the Toronto years was Marcel Pronovost, but he did have a few Toronto friends, one of whom was centre Pete Stemkowski. Terry enjoyed the young forward's company. They were both Ukrainian and hailed from Winnipeg. With Pat staying back in Union Lake this season, Terry rented a large hotel room on Jarvis Street. He would often invite "Stemmer" over after practice, and they would go to dinner and catch a movie.

Stemkowski was one of the few players who could make Terry laugh at his own expense. Often he would walk behind Terry, imitating the Uke's hunched-over gait. Stemkowski wasn't the only one who could find the Uke's funny bone. Marcel Pronovost reminisces, "Whenever Terry and I would be kibitzing and I wanted to get him going, I would imitate the manner in which he used to comb his hair. Because of his bad elbow, in the early Detroit years, he would bring his head back to the comb, he would move his head to comb his hair. Just to get him going, throughout our years together, I would imitate his head moving and I'd laugh and he'd swear!"

According to Marcel, "That last year in Toronto, Terry talked about Pat and the kids more than ever."

Terry also often went down to the Toronto Radio Artists' Club, a local Bay Street dining club bar nicknamed "The Track," because it was frequented by the workers and clients of the Toronto Stock Exchange. Max Applebie owned the club.

"Terry grew to be very close to Max even back in our Detroit years," Marcel recalls. "Max was very good to Terry. He often used to try to beef him up, take him for a Swedish massage, give us a plate of food before heading on the train."

Through November, the Leafs were playing well and so was Terry. When he beat the Habs, 5–1, on November 19, Punch came back with a recuperated Johnny Bower the next night in a 2–2 tie. Terry was playing so well that Imlach found himself defending his choice of Bower to an anxious press.

On Saturday, December 3, the Leafs beat the Red Wings, 5–2. Terry started the next night in Boston, an 8–3 win by the Leafs. Terry had mused, to himself and out loud, that his season had been too good to be true, and the few pangs of back pain he experienced after the Bruin game must have alarmed his optimism. The next day, he knew for certain when he woke up that his back was sore, but he didn't say anything to anybody. He figured he had a couple of days to rest before Wednesday's game in Montreal. Surely the pain would subside, and it did, somewhat, on Wednesday.

"Our goaltending is the reason we're in first place," Imlach announced. "Sawchuk has been fantastic. I think he's playing the best hockey in his career right now. Even better than he was playing with Detroit in the '50s."

"I feel great now," Terry said, "and I think I'm playing my best hockey in ten years." His spirits were so high that he mimicked his former walking style to journalists and teammates, saying, "If you'd been bending over for twenty years like I have, you'd probably be walking the same way!"

But the back pain returned during the game at the Forum. Two quick Canadien goals midway through the first period seemed to rattle Terry. Then he waved helplessly at a ninety-foot slap shot from the stick of Yvan Cournoyer that put the Habs up, 3–1. Something was wrong. After two more questionable goals in the second period, Bower took his place. After the 6–3 loss, Punch told the press Sawchuk's performance was of no concern to him. "The way he's played, he's entitled to an off night."

No sooner had Imlach cast this vote of confidence then, as Terry got into the shower in the Leafs' dressing room, a bolt of lower-back pain sent him crumpling to the floor. Defenceman Tim Horton rushed to his moaning teammate's aid and carried him out of the shower.

Terry spent a sleepless night on the train back to Toronto. When he dragged himself from the Leafs' dressing room at noon the next day, his ashen face was etched with pain.

"Going home, Uke?" someone asked.

"Wish I was," Terry answered. "I'm going into the hospital right now. That's where I'm going." As he shuffled out he added, "Sore back? I got no serious problem. I'll be back for Christmas."

In his bed at Toronto General Hospital, the pain increased as the day wore on. He was clearly worried when he spoke to the

Toronto Telegram's George Gross. "It's sore," he said. "It's getting sorer as the day progresses. I don't know whether to sit up or lie down. I just hope they'll be able to fix it without surgery.

"If I have to have another operation, it would finish me — at least for this season. It took me three months to come back after the operation last summer. Another operation could also finish me for good. Why did it have to happen to me just when I really wanted to play and things were going so good?

"I phoned my wife today. She cried. She felt sorry that these things always happen when things are going well for me. It's been a bad day for me. I just want to be by myself and think." As he concluded, he was on the verge of tears.

Imlach tried to keep a stiff upper lip. "He played too well to let a thing like this finish him. It may bother him for a while, but I'm sure he'll bounce back if it can be corrected. Of course, with back injuries, there's always an element of risk. But I'd bet he'll play again, just as well as he has so far this season."

For twelve days, Terry remained in hospital while doctors took x-rays and conducted a battery of tests. When he emerged on December 19, he was guardedly optimistic as he looked forward to a month of bed rest.

"They found some acute disk trouble, but the doctors think they caught it in time. They figure I may not need an operation. I'd rather not talk about it until later. It's the old stuff, the old operation. I guess it just needs plenty of rest."

Pat Sawchuk drove all night from Union Lake to Toronto with three-year-old Terry and five-year-old Debbie to attend the Leafs' annual Christmas skate at Maple Leaf Gardens for the players and families. "I decided to drive through the night because the kids could sleep on the way and there would be less traffic," she told journalist Bob Pennington. "There was also a promise they could skate here on Daddy's ice." When Pat produced a picture of twelve-year-old Jerry in goalie gear, Terry, standing at rinkside, piped up.

"The boy can skate. He's too good a skater to play in goal. I told him to tell his coach the only position he was *not* to play was goal. So he goes to the coach and tells him the only position he is to play in is goal. I was furious.

"No, I don't give him any advice," Terry said, "except to listen to his coach. If I told him things, the kid would only get confused. You get too much of that in hockey — Dad says one thing and the coach another. That's bad for a boy. I don't even go to see him play anymore because he freezes when I'm there."

Despite this quote, Pat says Terry did not approve of Jerry playing hockey. "He would rant and rave against it, refuse to give me money for his registration. If Terry was home, we would have to sneak out of the house, me and the kids, while Terry slept to go to Jerry's games. I don't know if he was jealous of Jerry, who was pretty good, or if he didn't want him to lead his kind of life, but he didn't like it at all."

Preparing to return to Michigan with Pat and the kids, Terry said he hoped to be able to resume skating on his return to Toronto on January 16 and to begin playing the first week of February.

"I don't recall him doing so much 'bed rest'," Pat says, "but he did laze around on the couch and watch a lot of TV. And the bar stool at the VFW, I would say, was in Terry's 'rest' category. Terry was not one who could stay in bed all day. He was not one to do himself any favours."

With Sawchuk and Bower both out of the Leaf lineup with back ailments — though Johnny's was much less serious — the goaltending assignments fell to the previous year's boy wonder, Bruce Gamble. But the Leafs began a free-fall in the standings during Terry's absence, dropping from first place to third in two weeks, winning just two games. When Terry returned to Toronto on January 16, the team was beginning a seven-game losing streak. Nothing seemed to work and the more they lost, the harder Imlach would push them.

"Punch was a pusher," Red Kelly said. "He liked to practise, practise, practise. In this respect, he had a real problem with some of the young players on the team who rebelled against him. We veterans understood what he was doing but the youngsters didn't appreciate his drill-sergeant mentality. That hurt the team."

If Terry had thought that sitting at a bar was going to cure his back, he was wrong. His back hadn't responded as quickly as he had hoped, and doctors prescribed a week of swimming and physiotherapy. But he wanted to begin skating.

"All this swimming is getting me down and besides, I don't think it's helping me anyways," he told coach Punch Imlach on January 23. Though he was supposed to be off skates for another two weeks, Sawchuk was itching to get back into action. "If I do that," he reasoned, "the season will almost be over before I get back."

Terry also pointed out that, whatever the Leafs' problems were, goaltending wasn't part of it. "I couldn't have played any better than these two guys (Gamble and Bower). I don't think our problems have been in goal." By February 12, when Terry first began to skate slowly, the Leafs were stuck in fifth place. The night before they had snapped a ten-game losing streak, but the pressures of the season had gotten to Imlach, and on February 18 he was in hospital, having been diagnosed with stress-related exhaustion.

Terry himself was about to experience an added dose of stress when Pat called him from Union Lake.

"I called Terry and told him I was pregnant. He didn't want to talk about it. Then he said, 'I don't care what you do, get rid of it!' And I said, 'What?' He said again, 'I don't care where you go, or what you do. I don't want to talk about it. *Just get rid of it!*' Then he slammed the phone down. But I refused to get an abortion. It was illegal. You went to butchers back then. Besides, I loved kids. Terry was quite upset with my decision. When we were together again, he hardly talked to me, or even for the rest of that year. That was just a mixed-up year!"

The affable King Clancy took over for Imlach behind the Leaf bench. "The younger players liked King and his 'rah-rah,' easy-going ways and they played hard for him, played up to their potential and we began to win again," said Red Kelly.

On Thursday, February 23, 1967, Terry suited up for his first start in eleven weeks, against the Red Wings in the Olympia. He didn't have long to wait to find out if his back would hold up. He survived a first-period collision with Gordie Howe and it loosened him up, boosted his confidence. He made key saves throughout the evening, especially in the third period, when he robbed Dean Prentice and Andy Bathgate of sure goals. His play was instrumental in the 4–2 Leaf win that stretched their undefeated streak to six games.

Two nights later, the Red Wings visited Maple Leaf Gardens. Terry again got the assignment. The goal light went on behind him in the second period, but it was a mistake. The goal judge's knee had accidentally hit the switch. Most of the 15,849 in attendance breathed a sigh of relief. Though the Wings pressed in the third period, Terry stopped every one of the thirty-nine shots he faced. His 4–0 shutout was number ninety-nine of his career.

He skated out as the game's first star, and later in the dressing room he said, "I've got my own Centennial project now. Play long enough and get a hundred shutouts."

As he put on his tie he observed, "I'm pretty thankful I can walk, let alone skate. Detroit doctors told my wife I'd be lucky to play hockey again after the spinal fusion. I thank the Lord I can still skate. Some things I've done bad but I must have done something good, too."

A week later, on March 4, Terry was in net at Maple Leaf Gardens to face the first-place Black Hawks. But it was Denis DeJordy in the Hawks' net who was overpowered. Terry hardly broke a sweat in the first period, as he faced only seven shots. The second frame wasn't much different, though he had to make one excellent kick save off a Bobby Hull slap shot.

"Ukey and I shared a lot of shutouts together," Marcel Pronovost recalls, "a lot of great moments together. As we went out for that third period, the whole team was very, very aware of Terry's possible hundredth shutout. He was close and we were prepared to bear down like a son of a bitch. We all knew. We were going to eat that puck."

The Leafs checked frantically in the third and when they had the puck, they rarely gave it up. There was tension in the air that belied the fact the Leafs were winning, 3–0. With three minutes left to go, Terry looked up at the clock and thought, "Well, if they get one, we'll try again next time."

But he faced only eight third-period shots and, with ten

seconds left in the game, the Gardens crowd counted down the seconds. With the puck in the Chicago end, Terry raised his arms wide in a V.

As the game ended, Terry's milestone was announced over the public-address system for the benefit of those few who weren't aware of Terry's feat. The crowd roared again. Terry accepted his kudos as he was chosen by Foster Hewitt as the game's first star.

Once in the dressing room, he received the plaudits of everyone. He couldn't stop smiling even though he tried to fight back his emotions as he undressed. Then he walked slowly around the room and shook the hand of every Leaf, thanking them. Behind him team executive Harold Ballard collected Terry's stick and that of Leaf captain George (The Chief) Armstrong, whose third-period goal was his 250th, for the Hockey Hall of Fame.

"Man, were they coming back tonight," Terry said of his teammates. "They were really checking for me."

Asked to summarize his feelings, he was at a loss for words. "I don't know what to say. I wasn't expecting this . . ." he repeated several times. Finally he smiled and said, "The first hundred are the hardest."

Marcel Pronovost praised Terry as "the greatest goalie I've ever seen." George Armstrong likened the milestone to "scoring 500 goals." But the Rocket and Gordie had achieved that milestone. This record, so unattainable, would probably be comparable to 1,000 goals.

That same night, a young boy in a wheelchair was guided into the Leaf dressing room, hoping to meet Terry. Bob Pulford was the first to notice and pushed the youngster towards Terry's corner. Sawchuk became quite animated, chatting and demonstrating the save he had made on Bobby Hull. With the team in a rush to catch the flight to Chicago for the next night's return match, Terry's sole concern was for little David Onley. Grabbing Pulford's stick, he wheeled the boy around the room, introduced him to each player, and insisted that each sign the stick.

Finally it was late and the team was rushing to the bus. Terry patted the boy on the head and told him to keep plugging, to keep exercising. The boy would never forget the shutout king's graciousness that night. That this side of Terry wasn't publicized irks Pronovost, even today.

The night after Terry chalked up his 100th shutout, Montreal's Rogatien Vachon recorded his first.

"Just ninety-nine more to get even with Sawchuk," joked the twenty-one-year-old.

Terry seemed to be back with a vengeance. His two goals allowed in the three games since his return lowered his season average to 2.04 — the lowest in the league. By March 13, the Leafs were in third place, two points ahead of the Habs, who, thanks to widespread injuries, were in the unfamiliar surroundings of the bottom half of the league. In Punch's first two games back, on March 12 and 15, the Leafs lost 5–0 in Chicago and 4–2 to the Wings. Toronto won their next two — beating Chicago, 9–5, and Detroit, 6–5 — but the results masked something ominous: Terry's goals-against average was climbing, and he wasn't feeling well. He sat out a key game against the Habs on March 22, a 5–3 loss.

At about this time, Uncle Nick in Chicago began to notice that there was something not quite right with his nephew.

"Every time he came in here to Chicago, I saw every game. He'd come over to the house, stay overnight sometimes, then I would drive him to the rink. But this one year in Toronto, he stopped coming for a while, he wasn't feeling good. He'd phone up and say he wasn't coming over. So, one day, I know he's in town, I said to my wife, 'Dorothy, I'm going downtown. I'm going to find out what's wrong with the kid.' He was my favourite nephew.

"So I go downtown and I meet Pronovost. Marcel Pronovost, they were pretty close friends. I asked Pronovost if something was wrong with Terry. 'Naw,' Pronovost said. 'He's just not feeling good, just not up to par, that's all.' So that was fine. Never did find out what was wrong."

On Tuesday, March 28, Terry, his skin drawn tight around his ribs, walked into the Leafs' trainer's room to weigh himself. When asked by a reporter how much he weighed, Terry mumbled, "One hundred and sixty-three and a half."

The next afternoon, *Globe and Mail* reporter Lou Cauz sought Terry out as he sat in the lobby of Montreal's Mount Royal Hotel. He was slated to start at the Forum that night. If his back was bothering him again, he wasn't saying, but he was despondent yet unusually talkative.

"Three more games, then the playoffs and that's it. Twenty years is a long time. I want to start spending more time with my family. You know, our seventh is on the way this summer."

When Cauz questioned his ability to turn his back on his $25,000 salary, Terry did not hesitate.

"Sure I would. I could go and work for my father-in-law at the golf course."

When Cauz asked him if he'd play for the Red Wings if given the opportunity, Terry naturally said he would. Suddenly, Cauz was on to a story.

In the game against the Canadiens, Terry played like an old man. He gave up large rebounds, bobbling the Canadiens' first five or six shots. The Habs threw twenty-five shots at him in that first period alone but came out tied, 2–2. At the first intermission, Terry told Punch that he wasn't feeling right, but he insisted on continuing. Jacques Plante, by now a broadcaster for Radio-Canada, was at a loss to explain Terry's play. "There's something the matter with him. He isn't handling anything cleanly. He's not hot. Perhaps he can't work up a sweat."

The second period wasn't any better. Yvan Cournoyer beat him cleanly at 4:34, and three minutes later, Terry lost sight of a rebound for the fourth Montreal goal. Punch muttered to himself that perhaps he should make a switch. When the Habs' John Ferguson was called for a delayed penalty halfway through the middle frame, Terry was very slow to skate to the Leaf bench for the extra attacker. Punch had seen enough; Bower played the last half of the game in a 5–3 Montreal win.

"It just wasn't my night," Terry said later. The next day Cauz sought Terry out. Terry spoke frankly to him again.

"I'm beat. I've lost a lot of weight. I don't know what I weigh, all I know is that I'm under 170 pounds." Terry continued to lament that he might be let go by the Leafs to the upcoming expansion draft. "They're not going to protect an old guy like me with a bad back. It'll be Bower or one of the younger guys." He again said he would play for Detroit if he had the opportunity.

On Friday morning, Cauz's story appeared in *The Globe and Mail* and was also picked up by other wire services. The head-lines were sensational: "Sawchuk Says He's Finished with Toronto", "Sawchuk Won't Return to Toronto", "Sawchuk Longs for Home". Later that day Cauz and other reporters were in Imlach's office while the Leaf coach was on the exercise bike. In stomped Sawchuk in his mask and full equipment, blind with rage, swinging his big goal stick menacingly at Cauz.

"You're trying to screw me!" Terry yelled repeatedly.

"Yeah, you give it to him, Ukey," Imlach said, laughing. "You tell him. Fucking reporters. They never get anything right!"

"You sure as hell did say those things to me, I've got every-thing here in my notes," Cauz yelled back.

The story visibly upset some of his teammates. "You'd think he would have at least waited until after the playoffs were done to say that," said one. Pat Sawchuk Milford today clearly remembers the mayhem that that story caused. "You know, that was all so blown out of context it was awful. Naturally, when the reporter asked Terry if he would like to play in Detroit, the answer was, 'Yes.' His friends were here, his family, his home. His answers were twisted to suit a story that was slanted a cer-tain way. He gave his all for Toronto. His loyalty was to the Leafs as long as he was a Leaf. It was all unfair."

On the final weekend of the season, the Leafs beat New York, 5–1, and Boston, 5–2. As in the two previous years, Johnny Bower played both games as Imlach prepared him for the playoffs. They ended the season in third place, two points behind Montreal and nineteen behind the Chicago Black Hawks, their first-round opponents.

The Maple Leafs holed up in Peterborough to practise and get away from the distractions of the city. In practise, Terry was twice hit on the left shoulder by blistering slap shots, leaving the area bruised and tender. No matter; Bower was the playoff goalie. Then a Pete Stemkowski slap shot broke Bower's little finger. Terry would again have to start in net for the semi-finals. Did he and the Leafs have a chance?

Terry expected to have his hands full against the Hawks, who'd set a league record with 264 goals.

At the five-minute mark of Game One, Chicago's Kenny Wharram took a shot from a bad angle that sneaked inside Terry's elbow, bringing the Chicago Stadium crowd to its feet. But the Leafs had come to play. They banged and bumped the Hawks at every opportunity and Frank Mahovlich tied the game almost two minutes later.

A little more than halfway through the period, Bobby Hull crashed through Terry's crease, jarring his mask just as Pierre Pilote was shooting. Terry didn't have a chance and it was now 2–1 Chicago. The Hawks shelled Terry, taking a 4–1 lead into the third. The teams exchanged goals to make it 5–2, and in the closing minutes of the game the crowd began to chant, "Good night, Terry!" Chicago coach Billy Reay spoke volumes when he said, "I thought we got the goaltending tonight."

The Ice Capades were booked into Chicago Stadium the next day, leaving the Leafs without practice ice. Undaunted, Punch flew his team back to Toronto for two days of practising. Prior to Game Two, Imlach defended his goaltender's performance. "I'm not going to criticize a goalkeeper who has 100 shutouts. It says in the book how good Sawchuk is, and I feel like the book says. He's been awful good a lot of times."

Tenacious forechecking by the Leafs was rewarded in Game Two when Pappin stole the puck in the corner, passed to Bob Pulford, who passed to Pete Stemkowski to put the Leafs up by one. Chicago's chance to even things up came when Eric Nesterenko broke in all alone on Terry. The Hawk put two dekes on Terry, went to his backhand, and fired, but Terry stayed with him, deflecting the puck wide with his stick. That cooled the crowd momentarily until Horton took a holding penalty and the awesome Hawk power play took the ice. Bobby Hull had two good chances and then Stan Mikita, the NHL scoring champ, was in all alone but Terry managed to snare the puck.

At an opportune play stoppage, Terry went to referee Vern

Buffey, and asked permission to get a strap on one of his leg pads fixed at the Leaf bench. The equipment "adjustment" was actually just a tactic to rest Terry's penalty killers. It worked. When play resumed a few minutes later, Dave Keon and George Armstrong were fresh, the penalty was killed off, and the Leafs snagged another goal courtesy of Keon towards the end of the period.

Armstrong gave the Leafs a second-period 3–0 lead and tireless checking kept the Hawks at bay. By the third period, the Hawks looked beaten until Terry, appearing a little sluggish, misplayed Stan Mikita's snap shot with half a period to go. Then Phil Esposito broke in alone. Terry came out to meet his attacker and stayed with him as Espo attempted to switch to the backhand after deking. But Terry was there to stop it. The Hawks threw thirty-four shots at the old Leaf goaltender, compared to twenty-four shots on Denis DeJordy, but the score remained 3–1 Toronto.

Billy Reay's postmortem had Sawchuk written all over it. "That one (save) on Nesterenko was great . . . If he had scored that goal it would have made all the difference in the world."

"I think I lost ten pounds standing out there," Terry softly said later.

The Hawks came out flying for Game Three and Terry had to stop two early blasts from Hull — one with his calf and one with the meat of the arm. In the other net, Glenn Hall got the call, but halfway through the first period, he was fooled by a Ron Ellis twenty-footer that put Toronto up, 1–0. The goal sparked the Leafs.

Mahovlich and Pappin gave the Leafs a 3–0 lead in the second period, leaving Mr. Goalie looking like he was all alone in his own end. Toronto began to play a physical game, zeroing in specifically on Bobby Hull, Stan Mikita, and Pierre Pilote. Their coverage was so complete that when Hull broke Terry's shutout with three and a half minutes left on the clock, the Hawks' reaction was more relief than celebration.

"Our guys made the ice look like a minefield out in front of me," said Terry after the 3–1 victory, in which he faced thirty-six shots, the same number as Hall. Terry and company had a

2–1 series lead, though Sawchuk's bruises and welts would have convinced anyone that his team was behind.

Two nights later, Reay blasted his team in a pre-game pep talk, and it paid off immediately. Ken Wharram took only nine seconds to put the puck by Terry. Toronto came back to tie it on a goal by Keon, only to have Pilote launch one through traffic to make it 2–1 Hawks. Horton tied the game barely a minute later; the wide-open play was hardly typical of playoff hockey. Four goals had been scored in barely ten minutes. The Leafs, lacking Chicago's firepower, realized they had to slow the game down. They tried to reassert the physical, punishing game that had worked in Game Three. It backfired as they took penalties. Playing short-handed, Terry had to come up big, and he did. He stopped Stan Mikita and Bill Hay on their respective breakaways, as well as Doug Jarrett's wrist shot. Terry's upper body absorbed two more Bobby Hull cannon shots.

In the third period, Terry tired visibly. His concentration was reduced in this, his fourth game in seven days. An uncontrolled rebound resulted in Chicago's third goal and, at the 8:48 mark, Bobby Hull wound up for another slap shot. Terry flinched visibly, preparing to take another body blast. Hull rang the shot along the ice and in off the post to make the score 4–2. It ended up 4–3 and the series was tied heading back to the Windy City.

Reporters asked Punch Imlach which goalie he was starting in the fifth game. "You guess which one and I'll use the other guy," Imlach quipped. At Terry's insistence, it was Bower. Today, Pierre Pilote recalls the Hawks' strategy in Game Five.

"Our goal was to really get at Bower. If we could get Bower out of there, we'd be all set. We knew we could beat Sawchuk. We all thought Terry couldn't see the puck anymore." Bower played the first period, was shaky, and was replaced by Sawchuk, who stymied the Hawk shooters over the last two periods for a Toronto 4–2 victory.

Pilote continues: "But a great player came up big. Sawchuk said, 'Okay. I'm gonna do it one more time.' He was like Frank Sinatra, he did it his way. It was unbelievable what he was stopping. Pucks that should have been in the net weren't. It was just totally unbelievable."

"There was a certain point in that game," Red Kelly says. "I forget how many minutes were left, five or six, and Chicago gave up. You could see it. They literally gave up. And my first impression was that these guys aren't champions. Champions don't give up until the final buzzer! When we saw that, we knew we had won, not only that game but the series. The last game of the series after that game was ours to win."

Pierre Pilote agrees: "Going to Toronto after that fifth game loss, we were defeated. Terry had taken the wind out of us."

In Game Six at Maple Leaf Gardens, the Chicagoans barely showed up. Terry made thirty-five saves but the Leafs were full of confidence and won the game easily, 3–1, to eliminate the NHL's most powerful team.

"Terry, you old son of a gun! You beat us!" smiled Stan Mikita while he shook Terry's hand in congratulations. But Sawchuk wasn't smiling. There was still another series to win.

Canada celebrated its centennial year in 1967, and the Stanley Cup Finals that year would be the last for the six-team league. The following year the NHL would double in size. How appropriate, then, that the two teams that had won eighteen of the past twenty-four Stanley Cups should meet in the last of the old-time finals.

"I've never seen Terry any better than he is right now," Marcel Pronovost told journalist Dick Beddoes. "When he's right, he just picks you up by the boot straps. Terry's put so much playoff money in my pockets, I got to go with him."

In Game One at the Forum, Terry got the start, but the Chicago series had taken its toll on him. He complained privately that he was tired. He moved slowly and played the same way. When the Habs scored their fifth goal on him with fifteen minutes left in the third period, Imlach replaced him with Bower. Getting his chance, Bower looked sharp the rest of the way, allowing only one more goal in the Canadiens' 6–2 romp.

Before the next game, Punch Imlach had stated, "Don't know who I'll start. They will decide themselves who'll play." Bower was hot in practice, so he earned the start.

Bower played an excellent game, stopping thirty-one shots and shutting out Montreal, 3–0, to even the series.

Game Three was more of the same, an end-to-end duel that went into double overtime. Bower stopped sixty of sixty-two shots and Bob Pulford's goal at the 8:26 mark gave the Leafs the game and a 2–1 series lead.

Bower was on a roll and the bruised and battered Sawchuk was content to sit on the sidelines and recover from the Chicago series. There is an oft-told tale that after practice on April 26, Terry went to his favourite bar on nearby Church Street and drank from five p.m. until closing time at one o'clock in the morning. He wasn't too worried about being hung over, since he didn't have to play the next day anyway, so the story goes.

The next day in the pre-game warmup, Johnny Bower stretched to stop a shot and tore a hamstring. Terry would have to play.

As the game started, Terry seemed fine, but at the twelve-minute mark of the first period, Ralph Backstrom beat him on a high backhand and then Beliveau banked another off Terry's skate to make it 2–0 Habs. They were fast and full of confidence, outshooting Toronto 19–11 in the first period.

In the second, Mike Walton put the Leafs on the board quickly, only to have Henri Richard beat Terry seconds later with a floater that, on other nights, Terry would have eaten. Ten minutes later, a Beliveau forty-footer fooled Terry to make the score 4–2, and another Backstrom backhand made it 5–2. Though Montreal barely outshot the Leafs, 40–37, over the game, the final score was a Montreal 6–2 rout.

"I've got one thing to say, gentlemen," Terry told reporters. "I just didn't have a good night."

Marcel Pronovost says the story of Terry's hangover doesn't wash. "There is no doubt in my mind that Terry had had a few drinks the night before, and even if he was out drinking till one o'clock in the morning, it still gives him lots of sleep. At our eleven o'clock workout he dons the pads, he's not that hung over, and at the game that night, he's fine. It's really just that he wasn't expecting to play."

The next day, a telegram arrived from a fan in the Maritimes who had sent congratulations to Terry after his 100th shutout. This time the note read, "How much did you get [to throw the game]?" The note stung Terry. It made him even more angry. And if Terry needed more motivation heading into Game Five at the Forum, the atmosphere in Montreal would provide it.

"Montreal thought they had us now," Pronovost recalls. "They thought they had Terry's number. They didn't know him very well. There was a lot of talk suddenly about Montreal winning the Stanley Cup and displaying it in the Quebec Pavilion at Expo '67 in Montreal. They already had a spot where they were going to display it. And we thought, 'No goddamn way! We're gonna display it in the Ontario Pavilion!'"

Prior to that Saturday afternoon game in Montreal, Punch took aside the man on whose shoulders the fate of the series now rested.

"We talked before the game," said Imlach. "I told him he had brought us this far and he had the records to prove he was a great clutch player. He was entitled to one bad game. I knew he could win for us as long as he played aggressively in goal. In other words, he had to go out and challenge the guys taking the shots. As Marcel Pronovost recalls, the Leafs got their inspiration going into Game Five from an unusual source.

"Frank Mahovlich was always as quiet as a mouse in the dressing room, but before we went on the ice that afternoon, the Big M stood up and yelled, 'We're gonna beat these guys today!' He marched out of the room and everybody charged out after him, and we did!"

"And the way Montreal started that game against Sawchuk, it looked as if they were happy he was around, figuring the two easy games they'd had against him gave them an automatic win. But they should have known Sawchuk by then."

On the first shift of Game Five, Ralph Backstrom broke in all alone on Terry, faked, then shot, only to have the shutout king kick the shot wide. A minute later, with the Habs buzzing around his net, Ukey charged out to greet Yvan Cournoyer, who was set up alone in the slot, for another big save. The Canadiens were all over the Leafs' zone, forcing Jim Pappin to take a penalty at the three-minute mark. On the ensuing power play, Sawchuk made stops on Beliveau, Cournoyer, and J. C. Tremblay. The Leafs killed off the penalty only to have Leon Rochefort bang home the first goal of the game at the six-minute mark. The thunderous roar of the crowd only strengthened Terry's resolve. The Canadiens thought they had broken the Sawchuk dam.

Despite being outshot 13–7, the Leafs went into the first intermission tied 1–1, thanks to Jim Pappin's goal on a weak wrist shot that Rogie Vachon should have had. The Leafs seemed to have taken control of the game.

In the second, Terry robbed Ralph Backstrom on a shot that he didn't even see. At the three-minute mark, Brian Conacher put the Leafs in front, but Red Kelly took an interference penalty at the halfway point in the period. Jean Beliveau was set up beautifully in the slot and let go a low slap shot, but Terry steered it wide with his skate. Suddenly big Marcel Pronovost carried the puck into the Canadiens' zone. His seemingly harmless forty-foot shot at Vachon sailed past the goalie's left foot and into the net. The Canadiens were stunned by the short-handed goal.

Dave Keon took a bouncing pass from Tim Horton deep in the Montreal end, deked Vachon, and stuffed it into the net. The Forum fell silent as the Leafs took a 4–1 lead.

Montreal coach Toe Blake replaced Vachon with Gump Worsley in an effort to shake up his team, but it didn't work. At the final buzzer, as the Leafs mobbed Terry, the Forum was three-quarters empty.

"Know what they say?" Tim Horton asked before Game Six. "Goalkeeping is like pitching. If Sawchuk is like [Sandy] Koufax tonight, we win. If he isn't, well, as they say in Montreal, 'c'est la guerre.'"

A calm permeated the Leaf dressing room as the players suited up. Imlach's "old pappies" knew what they had to do, and they also knew that Terry had to be on his game for them to have a chance. As Punch stoically addressed his troops, Terry sat quietly listening, looking down at the floor, focusing on the task at hand.

"We have to win this game tonight. If we go back to Montreal for a seventh game, all bets are off!" Imlach said. He didn't have to tell them it was slated for Thursday, a day on which the Leafs hadn't been able to win in these playoffs.

"Bill Gadsby played twenty seasons in this league and never won a Stanley Cup," Imlach continued. "You're sixty minutes away." He looked directly at the younger players. Then his gaze fell on the veterans. He chose his words carefully.

"Some of you have been with me for nine years. It's been said that I stuck with the old ones so long, we couldn't possibly win the Stanley Cup. For some of you, it's a farewell. Go out there and ram that puck down their goddamn throats!"

Terry took a deep breath, shoved his mask down his left pad by his knee, and led the team onto the ice, to a thunderous ovation from the Gardens crowd. Gump Worsley took his place in the Montreal net.

The Flying Frenchmen skated like the wind and, on his second shift, Habs' captain Jean Beliveau raced down the left wing and blasted a shot at Terry. Sawchuk deflected the shot away to his left with his pad and glove. And they kept coming. Cournoyer blasted a shot that Terry blocked with his left leg. Jacques Laperriere blasted one and Terry blocked it, then pounced on the rebound. A blocker stop on Backstrom, then a sideways dive to steal a sure goal from Beliveau. Then Leon Rochefort broke in alone and went to his backhand, but Terry snaked out a pad.

Sawchuk faced seventeen shots in the first period, while his Leafs launched only eleven at Gump Worsley. Both goalies were flawless as the period ended in a scoreless draw.

Early in the second period, Terry sprawled to stop a Bobby Rousseau drive. Then suddenly, after the six-minute mark, a Canadiens' error turned into a Toronto two-on-one against Worsley. Gump stopped Red Kelly's shot, but the rebound was banged in by Ron Ellis.

Down 1–0, the Canadiens stepped up the offensive pressure. Dick Duff's shot was stopped by Terry, and his second effort hit the post and stayed out. Terry stopped a Dave Balon riser, then shots by John Ferguson, Beliveau, and Ferguson again.

Leaf defenceman Larry Hillman slid across the crease to block a sure Cournoyer goal. For every Canadien there was a blue-shirted Leaf.

A Montreal penalty late in the period gave Terry and the Leafs a breather. Then, with both teams at full strength, Jim Pappin carried the puck deep into the left corner of the Montreal zone. His long cross-ice pass hit Stemkowski's right foot, and caromed off the right-hand goal post into the net before a sprawling Worsley could fall on it.

The Canadiens skated hard to start the third. The tension increased after Dick Duff stickhandled past Horton and Allan Stanley and beat Terry with a backhander through his legs. Suddenly the 2–1 Leaf lead was tenuous. Terry had to turn back shots from Ted Harris and J. C. Tremblay, and then a scary moment occurred at the six-minute mark. A tired and frustrated Henri Richard lobbed the puck over everyone's head towards the Leafs' goal. This was the kind of shot that could always handcuff Terry. This time the puck hit the ice ten feet in front of him and he reacted quickly and accurately enough to deflect that puck wide. The entire Leaf club, Terry included, breathed a sigh of relief.

The Canadiens were able to get a whistle with the puck in the Toronto end and fifty-five seconds left on the clock. Worsley was called to the bench in lieu of an extra attacker. The most important face-off of the year for either team took place in the circle to Terry's left. What happened next has been etched in the collective memory of Toronto Maple Leaf fans for thirty-one years: Stanley tied up Beliveau, Kelly got the puck and passed to Pulford, who passed to Armstrong, who skated over centre ice and deposited the puck from a hundred feet away into the Montreal net. The Toronto Maple Leafs, led by Terry Sawchuk, had won their fourth Stanley Cup of the 1960s. As the teams lined up for the customary handshakes, the Canadiens congratulated Terry especially.

Afterwards, Jean Beliveau said of Terry, "He came up with the key saves and gave them the time to get ahead. There were three or four shots in the early part of the game you could usually count on as goals."

Toe Blake summed up his feelings by saying, "This is the toughest series I ever lost."

In the dressing room afterwards, amid the jubilation, an exhausted, serene Terry Sawchuk watched his teammates celebrate the big win. Beside him was Johnny Bower. Both men dragged deeply on cigarettes and drank Coca-Cola.

"I'm too tired to dance around and I don't like champagne," Terry said. As usual, he was one of the last to shower and leave the dressing room. He snuck out of the Gardens through a back entrance, but some fans caught a glimpse of him and applauded. True to form, he didn't look back. He called Pat back in Michigan, then went out for a drink.

The Conn Smythe Trophy for the outstanding player in the playoffs was awarded to Dave Keon, the tireless checking centre. But, as Red Kelly recalls, "Terry probably would have won the Conn Smythe had he not had those two bad games against Montreal."

The next day, Pat took the kids out of school to join Terry for the Stanley Cup parade, the festivities at Nathan Phillips Square, and the party later at Stafford Smythe's place.

Even as they celebrated, it's not hard to imagine a bitter-sweet undertone to the festivities. The Leafs of 1967 were the last team to win the Stanley Cup in a six-team NHL. The next season would see the league double to twelve teams. In one month there would be an expansion draft to stock the new clubs, and many of the Leaf greybeards would be rewarded for their Cup win by being left exposed in the draft. Would one of the new teams want a Terry Sawchuk? And if they did, what would life be like for one of the game's greatest stars in a hockey-ignorant locale such as St. Louis or Oakland?

16

P UNCH Imlach and the rest of the Original Six GMs
would only be able to protect eleven skaters and one
goaltender from the NHL expansion draft of June 6,
1967. For Imlach, the question of which goalie to protect was
academic: he was loyal to Johnny Bower, who, although forty-
two, was still his hardest worker, the superior athlete, and who
had the steadier demeanour.

Still, not lost on him was Sawchuk's Stanley Cup performance. Despite Terry's infirmities, given the chance Imlach
would have both veteran netminders. As he'd tried to do with
Cheevers a few years before, Imlach initially tried to list Terry as
one of the eleven skaters. "Well, he can skate, can't he?" Punch
protested unsuccessfully at the draft, to the chuckles of all.

The expansion clubs would each choose a pair of goaltenders to open the draft. Clarence Campbell drew team names
from the Stanley Cup to determine the drafting order, and the
Los Angeles Kings got the first pick of netminders.

The Kings' owner, Canadian-born media tycoon Jack Kent
Cooke, stepped up to the microphone with the look of a
Cheshire cat. "Los Angeles draws Terry Sawchuk from Toronto,"
he said in a clear, unhesitating voice.

Imlach was still fuming at Cooke, who'd hired Leaf centre
Red Kelly as his coach. Even though Kelly had announced his

retirement and thought he had verbal permission to seek a coaching job, Punch still thought the Kings should have to draft Red. In the tenth round, Imlach decided to force the issue. He added Red Kelly's name to the Leafs' protected list.

The Kings were incensed, as was Kelly.

"We'll give them Kelly — for Sawchuk. We'll even throw in another goalie," Imlach retorted. But Cooke wasn't having any of it. In a postdraft deal the Leafs got the Kings' fifteenth-round draft choice, an unknown defenceman named Ken Block, for Kelly. And of course, Cooke kept Sawchuk.

Cooke had decided going into the draft that goaltending was to be a key factor that the expansion clubs had to address. And to him, a goalie who'd racked up 100 shutouts in the six-team NHL had to be more than lucky. "I felt I needed specialized help," Cooke said. "Sawchuk, I had to have. And I got him."

Other goalies drafted that afternoon included the Wings' Hank Bassen chosen by the Pittsburgh Penguins; Bernie Parent went to the Philadelphia Flyers from Boston; Montreal Vezina winner Charlie Hodge became an Oakland Seal; and the St. Louis Blues took a chance they might coax the legendary Glenn Hall out of retirement.

Starting with the third round, the teams drafted forwards and defencemen. The other five teams drafted veteran players in the twilight of their careers. The Kings, however, chose to go with youth, a manoeuvre that caused hockey experts to predict the Kings would finish "in last place or worse" in the West Division made up of the six new teams.

A week after the draft, the Sawchuk family German shepherd, Shadow, was struck by a motorcycle he had always had a penchant for chasing. Terry and Pat wrapped the dog in a blanket and drove him to a vet, where he was diagnosed with a broken hip. The hip was repaired and after a few days Shadow was brought home, but not before Terry had a run-in with those responsible.

"We pulled in at home from a drive and these motorcycles were in our driveway," eldest son Jerry says. "Dad told us all to stay in the car and he got out. Boy, we were all scared. Dad yelled at them about Shadow — and there were quite a few of

these biker guys — and Dad said to them, 'You might be able
to beat the shit out of me, but I guarantee you before you do, I
am going to be able to hurt one of you, and I'm gonna hurt you
good!' Dad went right at them — he would have taken them
all on, and probably died trying. Anyways, they took off with
Dad screaming at them that if they ever hurt the dog again, he'd
kill them!"

On the afternoon of June 15, 1967, Terry was tending to
Shadow on his back porch when the phone rang. It was a
Toronto reporter calling for his comment on having just been
awarded the J. P. Bickell Memorial Trophy as the Leafs' outstanding player in the past season.

"No kidding," Terry answered with surprise. "How do you
like that! That's a real honour. I wasn't even thinking about it."

It was a very small consolation prize for being left unpro-
tected by the Leafs. The Toronto media played up the irony of
the Leafs' letting their most valuable player go for nothing.
Terry, on the other hand, had seen it all before in 1964, when
Detroit let him go in the waiver draft after he was named team
MVP.

As Terry golfed that June with his former Bruin teammate
and current Kings GM Larry Regan, they discussed the young
team and Terry's contract. If Terry's hockey career was about to
be uprooted, his home life was a shambles as his incessant
drinking and abusive behaviour drove an ever-widening wedge
between him and his family. Drunk almost every day during
this off-season, he seemed to be at the mercy of his insecurities
about everything in his life. And when he vented, his family
was on the receiving end.

On a typical day in the summer of 1967, he and Louis, his
father, would head down to the VFW. Terry would take a sauna
for half an hour, then call for a bucket of beer on ice. Then he
would come home — "Sometimes on time to barbecue, sometimes to raise hell," Jerry Sawchuk says.

"We spent a great deal of our time in the kitchen, secure and
away from him," Pat says. "He'd come home, half crocked,
yelling, banging the front door, wanting to pick on the kids about
something or other. We would keep the door to the kitchen

closed. He'd be in the living room. And I would pray for him to just please pass out and leave us alone. A lot of the time, we lived in the kitchen."

Jerry even remembers Terry getting into a fistfight on the front lawn of Louis's house.

On July 2, 1967, Terry, who was uncharacteristically home with his family, sat in front of the television watching the movie *Ulysses*.

"I started getting labour pains and the movie had twenty to twenty-five minutes to go," Pat recalls. "I wanted to see the end, so during a commercial, I quietly went to take a bath, and then sat down to watch the rest of the movie. Now Terry still didn't like me, still didn't want this baby, but he slid down next to me on the couch and said, 'What's up?' I said, 'Well, as soon as the movie is over I think we should go to the hospital.' 'What! Why didn't you tell me! Come on we're going! I don't want to go through this crap again!'"

Terry drove Pat to the hospital in Pontiac and coldly dropped her off. She delivered their third son, Michael. Terry did not visit or inquire about his wife for the duration of her hospital stay. In fact, when Louis Sawchuk visited his daughter-in-law daily at the hospital, some assumed he was the father. Then the day arrived for Pat and Michael's ride home.

"Terry comes up to my room to pick me up. He doesn't say hello or anything, but he throws this bill on the bed for $26 or something. I had sent my mother some flowers. He ranted and raved about this bill until I was in tears. Then, for the walk to the car and the ride home, he doesn't say a word, doesn't look at the baby, nothing. We pull into the driveway, he gets out of the car, slams his door, and walks into the house.

"I had to get myself, my baby, and our things out of the car myself. This was the Terry I had to live with towards the end. Then he got back into the car, took off, and didn't come back till later that night."

Days later, the phone rang. Terry was in the house but Pat answered it. At the other end a female voice said, "Hello, is Terry there?"

"No, he's not, can I help you?" Pat asked sternly. The woman on the other end of the phone began sobbing. Pat immediately recognized the voice of a girl in Toronto she had met with the Leafs.

"I'm pregnant with Terry's kid!" the woman blurted out. "My husband has had a vasectomy so I can't say it's his kid. I have to talk to Terry!"

Pat was livid. Terry came into the room. Pat handed him the phone, saying, "There's somebody who wants to talk to you. It's one of your girlfriends." His face went white as Pat went into the other room to cry. After a few minutes, Terry came into the room apologizing.

She told him she wanted a divorce. He pleaded with her not to and reasoned that they were going to Los Angeles. They'd get a nice place on the beach. They could all move out there.

Incredibly, Pat agreed, after a time, to stay with him, to go to Los Angeles. To this day, she does not know what happened with the other woman's pregnancy, but she does point to a withdrawal from their bank account following this phone call that she can't account for.

Terry and Pat agreed to try to patch things over. He would go to the training camp in Guelph, then when he got settled in Los Angeles he would find a place to stay and fly them down.

Goaltender Wayne Rutledge, also picked up in the expansion draft, remembers meeting Terry, one of his idols, at the Guelph camp.

"He sure gave you the cold shoulder. He was established, not trying all that hard at camp, and we were all hustling like the dickens. If he was at a bar, say, after practice, and one of us other goalies came in, he would get up and leave, go drink someplace else."

Terry's old friend and Detroit teammate Johnny Wilson was the coach and general manager of the Kings' farm team, the Springfield Indians.

"Larry Regan asked me to sit in on Terry's contract session. We were shocked at his old Leaf contract from the year before — he had only made $18,000, something like that. We couldn't believe it — four Stanley Cups, four Vezinas, most valuable player to his team, and he was only making eighteen thousand! We had been signing unknown players for twenty, twenty-five thousand, and here we were about to call in the greatest goalie the game had ever seen. And he had just won the Leafs the Stanley Cup!

"So Terry comes in and Larry offers him a three-year deal for $40,000 the first year, $38,000 the second, $35,000 the third, something like that. Terry sat kind of stunned for a second and his eyes filled with tears and he said, 'I've never seen that much money in my life.' The three of us sat there — kind of choked up, you know. It was awkward. Three grown men trying not to cry. Terry was very touched. As he left the room, he couldn't thank us enough. Then we went down to the Legion together and had a few beers. Terry could always find a Legion."

Jiggs McDonald, the Kings' play-by-play announcer, tells a story that Terry was able to add to his earnings at the expense of his rookie teammates.

"Larry Regan had a rule that no player was to have a car at training camp, but Terry did. Now because I was the advance man, Cooke had wanted me to find food and lodging for nine dollars a man. I was able to bring it in at $9.25 a man, much to Cooke's disdain, but we had to eat by this golf course out near Kitchener and Ukey, with the only car, charged each player taxi fare. He really made some money. And Regan didn't try to stop him, explaining that Terry had been a pro a long time and was the Kings' number-one man."

Jack Kent Cooke idolized Terry Sawchuk and, before each training camp session, Cooke would lace up the skates as the Zamboni was leaving the ice. He'd go to the dressing room, look in and say, "Mr. Sawchuk, are you ready?" Terry would skate out in full gear and the owner would take shot after shot, trying to score. Cooke would even try to distract Terry, saying Pat was up in the stands, but still he couldn't score. After five practices, Terry, bored with Cooke's childhood fantasy of scoring on the great Sawchuk, let one in.

"Cooke tore a strip off Terry," Jiggs McDonald says, "really letting him have it. 'Don't you ever let up, not ever!' He really lit into him big time. With that goal, Cooke left the ice, satisfied that he had finally scored on his prized acquisition, and never tried again."

As the Kings broke camp to fly to Los Angeles, Terry's backup, Wayne Rutledge, still hadn't signed a contract. "I was holding out for $12,000," he says. Rutledge recalls the Kings' being in total disarray. "We practised on an ice pad in Burbank, north of L.A., and also in Long Beach. We were twenty guys in five cars, and nobody knew where the hell we were going. The dressing rooms were like large washrooms with no seats. Between practices, the trainers had to dry our equipment on this patio in the sun. We often went out to practise in still-wet equipment. It was all very poorly organized."

With Terry in his nets, Cooke had an ill-conceived idea that the Kings would win the Stanley Cup. Red Kelly publicly hoped that he could get forty games out of Terry. "If that could happen, we'll be right in there!" he predicted. It didn't matter that Terry hadn't played forty games in any of the last three years, making only twenty-eight appearances in 1966–67.

True to form, at the last practice in Long Beach before the season opener, Terry injured his right elbow. He was rushed to the trainer's room and ice was hastily applied to the injury. Wayne Rutledge picks up the story.

"Jack hosted a media party at his Bel Air mansion the night after that last practice. All the Lakers [basketball players] and the media were there. Terry showed up with his arm in a sling. He knew that Regan hadn't signed me yet and he told me, 'You got 'em now, kid. They have to sign you now. You'll be starting the home opener.' Jack's jaw dropped four feet when he saw Terry with his arm in a sling."

Rutledge finally signed prior to the season opener and, as he prepared to step on the ice, the wall that Terry had put up between them quickly came down. Smiling at the nervous rookie, he patted him on the back and gave him encouragement.

Rutledge won the Kings' first game ever by a score of 4–2 over Philadelphia. They beat the Minnesota North Stars at home, then tied both Oakland and St. Louis on the road.

"After our first four games when I held my own, I think Terry relaxed substantially," Rutledge says. "I think until then he felt the weight of the whole organization on his shoulders, with the media hype about him and all."

After first arriving in Los Angeles, Terry, as well as most of the single King players, lived in a hotel not too far from the Los Angeles Sports Arena, their home ice until the opening of the Fabulous Forum, which was slated for New Year's Eve. Before long, Sawchuk rented a house in Hermosa Beach and invited assistant trainer Danny Wood, who'd been staying in the hotel room next to Terry's, to move in.

"What I recall was that Terry liked to sit in his shorts, have a beer, and quietly watch people go up and down the boardwalk or the beach. When I'd see him sitting there, I wondered what he was thinking. He never, never talked about his past.

"He did talk about Jack Adams once with a certain degree of disdain, and only about the fact that after three years in the league, Adams had made him lose weight. He was bitter about that, he resented that. He felt it hurt his career."

In his first game as a King, Terry beat the struggling Black Hawks, 5–3, but then lost to the Leafs, 4–2. "Before that game, Terry went up to Punch Imlach and embraced him with such affection that the two men were crying," Jiggs McDonald says. "Terry told me that after the birth of his kid in August, Punch had deposited a thousand dollars into a bank account for the child. He was really touched by the gesture."

Two games later, Terry made his debut in Los Angeles against the visiting New York Rangers, who shelled him, 6–1. Terry had won only one of four games.

"I don't know what it was," Rutledge says, "but the guys seemed to try harder when I was in net. I don't know if they relaxed in games with Terry behind them because they figured, 'Ah, we've got the best in net. If we screw up, he'll stop them,' or if the guys figured I needed more protection, but that seemed to be an early pattern."

Through the middle of November, the two goalies had played the same number of games, but Rutledge had six victories to Terry's three. Never a media darling, Terry began to catch heat from Los Angeles hockey writer Bill Libby.

"Bill Libby liked the underdog, and it was clear he did not like Terry. If he could slant a story against Terry, he did," Wayne Rutledge says. "Even if Terry played a great game, Libby wouldn't write it up that way. And he would harp about Terry not being cooperative with the press."

"Terry was never a great press personality," Jiggs McDonald says. "But you got to know him, and he would say, 'What do you want,' or 'Meet me here after,' or sometimes he would even seek me out. Sometimes he'd tell me to sit beside him on the bus or at the airport. He knew I was raw, young, and every now and then he would really help me out — always on his terms, but if you treated him with respect, he eventually gave it back, but always on his terms."

"Bill Libby did not know his hockey," Red Kelly says. "Sometimes he wrote things right off the wall and you'd shake your head wondering what planet he was on."

Pat and the kids joined Terry in Los Angeles later that fall. "I refused to get on the plane until Michael was baptized," Pat says. "What an entourage we were — me, seven kids, Shadow our dog — they wouldn't let on the plane because they were afraid of him. Jerry went and put Shadow in a cage. At Hermosa Beach, the house was just gorgeous. The beach, the location, the house were gorgeous!"

Sharyn Rutledge, Wayne's wife, said the Sawchuk home became the Kings' social hub. "A lot of us lived in apartments in L.A., and that was no fun, so we often went to Terry and Pat's for beach parties."

Jiggs McDonald also recalls Terry coming to practice one morning with a bag of brown stuff he'd found on his front yard. "A car had driven by one night and he'd heard this thing land on the front yard. We told him it was marijuana. He didn't know what to do with it so the guys said, 'Why don't you try it?' He said, 'Oh God, no, I could never do that.' Knowing Terry, he probably sold it."

In early December, the Kings visited aging Madison Square Garden, where they lost to their hosts, 4–2. After the game, Terry taught Danny Wood a lesson. Almost everyone had left, and the young trainer was spreading the players' equipment on the floor to dry, as the team was not flying out until later the next day. Terry began repacking his equipment in his bag.

"Uke, it's okay," Wood said. "I'll come by in the morning and repack all the bags, don't worry about it."

Terry stopped, looked at the young man, and said, "You trainers don't talk much in this league, do you?"

"Why, what's wrong?"

"Woodsie, shut the light and come outside with me for five minutes." Standing by the side of the rink, Terry struck up a conversation with some of the rink attendants. On a couple of occasions, Wood tried to re-enter the dressing room, but Terry stopped him. "Give it five minutes."

Finally, the goaltender said it was time and together they headed back to the dressing room. Terry stopped at the door and said, "I'll hit the light and you open the door fast."

"When I opened that door," Danny Wood says today, still incredulous, "there were rats all over the equipment. They scattered quick, went up into the dark ceiling rafters, you could see the reflection of all of their eyes. They apparently would chew all the palms out of the gloves, because of the salt from the players' sweaty hands. Terry said that if I insisted on leaving equipment out to dry, we should leave the lights on all night."

On the night before Christmas Eve, Terry gave a rare glimpse of his ability to do something thoughtful for his family. Daughter Carol Ann remembers, "That Christmas, Dad had a truckload of crushed ice dumped on our front porch and all of us kids went crazy throwing ice balls in the middle of the night. We were used to seeing snow at Christmastime. I guess he wanted us to feel at home."

"You know, Terry didn't want our last baby, Michael," Pat says. "But by gosh, in L.A., he loved him. 'That's my boy,' he'd say. We'd put Michael on the floor, on a blanket and he'd move his arms to keep beat with the music, you know. It got that Terry got such a kick out of it, that he was always putting Michael on the floor, turning on the stereo, then howling with laughter. And this was his 'unwanted child!'"

Injuries began to keep Terry out of the lineup. During one midseason stretch, Terry played one game to Wayne Rutledge's four. Jiggs McDonald recalls Red Kelly often saying, "Terry's not ready. I'm resting him."

"Terry refused to get new equipment," Danny Wood says. "He wore the same belly pad and shoulder pads he'd had with Detroit in the '50s. As a consequence, he was always hurt and bruised. His bad elbow bothered him the whole year, it was a mess.

"As a physical specimen, he was a disaster! His shoulder looked like it had been broken and never set right. His bad arm was three or four inches shorter than the other. He'd walk all stooped over, hobbling in and out of the rink. Yet as soon as he got on the ice, he'd skate around like he was just a kid. I used to think it's too bad Terry couldn't be on his skates twenty-four hours a day. He seemed to be in less pain."

According to Wood, veterans from opposing teams would approach him and ask about Terry's health. "It got that I could see them coming a mile away and I would answer them before they would even ask. Everybody in the league wanted to know how Terry was, what he was thinking, personal stuff. There was amazing respect and kinship for him."

If they'd thought to ask Pat, she would have told them of a disturbing turn in Terry. "The drinking was more than any of us could tolerate. He was now drinking the day before a game which he had never done before in my presence, ever. He once hit Carol Ann so hard across the face that I had to keep her out of school for a couple of days because you could see the hand imprint. This was just a seven-year-old kid, for gosh sakes. 'She was pissing me off,' he'd grumble. I was their protector but I couldn't be there for them all the time."

On December 30, 1967, the Fabulous Forum opened with all the trappings of a Hollywood premiere. Canadian-born actor Lorne Greene acted as master of ceremonies for the pre-game show. The Flyers spoiled the party by winning the game, 2–0, but hockey had arrived in Hollywood and many television and movie stars began to frequent the games — Danny Thomas, Glenn Ford, Fred MacMurray, Peter Falk, and Jack Lemmon, to name a few. Donna Douglas of the TV series *The Beverly Hillbillies* had dated a couple of the Kings' players and celebrities were soon being escorted through the Kings' dressing room by Jack Kent Cooke.

"Terry did not like to be bothered after a game till he was ready," says Danny Wood, "you know, undressed and that. He didn't care if the president of the United States was in the room. So, in comes Elvis Presley with Jack, and as they're coming through, the players are all getting up, stepping forward to shake his hand. Now they head towards Terry. I'm watching from the corner and I'm holding my breath, 'cause Terry's not 'ready.' I thought he'd be liable to tell Cooke and Elvis off, and we'd all be in a pickle.

"The pair reach Terry, and Cooke introduced the king of rock and roll to the shutout king. Terry looked up slowly, reached out, and shook Presley's hand. 'Terry, it's a real honour for me to be meeting you,' Elvis said.

"'Same here,' Terry answered. Everyone in the dressing room let out a sigh of relief."

As the season progressed, Wayne Rutledge was getting more and more of the goaltending chores.

Red Kelly knew and understood Terry better than anyone associated with the Kings. He knew that his star had a lot of hard miles on him. The team was playing well with Rutledge in net and he recognized that Terry's value to the team would come down the stretch and into the playoffs, so he excused Terry from practices more frequently, as Danny Wood became the second practice goalie.

On January 28, 1968, Terry recorded the 101st shutout of his career by blanking the Flyers in Philadelphia, 2–0. After the game, he and Rutledge were in a coffee shop, having a few beers. A fan began to give Terry a hard time. "The next thing you know," Rutledge says, "they're outside dancing around like two banty roosters. Suddenly, the other guy is flat out cold, and Terry's saying, 'Did I hit him? I hit him! I showed him not to mess with me! Did I hit him?' Uke didn't know till the day he died that my brother-in-law, Dale Rolfe, had decked the guy. He thought he had done it."

When the Kings headed into Chicago to face Bobby Hull and company on February 4, a family tragedy sent Wayne Rutledge

and his brother-in-law, Dale Rolfe, back to Ontario. The Kings
sent word to the Hawks that they were carrying only one
goalie, but the Hawks were not able to find a backup.

"Ah, use our practice goalie," Terry joked in the dressing
room before the game. Red Kelly thought the idea was as good
as any and he told Danny Wood that his name would be on the
game sheet. Shocked, Wood tried to reassure himself that
nothing would happen to Sawchuk and all would be well.

In the second period, Chicago's Pit Martin let fly with a
booming slap shot that struck Terry flush on the face, sending
him down to the ice. Terry was cut badly because his mask had
jammed against his face and cracked in two places. Trainer
Norm Mackie was summoned onto the ice. On the bench, Danny
Wood was panic-stricken, as Sawchuk was brought over so the
damage could be assessed. Terry's eyes were swelling shut
with the accumulating blood. Terry looked at Wood and said
with a smirk, "Well, it looks like it's your turn to go."

"Holy geez, Uke," Wood answered, "I'm not going in there,
guys like Bobby Hull, Mikita, Wharram shooting at me."

"Don't worry about it," Terry said calmly. "I've already talked
to them. They will not shoot the puck hard, and they'll keep
them open," meaning no screen shots. Wood saw his life flash
before his eyes after he tried to envision himself facing a Bobby
Hull slap shot.

The referees began to press Red Kelly to decide whether
Sawchuk would continue or not. Meanwhile Danny Wood
moved to the end of the bench, trying to be inconspicuous.
Sawchuk caught this and spoke up: "Ah, this is killing me. I've
got to get my equipment off. Come on, Danny." Wood, his back
to Terry, could not see his impish smirk.

Finally, Terry put Wood out of his misery, putting on his same
cracked mask, skating past the assistant trainer, and saying
with a wink, "Oh, I'll finish, kid. You missed your big chance!"

"He played the rest of the game with one eye," Danny Wood
marvels today, "and talk about your code of ethics. It was a
close game at that point, but the Hawks deliberately let up. He
was in a bad way and they deliberately turned it down a notch.
No more slap shots, no more boomers."

By the time the Kings had landed in L.A. the next day, both Terry's eyes were swollen shut. He was admitted to Daniel Freeman Hospital and was out of the lineup for several days.

"After the Chicago game, we realized Terry's mask was cracked," Danny Wood says. "He had another one but he said to me, 'See if you can fix that mask up.' I went home and got some fibreglass and worked on it that night. Terry went out to practice with it the next day and he came off and said to me with a smirk, 'You'd better stick to hockey. Repair work isn't your bag.'"

As the repair job hadn't taken, they called Lefty Wilson and got another one flown down. Danny approached Terry about the broken mask. "Gee, Terry, if ah, you're not going to do anything with that mask, ah, I'd consider it an honour if you'd let me have it?"

"Oh ya, another souvenir collector?" Terry joked.

Danny stammered something in his defence, but Sawchuk interrupted him. "Look, you cared enough about it that you tried to fix it so, sure, it's yours." He autographed the inside of it and handed it to the delighted trainer.

Terry had only played in twenty-five of the team's first sixty games, but Red Kelly still had faith in him.

Playing all the games down the stretch, Terry and the Kings started March badly by losing three of four games.

Danny Wood recalls the last of these, a 3–1 loss in Pittsburgh.

"Terry took a nasty shot in the mouth and I went out. There was a lot of blood and he said, 'Well, how's it look?' I said, 'Well, it's a good thing you took your whole lower dentures out.' He said, 'I don't have a whole lower denture, just a partial plate.' So I said, 'Well, you'll need a whole one now.' Whatever teeth he had were gone. We looked around on the ice but then he figured, 'Ah, I musta swallowed 'em. Just stop the bleeding. We got a game to finish.' And he did, no problem. That was Terry Sawchuk."

Jiggs McDonald vividly remembers an incident that night in Pittsburgh that is indicative of Sawchuk's family troubles and the degree to which they were kept secret.

"Ed Fitkin, my broadcast partner, and I could hear Terry in the next hotel room yelling and screaming at Pat on the phone about one thing or another. He was just livid. Suddenly we could hear the furniture start to be moved and then things were slamming against the walls, crashing and smashing. What a mess that room was. It was quietly paid for by the team but oh, what a night that was! It was hushed up and never spoken about again. But I don't imagine Larry Regan or Mr. Cooke were impressed."

The next night, March 10, he went into Madison Square Garden and played one of the best games of the season, beating the Rangers, 4–3. The performance left New York general manager and coach Emile Francis shaking his head in amazement. "He may have been as good tonight as he was last spring. He's still amazing."

The New York win was the start of a seven-game undefeated streak that vaulted the Kings to the top of the West Division alongside Philadelphia. Terry got stronger in each game, one of which was a scoreless tie with Philadelphia, forced by damage to the roof of their arena to play their home games in the rink of their Quebec City farm club — for the 102nd shutout of his career.

"Terry Sawchuk . . . has returned to his greatness in recent games," commented an article in the *Pasadena Star News* on March 18, after the Kings beat the North Stars, 2–1. "This can't have been more clearly demonstrated in the two tests at Quebec and Minnesota. Sawchuk was brilliant and cool."

Of the last fourteen games, Terry played twelve. Los Angeles ended up second in the West, a single point behind the Philadelphia Flyers. Red Kelly was optimistic at the outset of the playoffs, mentioning that his Kings had the best record of all the expansion teams in games against the established clubs. But their first-round opponent, the Minnesota North Stars, had won six and lost only two of the ten meetings with L.A.

Working in the Kings' favour was the fact their 200 goals were tops in the West, while the Stars had allowed the most goals in the division, 226. And the Kings had Sawchuk. In a *Sports Illustrated* story, Terry laughed when it was suggested he was entering the playoffs on a high note, as he had done the previous year with Toronto.

"I haven't even thought of that. The fact is, I'm finally in good shape. That's all there is to it."

The assassination of Martin Luther King, Jr., delayed the start of the Kings–Minnesota series. When it did begin, both teams were lethargic as Terry faced thirty-one shots en route to a 2–1 victory. Terry faced only eighteen shots in Game Two, as he picked up the twelfth playoff shutout of his career. Minnesota general manager Wren Blair said, "I'll bet he's never had such an easy couple of games. We must have helped Sawchuk to another year."

Back in Minnesota for Game Three, the North Stars put five goals past Terry in the first two periods. Red put Rutledge between the pipes in the hopes of shaking up his troops and resting the veteran, but the Stars tallied twice more for a 7–5 victory.

Red came back with the Uke for Game Four in a hard-fought contest in which the Stars prevailed 3–2 and tied the series.

A bug kept Terry out of the lineup for Game Five and Rutledge made twenty-seven saves in a 3–2 victory. Back in Minnesota, the Kings had the series all but wrapped up with a 3–1 third-period lead. But a fluke goal got past Rutledge to send the game into overtime, which was won by Minnesota at the 9:11 mark.

Red Kelly's mind was made up at the end of the sixth game that Sawchuk would play the deciding seventh game of the series.

"Wayne is a good guy, and had played some good goal, but he was no Terry Sawchuk," Kelly said. "I had to go with Ukey. If he's on his game at all, Minnesota knew they might just as well stay home. And I figured he'd come up big for this seventh game."

"I honestly believed that I was going to be playing," said Rutledge, "and so did my teammates, and for that matter, so did Terry. I think he was shocked that I didn't get the start. I think our guys were let down a bit."

It was the Kings who came out flat and when the first period was over, the North Stars had a 3–1 lead. Eddie Joyal closed the gap with a goal at 6:12 of the second. What followed was a total L.A. collapse. The Stars potted five goals in eight minutes en route to a 9–4 pasting. Sawchuk was getting no support at all from his teammates.

After the last couple of goals, the Forum fans booed Terry and threw refuse on the ice around him. On the bench, Wayne Rutledge recalls seeing some of the players turn around to look at Red Kelly, beseeching him to pull Sawchuk. "But one thing about Red," Rutledge says, "he very rarely pulled you out of a game. And Terry never pulled himself."

"I was never so disappointed in Terry as I was that night," Kelly says. "I felt that he let me down and the team down. The loss wasn't all his fault but it was *the* big game and he missed it, really. That was a game made for Ukey. Seventh game and all, and he disappointed me."

Terry left the rink that night bitterly disappointed in himself, but also angry at the L.A. fans. They couldn't understand it just hadn't been his night.

As Terry got into his car, he knew he needed a drink, two at least. Then, perhaps, he'd stop by his lady friend's for a nightcap. Perhaps that would help take some of the sting away from this night. Then, he'd go home to his big beautiful home at Hermosa, its rent paid for by the Los Angeles Kings. At least, he thought, he still had that.

17

LAST DAYS IN DETROIT

DESPITE the beauty of the California sun, the boardwalk, and the Pacific Ocean right in their backyard,
Pat found that the key to surviving life with Terry now
was to completely immerse herself in the lives of her children.
Sometimes even that was not easy.

"My kids and I had a great time; the boardwalk behind the
house was called the 'strand' and there were these large swings
by the water that when you got them going, it looked like you
were going right in the ocean. I remember, though, I had to
watch Jerry, because he always wanted to skip school and go
surfing. And he and his father got into the biggest fight in the
world there, and that's when I called the cops on Terry."

"I always was the kid in the house who was grounded the
whole summer," Jerry says. "Sometimes I deserved it, sometimes not. By the time we got to California, after putting up
with his bullshit for so long, I started fighting back."

"I was putting all the kids to bed," Pat continues, "when
Jerry comes up and asks if he can have a piece of cheese. I say
yes, but keep it hidden, so the other kids don't see it. I'm
trying to get them to bed. Next thing you know, Terry comes in
the house, loaded to the gills, hardly able to stand, wanting to
pick a fight, and he starts yelling at Jerry, about this piece of
cheese that he tucked in his shirt pocket. I mean, it got that

Terry would pick a fight over the colour of the moon. Anyways, he starts whacking Jerry around and hitting him and Jerry's fighting back."

"I had him so mad," Jerry continues, "that he chased me outside for three blocks in his underpants. I was faster than him and the harder he ran to get me, the more I was laughing at him."

Terry stormed back into the house and locked all the doors. "The son of a bitch, he can stay outside!" he boomed.

"He can't stay outside, he's fourteen years old!" Pat pleaded.

"He can stay outside, for putting food in his pocket!" Terry went into their bedroom and passed out, while Pat had settled the other kids and made herself scarce. She combed the immediate neighbourhood, but could find no trace of Jerry. She returned home and unlocked his bedroom window.

"I certainly disliked him," Jerry says, "yet I was too afraid to hate him, because at that time, we would accept whatever morsel of kindness he would offer."

"Terry was a total ass in California," Pat says. "I was at some party, for team wives or something, and I came home early. Terry is downstairs with this girl, they're drinking in front of the children. There was also this elderly gentleman there, from down the street, whom we had befriended and who had just lost his wife. Anyways, Terry tries to tell me that the girl is this gentleman's friend, not his, but the man turned to Terry and said, 'Oh, no, Terry, she's not my friend,' and walked out. But at that point, I really didn't care anymore."

In early September, a reporter from the *South Bay Daily Breeze* visited the Sawchuk compound. Terry donned his jogging suit and sneakers, while telling the reporter, "With seven kids, we run into just about every type of person. Our daughter, Debbie, spends time at the psychedelic shops in Hermosa and I guess she knows just about every hippie in this city. We're just like any other family down here. We have neighbours, real good neighbours, and the kids are always bringing their friends over."

He went on to describe Jerry, then a Bantam goalie who occasionally played forward. "Jerry got to use one of Bobby

Hull's sticks one time. He got three goals. He shot one from way back that must have been going a hundred miles an hour, just like Bobby. The other two were close-in shots that fooled the goalie. He really likes hockey. So do all the kids. Little Terry wants to be a surfer."

Uke told the reporter that he often ran the beach, surfed, played volleyball, fished, and golfed to keep in shape. Terry continued, "The weather is wonderful. We've had trouble with some of the summer crowd but this is an ideal place. I like the fishing. It beats being a newspaper reporter."

Terry posed for a picture in their basement recreation room with him jogging on the spot, smiling, with the family on a couch next to him. Another picture taken on the beach showed father and son, with Terry bending forward holding his mask and Jerry donning his Dad's gloves and stick. To the untrained eye, father and son were sharing one of many warm exchanges of goaltending knowledge.

"If you look at Jerry," Pat says, "he's looking at his dad with a hidden 'You're such a jerk' smirk. Jerry really has an inside laugh about him."

"The thing that really bothers me about him to this day," Jerry says, "is the fact that he only saw me play hockey a couple of times, ever. Other hockey players saw and took their kids to games regularly. He had no excuse."

Terry told the reporter, "This is the first summer in a number of years that I haven't worked. The budget is kind of low, but I feel great. I'm ready to go to camp."

Terry would encounter a markedly different reception from management when he arrived at the Kings' September 1968 training camp in Barrie, Ontario.

"Jack Kent Cooke had certainly soured over Terry," Jiggs McDonald says. "Terry knew that the writing was on the wall."

Larry Regan had been shopping Terry around since the June draft, but had found no satisfactory deal. He got a nibble from Toronto's Stafford Smythe, who had offered a straight cash deal of $20,000. But Cooke wanted a player in return, not cash.

The Kings had prepared to move Terry, having obtained goalie Gerry Desjardins. Red Kelly told management that whenever a deal was made, he wanted to be the one to break the news to his old friend and teammate. "The only thing I wanted, was to be the one to tell him," Kelly says. "After all of our years together, I felt I owed him that much."

On Thursday, October 10, 1968, Terry was in Winnipeg for an exhibition game against the Canadian National Team. Red Kelly called Terry aside to tell him he'd been traded to Detroit.

"He cried," Red continues. "I tried to explain to him that he would be better off, going back to a more established team, like the Wings, that he would have a better shot at a Stanley Cup. He cried. It was a sad day for both of us."

In exchange for Sawchuk the Wings gave up Jimmy Peters, a fringe player who had amassed only eleven points in forty-five games for Detroit the previous season. Peters, the son of Terry's former teammate by the same name, had been relegated to Detroit's farm team at Fort Worth. Terry's star seemed to have fallen extensively.

"After his meeting with Red, Terry hung around for like thirty seconds," Jiggs McDonald says. "His head was down, shoulders slumped forward. He looked like a beaten man. I felt so sorry for him."

Wings' general Manager Sid Abel professed to be pleased to have Sawchuk on the team for the third time, but coach Bill Gadsby didn't share his enthusiasm.

"That was the worst situation in hockey. Having three goalies — Ukey, Roger Crozier, and Roy Edwards — was a nightmare because only one could play and the other two were sitting around. And at this time, Roger Crozier is in his prime, so how much space does that leave for the other two, both still fine goalies?"

As Terry reported immediately to the Red Wings and took up residence at the Sawchuks' home on Golfside Drive, the responsibility of moving seven children and a dog rested squarely on Pat's shoulders.

"I closed down the house at Hermosa Beach by myself, sent three kids and a dog on an airplane, then drove myself and the four other kids from California to Michigan. What a haul! Poor little Terry was getting sick as a dog. He was lying on the floor in the back seat, getting sicker and sicker. To tell you the truth, we all weren't feeling the greatest.

"A freak snowstorm in Albuquerque, New Mexico, stopped us. I decided to call a doctor and I described to him all our symptoms. He says, 'If it is what I think it is, you're all lucky to be alive.' The exhaust had a hairline fracture and the fumes were seeping up into the car. What saved us was I'd open the window vent to smoke.

"I got everybody out of that car quick. We all went to a motel room, and showered. Some lady brought us some soup. The car was fixed, the symptoms lifted after a good night's sleep and we were on our way again."

For the first time in his career, Terry would be joining a team that was not all that sure it needed him. The acrobatic Roger Crozier had now developed into a first-rate goalie, a Calder winner as top rookie in 1964–65, the year Terry had left. In the 1965–66 Stanley Cup final against Montreal, he had played gallantly in a losing cause and won the Conn Smythe Trophy as the top playoff performer.

Roy Edwards was in his tenth professional season but had only cracked an NHL lineup the previous year with the Wings. His arrival was timely; he played in the lion's share of the games after Crozier had been troubled by stomach and pancreas flare-ups.

It was a credit to Terry and the Wings' organization that they included him in their plans, though sparingly. Still, they did use Terry occasionally and, heading into L.A. for a November 14 game against the Kings, Gadsby gave Sawchuk the start, sensing Terry might get himself psyched up for this game against his former team.

In the first period, the Wings built up a 3–1 lead over the goalie that had replaced Terry, Gerry Desjardins. In the second period, the Kings fired sixteen shots at Terry but he was up to the task, turning them all aside as Frank Mahovlich increased the Wings' lead to four.

Garry Unger extended Detroit's lead to 5–0 in the third period before the Kings finally beat Terry, twice. The Forum crowd, which months before had booed Terry so badly that veteran newsmen described it as the worst abuse they had ever seen an athlete take, cheered him this night.

"Did you hear them tonight?" Sawchuk said afterwards. "They cheered, eh? That's different. They didn't boo me tonight."

Urged on by Wing management, Terry began to take an interest in young Crozier. Due to nerves, illness, or injury, Roger had only played in thirty-four games in the 1967–68 season, a far cry from the fifty-eight games of the year before. This past summer, he had retreated to his home in Bracebridge, Ontario, to work for a warehouse company and to find more calm for his frayed nerves. He once told journalist Jim Hunt that he worried constantly during hockey season about his perform-ance and keeping his job. Crozier was a man hindered by self-doubt and the Wings hoped Terry could help the boy's confidence.

"Ya, Ukey helped Roger out quite a bit," Bill Gadsby says. "I never saw them talk off the ice but on the ice they would often discuss things. As a matter of fact I often saw Roger and Roy Edwards huddled with Terry around a net. Goaltenders would tell each other things that they'd never tell me, as their coach. Roger calmed down significantly because of it and was a better goalie. Both goalies benefited from Terry's presence."

"The family," Pat says, "was more relaxed when Terry was on the road, I'm sorry to say. The children were happier. When it came time for Terry to come home, the tension would start. The kids would kind of line up on the couch and wait for him to come through the door. Sometimes he'd bring them presents but most times, God knew what mood he'd be in, it was too frequently nasty. He would bang the front door open and decide who or what to pick on. This ranting would go on until he finally fell asleep.

"The kids would get stomachaches when they knew their Dad was coming home, especially Kathy. She was a very quiet, emotional kid. When she was five, I took her to the doctor and she was diagnosed as having a nervous stomach. The ensuing years with her father sure didn't help it."

Verbal abuse had become his specialty, though he didn't hesitate to hit the children if he felt they'd misbehaved. Pat had so far in their lives been able to act as a buffer, shielding or rebuilding these seven fragile personalities. Yet Jerry, the oldest, was slowly becoming the man of the house. He was very close to his mother and perhaps herein lay part of the puzzle as to why Terry picked on him the most, a certain jealousy at having his place usurped by his son.

Terry saw himself in his eldest son. He compared Jerry's close, warm, hugging relationship with Pat to his own cold youth with his mother and he was envious to the point of constant anger. Whenever Terry came home, it was always to a mother, not a wife. He was angry at this love of Pat's being shared with his children. He was angry that he had never experienced and felt such love in his childhood. He was even angry about the past love that his mother lavished on his children before her death.

It was the root of the Terry Sawchuk psychological puzzle. Certainly there were many other aspects that figured into his troubled psyche, like Mitch's death, his father's timid personality and absenteeism when Terry was a child, the stress of his hockey career — the high level of play he demanded of himself and his unsure, self-doubting ego — the unbelievable array of physical injuries he had endured, his deepening depression that was caused by and fed his alcoholism, and his constant inability to control his home and professional lives at the same time.

But at the centre was this deep-rooted jealousy and anger that was directed at the only logical outlet available to him: his family. Instead of seeing his family as something good he had accomplished with his life, he was instead reminded of what he had lacked.

As Christmas of 1968 approached, Terry was completely in his own world, almost oblivious to his own family and the legions of Terry Sawchuk fans.

"Terry would get lots of requests from fans for his autograph, like, you know, 'All little Johnny wants for Christmas is a Terry Sawchuk autograph card or picture.' And there would be a hundred of these, and I'd say, 'Would you sit down and sign these?' and he'd sit down and sign two! Two! What good does two do in a pile of a hundred or more! He got so hard-nosed about things. So I would sit down and sign all these things for him. I hate to say it but a lot of Terry Sawchuk autographed pictures were his wife's signature. But that's what Terry got to be like."

On a cold winter evening in late December, Terry came home after another afternoon of drinking. As he staggered towards the front door, he noticed a gum wrapper in a bush and he turned livid with anger. Charging into the house, he was screaming, wanting to know who left the gum wrapper in the bush outside. In their beds sleeping, the seven Sawchuk children opened their eyes instantly. It was a reflex action. Some of them began to shake nervously, all wondered what scene of horror was about to take place. One of them hid in a closet. They didn't have long to wait as Terry barged into all their rooms, screaming at them, wanting to know who'd left the gum wrapper in the bush. His eyes were bulging and the large vein on his forehead was pulsing with rage.

Flying out of her bedroom, Pat attempted to intervene and calm the children but instead acted as a catalyst for Terry's fury. Turning his rage on her, he screamed, "What kind of fucking housewife are you! Can't you control this household! There's garbage all over the fuckin' place! This place is a fuckin' pigsty! Can't you do anything right! What the fuck good are ya!" And so on and on it went.

Pat attempted to explain and reason with Terry about the measly gum wrapper, but Terry was out of control. He grabbed Pat and began pushing her around. The children were all crying, screaming, shaking, and recoiling in fear. Pat was attempting to defend herself, when suddenly Terry grabbed her and dragged her towards the front door, and outside into the frosty winter air, threw her down, walked back into the house, slammed the door shut, and locked it.

Terry turned to his children. "If any of you opens that door to let her in," Terry screamed at them, "the same thing is going to happen to you! Don't you dare open that door! Got it?" The kids stared at him shaking, crying, yelling for their mother. They obeyed him out of pure fear. Terry staggered into his bedroom.

"It was a cold night," Pat continues. "So I quickly walked to my parents' place, since they were always home. But would you believe it, this particular night they weren't! So I walked back to the house. I only had shirtsleeves and it was so cold, but it got to the point where I didn't give a damn if I died. By the time I got back, Terry had passed out. One of the older kids had then unlocked the garage door and I got in."

The next day Terry was completely apologetic. But Pat was nearing the end of her rope.

As 1969 began, there was more of the same, Terry drinking, then ranting and raving about something insignificant, and traumatizing Pat and the children. "By this time," Pat says, "Terry didn't care about us. All he did was drink, drink, drink, then come home and rant and rave."

The animosity between Pat and Terry culminated one night when Terry chased Pat into their kitchen. In a rage, he wrapped his hands around her throat and backed her against the kitchen cupboards. Pat managed to escape the situation and finally came to the conclusion that something had to be done.

Hiring a lawyer, she swore out a legal complaint. In the presence of the police, Terry was informed that Pat was filing for separation and divorce and wanted him out of the house.

"I wanted the police there because I didn't know how he would react. I was afraid for my life. But he packed up meekly and mildly, and quietly walked out of the house. He knew I was right. He knew it was time."

That night in January, Terry was slated to be the starting goalie in a game for the Wings. Coach Bill Gadsby recalls that night.

"I had a team meeting before the game and I says, 'Ukey, you'll be the starting goalie,' and I go over the rest of the lineup and stuff. Afterwards, Terry says, 'Bill, can I see you for a second?' so we go to the side and he says, 'Ah, I just got served with divorce papers and I'm really not in a frame of mind to play.' I say, 'That's okay, Uke, no problem.'

"So I go back out to the team and I say, 'Guys, there's been a change of plans. Ukey's gonna sit this one out, so Roger will start and Roy Edwards will be the backup.' Then Crozier comes up to me and says, 'Ah, Bill, can I see you?' We go to the

side and Crozier says, 'Bill, I'd rather not play, I had a bad pan-
creatic bout through the night and I'm really not feeling good.'
I say okay and I go to Roy to tell him he's starting, with Roger
as his backup.

"If he (Roy) would have said, 'Bill, can I speak to you for a
second?' I think I woulda pulled my hair out. Here I had three
goalies but in the end, I barely had one! For a second there,
I thought I might have to put Lefty Wilson in!"

When the 1968–69 season was over, the Red Wings were out
of the playoffs for the third year in a row. Although his 2.62
goals-against average was his lowest in four years, Terry
appeared in only thirteen games, and for the first time in his
career he failed to earn a single shutout.

Alex Delvecchio noticed a distinct change in the on-ice Terry
this year. "For the first time in his career, the pressure was off
Terry. I think he liked the role of backup. He was near the end
of his career and had accepted his destiny, so to speak. He
liked his salary and now he didn't have to work all that hard
for it. I found him almost happy in that last year here in
Detroit. He seemed more relaxed."

Lefty Wilson concurs. "I found the Uke to be kind of happy
that year. Shit, I remember when Gadsby would announce
which goalie was playing, the other two would laugh like
bastards. And I remember Ukey laughing at the other two
(Crozier and Edwards) if he didn't have to dress. I remember
him kibitzing."

The pressures of hockey had finally ceased for Terry. No
longer did he have to worry about being number one. With
fewer games came fewer injuries. He began to enjoy hockey
again, no longer a hostage to it. He was also no longer the star
and so the press left him alone.

In his personal life, it could be argued that Terry's separation from his family was also somewhat of a tonic for his
troubled psyche. No longer seeing Pat and the kids, he was no
longer reminded of his own troubled youth, his own lack of
motherly love. He was no longer jealous. He was no longer
angry at what they represented. And he did not have to feel
remorse or regret for his tirades since they no longer happened.

Much as he loved his family, "out of sight, out of mind" certainly held true.

As the season came to an abrupt end, Terry knew that a divorce from Pat loomed ahead. He did think of his children, and contemplated doing something special with them.

Suddenly, on June 20, 1969, his future and that of his family became a little bit more clouded when Terry was traded to the New York Rangers. The physical distance between him and his family was about to increase dramatically and so inevitably would the emotional distance.

18

TO CATCH A FALLING STAR

THROUGH the summer of 1969 there was no contact between Pat and Terry, who also had not seen or talked to his seven children. It was a period of calm and healing for Pat and the kids. No more late evening drunken tirades, no more arguing, no more hiding, no more being frightened, no more sick stomachs.

Pat describes the divorce proceedings.

"They put Terry and me alone in this room, like they do for all couples, you know, to make sure that this is what they really want to do. And there we were, face to face. He came around the table, got on his knees beside me, and begged me not to divorce him.

"I looked straight ahead. I couldn't look at him. I just couldn't look at him. And I said, with all the strength I could muster, 'I have to, Terry, I have to. I can't take life with you anymore. I just can't anymore.' But he was doing a good job on me and I almost gave in. Almost. But I had to, for my sake and the sake of our seven children, I had to divorce him."

The divorce was granted on the grounds of "extreme and repeated cruelty." Finally, Terry had lost the only woman he had truly loved. Despite all his anger, his misbehaviour, his womanizing and drinking ways, his inability to show affection, he did love Pat and the kids with all his heart. And they, in turn, deep down, loved him back, but they couldn't live with him anymore.

Pat and the kids continued to live in the house on Golfside Drive. And though Terry had moved in with his father, he still had to continue to make support payments. Even now, Terry's frugality reared its ugly head.

"Terry's lawyer had offered, before the divorce was final, to have Terry pay $25 a month per child," Pat recalls. "I still wasn't working at the time and so that left me with $150 a month with which to dress and feed seven kids, not to mention the house mortgage payments, electrical bills, and property taxes. And because Terry had replaced our broken-down refrigerator, my lawyer thought we should accept Terry's payment offer. I couldn't believe it! Of course that was not even near good enough and we came to terms on a more reasonable monthly payment. I'm sure it must have just about killed Terry to part with his money, even if it was for his kids."

Later on that summer, Terry took the six oldest kids and Jerry's friend Ronny on an overnight visit to the Cedar Point Amusement Park in nearby Ohio. The trip is remembered fondly by all the kids today, especially Terry Jr., who was almost six years old at the time.

"That is my best memory of my Dad. I told him I wanted to go on the giant Ferris wheel and when we got to it, the lineup was like a hundred yards long. We waited and waited. When we finally got to the front, the gentleman who ran the ride had me stand by this measuring stick and it turned out I was an inch too short. Dad then told the man he wasn't leaving until he and I got on the ride. They argued back and forth for five minutes until someone in the crowd recognized my father. At this point the gentleman finally agreed to let us ride the wheel."

For Jerry, the trip meant another occasion to come to loggerheads with his Dad. "When we were in the hotel room later, he started giving me a hard time. I gave it right back to him and demanded he take me home. My friend Ronny just about messed his pants when I stood up to Dad, but even though we argued, there was beginning to be a different respect built between us. That's where I first noticed it."

The 1969–70 season was Terry's twentieth full season in the NHL. It was hard to fathom that, after everything that Terry had gone through in his life, he could still crack an NHL lineup as he approached the age of forty. His contemporaries — Hall, Worsley, and Plante — from the 1950s were also still figuring in the plans of their respective teams, but by and large they had taken better care of themselves over the years. It was a testament to Sawchuk's talent, determination, and stubborn will that he had reached this point. Ranger general manager and coach Emile Francis still felt Terry had a game or two left in him, as he told *Hockey World* magazine before the season began.

"(Sawchuk's presence) will give Ed Giacomin something to think about. With Sawchuk around, I will have flexibility, particularly at playoff time."

"I felt coming into that season that Giacomin had played too much the season before," Francis says, "so now I brought Terry in to act as a stabilizer. I felt that if I could get ten to twelve games out of him that it would be enough to give Eddie an occasional rest, maybe keep him fresher for the playoffs, and maybe Eddie could learn a thing or two."

At training camp, Sawchuk was enthusiastic. Emile Francis remembered Terry giving an almost youthful effort. Fully aware that his role with the Rangers was limited, Terry was happy — as happy as Terry could be. He began arriving at the rink earlier than he had in years for games and practices.

"All his life," Pat says, "Terry had never been a clotheshorse. He'd wear something till it fell apart. In the past, he would buy his suits and I would buy the rest, with his approval, and his tastes were rather boring when it came to clothes. After the divorce, he must have gotten the word from his pals — 'Spruce up! You're single!' He soon began to sport leather boots, new clothes, sports jackets. After all, he was in New York, the fashion capital."

Reunited with his Toronto teammate, Ron Stewart, the two men rented a house together at 58 Bay Street in Long Beach, on the southeastern portion of Long Island, away from the distractions of Manhattan. Emile Francis and most of his players lived in the island's quiet communities for the winter. The two old friends agreed that their place perfectly suited their needs for peace, quiet, and anonymity.

As the season began, Terry would again clash with a hockey writer who had a vendetta: *New York Times* reporter Gerald Eskenazi.

"I remember a particular reporter, I think it was Eskenazi," Francis says, "who had given Terry a few printed shots in the press, who came into the dressing room after one of our early games and asked Terry a question. Let's just say that Terry's response was not printable."

When Terry got to New York he stopped making his child-support payments. Pat got a job at her dad's golf course, but soon the bills weren't being paid. The electricity was shut off. "I had to act fast," says Pat. "So I took that fur coat that Terry had gotten for me, the one I swear had really been for his girl-friend, and young Kathy and I went to downtown Detroit to some hockshop and pawned it.

"Boy, were we scared! I mean, nobody went downtown, much less a woman and a young daughter. But that is how I got our electricity turned on. Then the mortgage payments on the house fell behind; we were gonna lose the house, too. My dad said it was even in the paper. So finally I called the Rangers and spoke to Emile Francis and told him the story about the fur coat, the electricity, the mortgage, all of it. It didn't take very long for a cheque to be in the mail. We were okay after that."

Wayne Rutledge recalls a very upbeat and enthusiastic Terry Sawchuk that year. "You know, I'd see Terry on the ice or after a game and he'd be happy. He'd say, 'Wayne, it's a great life. I get a good paycheque, I play maybe a game or two a month. It's great!' You know, he looked like he was just starting to come out of his shell. He'd always seek me out to talk. He seemed really upbeat, like he had no more pressure and he could finally relax, which was something he was never good at."

"I had no qualms about Terry whatsoever that year," Emile Francis says. "He practised hard, I recall, because he knew I was from the old school and I never tolerated anybody slacking off, dogging it, whether it was my top scorer or Terry Sawchuk. Reports that he didn't practise hard or that I was disappointed in his play is hogwash. I was glad to have him on my team."

But Terry was certainly still moody and there could be no doubt that if a player took a high shot in practice, Terry would make no attempt to save that player's next shot or even step out of the net.

On December 2, he was severely bruised and cut on the leg by a collision with teammate Real Lemieux that forced him not to dress for a couple of games. That was okay, he thought. He didn't have to play, anyway.

By Christmas, the Rangers were hot and in first place for six weeks now. On Christmas morning, the Rangers had a practice which drew a lot of vacationing school children. As the eager kids waited for the Rangers to leave the arena, most of them wanted autographs. Most of the players stopped to sign but Terry walked right past, telling one boy, "You don't want my autograph, I'm washed up."

Through January, Giacomin was cruising along nicely in goal and a contented Sawchuk looked on with glee. Still, when called upon, he played well. On February 1, he started against the Pittsburgh Penguins at Madison Square Garden. As the game progressed, Terry held the Penguins off the scoreboard and the Rangers built up a lead. By the third period, the Rangers knew another Sawchuk shutout was in the offing. They dug down deep and gave Terry extra effort just as all his pirates had done down through the years on his way to this, his 103rd shutout.

As the buzzer sounded, Terry raised his arms up in a V and his teammates all jumped onto the ice to congratulate him. Defenceman Brad Park was the first to reach him and he kissed Ukey's forehead — an unusual but touching tribute to one of hockey's legends.

"We wanted to show he was not washed up," Park said, "as some guys have been saying. I don't think we tried extra hard on defence to protect him, though. Well, maybe we did just a bit. We know what he can do, and we wanted everyone else to see what he can do. We like Terry. He's the kind of guy you like to play for. He's always encouraging the younger guys."

Emile Francis fondly remembers the night. "Any night of a Sawchuk shutout was magical. Terry played well that night, real well, and the team and I were darn proud of him, and I told him so."

Ed Giacomin recalled that magical night to broadcaster Dick Irvin. "I know he (Terry) always hated the press. After his 103rd shutout, when the press came to talk to him afterwards, he jumped all over them. He told them where they could all go and yelled at them, 'Where were you guys the last twenty, thirty, or forty games!'

"I was in shock. When they left, I told him I could never do anything like that and all he said was, 'You'll understand someday.' I never got the opportunity to really understand, though."

Though he felt better than he had in years, Terry knew his NHL days were numbered. But whether he was playing or not, his presence could still evoke awe and charisma, especially among goaltenders. In famed broadcaster and author Dick Irvin, Jr.'s 1995 book *In the Crease*, Phil Myre relived his brush with Terry Sawchuk in that 1969–70 season.

"I idolized Terry Sawchuk. Whenever I could play hockey as a kid, whether it was on an outdoor rink or on the street, I was always Terry Sawchuk. I used to go down to our basement at six o'clock in the morning and throw balls against the wall and when I stopped them coming back, I was always Terry Sawchuk.

"When I was brought up by Montreal, I played my first game in the NHL against the Rangers in Madison Square Garden. Terry Sawchuk was with the Rangers.

"He was backing up Ed Giacomin. I remember in warmup sneaking glances at Sawchuk. I couldn't believe I was on the ice at the same time as he was, in the same game. Giacomin played that night and we got beat 2–0. There I was, twenty years old and playing my first game for the Montreal Canadiens and I felt I had played well.

"In those days in New York, both teams went out the same gate to get to their dressing room. When the game ended, I was skating down the ice to go out the gate and I see Terry Sawchuk standing there. I didn't realize it right away but he was waiting for me. I had never talked to Terry Sawchuk and he didn't know he had been my idol. So he waited for me and when I got to the gate, he patted me on the ass with his stick and said, 'Good game, kid! Keep playing that way and you'll be a hell-of-a player!' I couldn't believe it! It was one of the greatest moments of my life and it was so motivating for me!"

The Rangers stayed in first place until the beginning of March, when a rash of injuries finally caught up to them. They very narrowly edged out the Canadiens for the fourth and final playoff spot. The teams ended up with identical 38–22–16 records, but New York had scored more goals and therefore qualified. In twenty-two years, the Canadiens had never missed the playoffs and it took until Terry's twenty-first season for it to happen.

In eight appearances, Terry won three, lost only once, and tied twice. His goals-against average was 2.91.

Terry received shocking news from home on the eve of the playoffs. His father, Louis, had been involved in a near-fatal auto accident. The seventy-one-year-old lay in a Pontiac hospital in a body cast. Terry was concerned, though he was told his father was in serious but stable condition.

In their semifinal series, the Rangers faced the Big Bad Bruins, who had been narrowly squeezed out of first place by Chicago.

Still, with injuries to key players and top defencemen Brad Park and Jim Neilson playing hurt, Giacomin faced a barrage of rubber. When the score reached 7–1 for Boston, Emile Francis had seen enough and gave Terry the nod to play the third. Terry allowed only one goal in the period, enough to convince the "Cat" that Terry should start the next game.

Through most of Game Two, it looked like the strategy would work. Sawchuk held his own and made some fine saves in maintaining a 2–2 tie until late in the second period. Then Johnny Bucyk beat him from a tough angle and the wind seemed to go out of his sails. Despite his best effort, the Bruins dominated en route to a 5–3 victory and a 2–0 series lead.

"Terry played a fine game but we came up short," Francis

recalls. "But it got our team thinking and maybe gave Eddie (Giacomin) something to think about. His playoff record had not been the best up to that point." Indeed, the Rangers had now lost ten playoff games in a row.

The Rangers bounced back, winning the next two games with a resurgent Giacomin in the nets.

Writer Scott Young ran into Terry in a Boston hotel lobby at this time as Sawchuk sat talking to Bill Gadsby.

"We talked for just a moment," Young later wrote, "and then I left, but I left thinking that Sawchuk was looking better than he had for years. His face was not as drawn. Some long-standing worry seemed to have been lifted. I thought, 'Perhaps it's because he hasn't played much this year.'"

Back at the Boston Garden for Game Five, the Rangers had the Bruins on the ropes, 2–1, going into the third. But by the eight-minute mark of the third, a pair of Phil Esposito goals put the Bruins ahead and gave them the momentum. Emile Francis turned to Terry and nodded. The veteran knew exactly what his boss wanted from him — a delay. Donning his mask and gear as slowly as possible, he went into the net to warm up. Normally, Terry needed only a few shots to be ready, but this time he took all the shots he could in order to give his teammates a breather. Finally hassled by the referee, Terry slowly indicated he was ready. At the first opportunity, Brad Park iced the puck and Giacomin resumed his place in the net. As Terry made his way towards the bench, the players tapped his pads in the standard show of respect to a goaltender.

Sitting down, neither he nor anyone else realized that he had just made his last NHL appearance. Coincidentally, his first game had been against Boston, back on January 8, 1950. Today's date: April 14, 1970.

The Bruins did not score again but still held on to win. They eliminated the Rangers in New York with a 4–1 victory in Game Six. The Bruins would then sweep Chicago and St. Louis to win the Stanley Cup on Bobby Orr's dramatic overtime goal against Glenn Hall. In the famous photograph of this goal, Orr, parallel to the ice, seems to be flying through the air.

The day after the Rangers were eliminated, Terry saw Emile

Francis in his office at Madison Square Garden. His first priority, he said, was to fly up to Detroit to see his father in hospital. The talk was short and amiable. There was no talk of next year's plans or Terry's position with the team.

Once back in Detroit, Terry visited his father regularly. His condition, though stable, was not improving. The blood circulation in his legs was poor and, if it did not improve, doctors feared they might have to amputate both of Louis's lower legs. Pat Sawchuk was concerned as well and visited her ex-father-in-law often. On one such occasion, she bumped into Terry. She clearly recalls their last meeting.

"While visiting with Terry's dad, Terry and I talked at the hospital for a couple of hours. Then afterwards we decided to pick up the kids and go out for supper. Sid Abel owned a Holiday Inn and that's where we went. He hadn't seen all the kids together in a while so we had a nice visit. I'd say he was in good spirits. He joked with the kids and teased the girls. He said later, in the summer, he wanted to take all of the kids on a trip to Florida. I would go along to help take care of them. Maybe he thought we might reconcile.

"We had a nice meal, then he kissed the kids good-bye."

This occasion is the only memory that Michael, then three years old, has of his father. "I remember as we were leaving that place, that restaurant, there was this great big barrel of Tootsie Rolls. Dad lifted me up, held me upside down by the ankles, and told me to grab as many Tootsie Rolls as I could. That is the only memory I have of my father, but I'll never forget it."

As they left the restaurant, Terry and Pat didn't doubt they'd talk again. After his short stint back in Michigan, he decided to return to New York to pick up his car and drive it home. He also wanted to clear his belongings out of the house he rented with Ron Stewart. Terry landed back in New York on the afternoon of April 29.

It would be later reported that at this point, he was severely depressed after an "unsuccessful reconciliation attempt" with Pat. Yet all signs show that getting back together with Pat was never discussed. Still, there was no doubt Terry wanted more than mere friendship from Pat, and perhaps this bothered him.

As well, his father's condition no doubt weighed more heavily on his mind.

That evening, Terry went to his closest New York friend Ben Weiner's place for supper. Weiner was the manager of Cooky's Steak Pub in the Green Acres Shopping Center in Valley Stream, Long Island. Sensing his friend was somewhat down, Weiner suggested they go to E & J's Pub, a local bar they frequently patronized along with many Rangers and members of the Knicks basketball team. Ron Stewart was already there, asking bartender Joe Craine if he knew of someone who cleaned furnaces. He'd had a few drinks and was about to leave when Weiner and Terry came in, so the three men sat together and talked. Soon the subject of their moving out of their rented digs came up. Stewart mentioned that they would have to clean the place up, to leave it as they received it the previous fall.

Sawchuk, who was in a snarly mood, laughed off the suggestion, but Stewart persisted.

"We've got to get busy," he said.

"To hell with it!" Sawchuk retorted.

"No, Terry," Stewart continued. "We've got to get the house back into the shape the owner gave it to us."

But Terry would have none of it. He was not in the mood to discuss responsibility. When the talk turned to money and unpaid bills, Sawchuk began to lose his perspective. Stewart informed his roommate that he had paid the phone bill and other assorted bills, totalling one hundred and eighty-four dollars and change. Terry's blood began to boil. He pulled a roll of money out of his pocket, handed Stewart $190 and told him to shove it. "I ought to cut your fucking head off!" Terry shouted, taking a swing at Stewart but instead hitting a local man, a garbage collector, seated nearby. A scuffle broke out which was broken up by Weiner and others in the bar.

Stewart, realizing his friend was out of control, bolted out of the bar, but Sawchuk was close behind and the wrestling match resumed on the sidewalk outside. No punches were landed as Stewart was able to grab Terry's arms. Ben Weiner and others again pulled Sawchuk off Stewart. Terry was still livid, out of control. Stewart climbed into his car and drove back to their house. In the meantime, Weiner was able to talk Terry into re-entering the bar to calm down. After finishing another drink, Terry decided to leave. He was still in an ugly mood.

"I'm going to bed . . . but before I do I'm going to find that bastard!" He stormed out of the bar towards his car. Weiner, very concerned about Terry's state of mind, decided to follow Terry home. Ron Stewart was in the backyard when Terry arrived. It was pitch black.

Terry immediately resumed his verbal and physical attack on Stewart. Stewart could not understand what had gotten into the goaltender. Rosemary Sasso, a twenty-four-year-old Canadian-born nurse and a friend of Stewart's, heard the commotion and came out of the house via a set of stairs. Her presence temporarily halted Terry's attack, but soon Terry was after Stewart again. She attempted to physically intervene but Stewart instructed her to get back into the house. She hesitated just as Ben Weiner arrived.

Weiner yelled at Sasso to get into the house, then grabbed Terry by the waist, attempting to pull him away. In the melee, Stewart backed away and tripped over an overturned metal barbecue pit that had fallen the day before. As Stewart fell backwards, Sawchuk — with Weiner wrapped around his waist — fell forward on top of Stewart. In the fall, Terry's stomach landed hard on Ron's extended knee. Terry cried out in pain and fell down himself, clutching his stomach.

"I've been hurt, I've got a terrible pain!" Terry screamed. Stewart wondered if Terry was just faking the injury but soon realized the severity of the situation and called Rosemary out of the house. She quickly examined Terry. Stewart instructed her to go into the house and call Dr. Denis Nicholson, a Long Beach physician who cared for many of the Rangers and their families. Terry screamed out that he didn't want a doctor.

Sasso followed Stewart's instructions and, very quickly, Nicholson was on the scene. The doctor found Sawchuk in horrible pain and in shock.

"He was pale," the doctor later publicly related, "and had extremely low blood pressure. The shock must have been from the pain."

Nicholson suggested that an ambulance be called. Terry was adamant that he did not want or need to go to the hospital.

Stewart persuaded his long-time friend to go to the hospital. Terry was in no position to disagree. He was loaded into the ambulance, as his worried friends looked on.

19

LOVE, PAT AND THE KIDS

"**Y**OU guys are crazy," Terry repeated as he waited with Ron Stewart and Ben Weiner in a room at Long Beach Memorial Hospital. "There's nothing wrong with me!" Terry was pale as he was examined at eleven p.m. An initial exam revealed extreme tenderness in the upper right part of his abdomen. He was short of breath and had low blood pressure, yet the x-rays showed nothing. Terry was admitted and an intravenous tube was inserted in his arm. Ron Stewart stayed at the hospital that night to be with Terry. It was a restless, worrisome night for both men.

By morning, things looked better. The pain in Terry's lower abdomen had decreased, though he continued to wince each time he moved. He admitted to the attending physician that it still hurt in the upper right corner of his abdomen, that it was tender. Stewart left the hospital to organize the handing-over of the house to its owner. Rosemary Sasso, who had once been a nurse at Long Beach Memorial, helped Ron with the final cleanup.

On May 1, doctors decided to operate on Terry after the upper abdominal pain intensified. A deep laceration was found on the underside of the liver; it compromised the gall bladder and the *porta hepatis* — the liver's main area into which blood enters through the main artery and from which bile leaves through its main duct.

The surgeon, Dr. Weitzman, removed Terry's now-useless gall bladder. The surgeon did not suture the lacerated area for fear of hitting the main vein. He instead inserted drains to remove unwanted blood and bile and felt the area would heal itself. Terry was then closed up, given three units of blood, and moved from the recovery room into the intensive-care unit.

In the meantime, Ron Stewart had received word from his home in Barrie, Ontario, that a family member had taken ill. He had to return. Visiting Terry before leaving, Stewart felt confident that the removal of the gall bladder had solved the problem. Ron told Terry he had to leave for a few days but that he would return.

By the time Stewart returned, Terry was able to tolerate clear fluids by mouth and was given an additional unit of blood. He was out of intensive care.

He was visited often by Ben Weiner and Dr. Nicholson. Terry told the doctor repeatedly that the blame for the accident rested solely on his shoulders, not Ron Stewart's.

His condition continued to improve over the next several days though he still had pain in the vicinity of the area where the liver is located. His status was still guarded, even eleven days after the injury, but there was strong cause for optimism when the drainage tubes were clamped and Terry felt no further discomfort.

At two-thirty a.m. on Monday, May 11, Terry began to complain of severe abdominal pain and his heart rate shot up. His stomach dressing began to bleed and his blood pressure dropped. He was transferred back into the intensive-care unit and given two units of whole blood, which immediately helped his condition. On Thursday, May 14, he was given an additional two units of blood, but the next day he took another turn for the worse. When fresh whole blood began to pass through the drainage tubes, a second exploratory operation was immediately performed on his liver.

Doctors found extensive bleeding and clotting, and removed almost 1,200 cubic centimetres of fresh clotted blood. As well, due to the extensive clotting, some liver tissue was dead or dying. Surgeons could not locate the source of the bleeding and opted to wrap the liver with a part of abdominal tissue called the *omentum*, a common practice used to help localize bleeding. Two drains were installed in this area and, as the surgery ended, Terry's condition was downgraded to poor.

Terry's situation became more complicated. Until now, Terry had wanted to keep the whole affair a secret. He did not want word to get out to the Rangers, to his family, or to his father in hospital up in Pontiac. Besides, Terry knew the police had done a preliminary investigation of the incident and ruled the whole affair "horseplay." Terry had taken responsibility and wanted the whole affair to die there.

Somehow or other, Terry's brother Gerald was notified of Terry's condition. Terry found the whole thing embarrassing. He just wanted to get better and get out.

Gerald, his wife Joan, and Terry's son Jerry flew down to New York. Listed as the legal next of kin, Gerald arrived to find Terry was doing much better. In fact, the day after the operation Terry was noted to be alert and cooperative with a stable pulse and blood pressure, though he still experienced moments of weakness.

"Gerald and Joanie called us," Pat says. "They said he was in hospital and that he'd had his gall bladder removed, and we were left with the impression that it wasn't that serious. I was sorry he was in the hospital but I thought he'd be okay."

"When I walked into his hospital room, I walked right past Dad," Jerry recalls. "I hardly recognized him. He was so thin and haggard-looking."

On the same day that Terry had gone into surgery for the second time, Ranger coach/GM Emile Francis was in Quebec City. During the second period of a Junior game, Francis was paged. He went to the arena office and took a call from a doctor at Long Beach Memorial Hospital.

"I have one of your players here," the doctor explained, "who is in serious condition and may not make it through the night."

Incredulous, Francis demanded to know who. Terry Sawchuk, the doctor said.

"He's in very serious condition," the doctor continued.

"Can you tell me what the problem is?"

"Well, he's had an accident."

"What kind of accident?" Emile asked.

"Well, I'm sworn to secrecy. I can't tell you."

"You may as well tell me, 'cause I'm gonna find out anyways."

"No, I can't tell you. I agreed not to tell you what the problem is."

Francis thanked the doctor for notifying him and flew out the next morning. He drove straight to the hospital, which was three blocks from the Francis home. At the information desk, the Ranger boss was told that Sawchuk was indeed a patient there but that he was in the intensive-care unit, and only family were allowed in.

"I look over my shoulder and I see 'Intensive Care,'" Francis says today, "so I just walk away from the desk. I look around, then just walk right straight into the ICU ward. There are a lot of empty beds but I look way down the end and I see him there. I walk up to his bed and he looks at me and says, 'What are you doing here?' I laughed and said, 'Terry, better than what am I doing here? What are *you* doing here?' And he told me about the fight and all that. And he said he and Stewie wanted to keep it quiet because they didn't want me to find out. But most of all, Terry said, 'It wasn't Stewie's fault. I precipitated everything. It wasn't his fault at all.'"

Emile found his goaltender's spirits high, but the meeting was interrupted by moments of sudden weakness and near-unconsciousness.

Son Jerry recalls, "From where we stayed, it was far enough from the hospital, but I would walk to go and see Dad. We had some nice talks. In fact we had a real nice talk about my playing hockey, how much I liked it, my being a goaltender. We had a real discussion about it."

By the third week in May, word had leaked to the New York media that a prominent athlete lay ill in a hospital. A reporter with the *New York Daily News* tracked the story down, but when he presented it to his superiors, they balked, opting to spike the story. Miffed, the reporter went over to *The New York Times* and handed the story to an appreciative Gerald Eskenazi, who was only too happy to break the story on May 22. By this time, Terry had been removed from the intensive-care unit but was still headline material.

The hospital switchboard was swamped with calls. Reporters who got through to the nursing station on Terry's floor were told that Mr. Sawchuk was too ill to receive phone calls or visitors. The Rangers' offices were equally hectic, though Eskenazi quoted Francis as saying that Terry's surgery would not necessarily prevent him from playing hockey next year.

Caught off guard by a reporter in his hometown of Barrie, Stewart feigned lack of knowledge of the Sawchuk incident and his involvement.

"It's news to me. I'm going to phone New York and see how it (rumour of his involvement) got started."

Did he recall "wrestling" with Sawchuk on April 29?

"I certainly do not. Offhand, I can't recall what I did on that day. How could a story like that get started?"

Terry had a surprise visitor at his hospital room, a self-proclaimed New York Ranger fan calling herself Shirley Walton. She said she had come to see for herself how he was. She had brought him flowers and he seemed pleased to have a visitor even though he was weak. As she asked him questions, Terry answered without hesitating, eager for conversation.

"It was just a fluke," Terry told her of the accident that had been reported in that day's newspaper. "A complete fluke accident. Those writers, they'll do anything to make up those stories." Terry reminisced about his year as an L.A. King, and talked about his hospital stay.

"I can't even tell you if this is a good hospital or not. I've been so doped up for so long, I don't know. They still don't know if I'll recover from this. And it was so bad for a while that I really didn't care. I'm still full of tubes and my back is bothering me from lying here so long."

Terry boasted about Jerry, his son. "The oldest, he's almost sixteen. And he's a pretty darn good goalie."

Terry lamented the fact that his hospitalization had hit the media. Walton mentioned the speculation that he might be traded to St. Louis before the next season. Terry shook his head and raised a pencil-thin arm, answering, "I'm retired, man. Look at me. I can never come back from this!"

The visit ended with Terry shaking her hand and giving her a toothless, trusting smile. "Well, I hope I see you again sometime," he said, "but not in this place."

The next day, a headline in *The Toronto Star* read, "Terry Sawchuk: 'Can Never Come Back from This.'" The story was written by New York writer Shirley Fischler, wife of hockey writer Stan Fischler. She had used her maiden name, Walton, to trick Terry into giving an interview. She wrote that when she saw him lonely, ill, and weak, she was suddenly sorry that she had gone to see him, "But I had an assignment."

During the same weekend of May 23–25, Jerry Sawchuk visited his ailing father. Jerry handed his father a nice card from his mother, and pictures of the seven kids. She wrote that she was praying for him and for a speedy recovery. She signed the card, "Love, Pat and the kids."

Terry was glad to see his son, the card, and pictures. He perked up during Jerry's visits and the two joked around. Terry had been taken out of intensive care the day before and put in a semiprivate room. His condition was improved and stable. He was slowly walking around. It seemed possible that the worst was behind him, his only complaint being a sore back.

Suddenly on Wednesday, May 27, Terry spiked a temperature and he was immediately given antibiotics. A chest x-ray revealed a slight build-up of fluid in the right lung, a condition that had existed for the past twelve days. The next day he was beset by extreme pain in the liver area again. His pulse raced and his skin looked grey. Most of all, he was draining pure blood again. He was given three more units of blood and doctors hoped, as before, that the problem would correct itself. Terry was placed back on the critical list.

"Terry was getting worse," Emile Francis says, "and I said, 'Terry, we're gonna get something done now, and it's gonna be done real fast.' So I called our team doctors in New York and got them conferring with the hospital doctors, and convinced them to move Terry to New York Hospital because it had more advanced equipment for Terry's problem. There were two specialists we wanted Terry to see, so the hospital doctors said, 'Okay.'"

Emile Francis was at the hospital at seven o'clock the next morning. The news was good. Terry had spent a stable night and the doctors at Long Beach gave the okay to transfer him to New York Hospital. Francis got into the back of the ambulance with Terry for the ride to Manhattan. Halfway into New York, Terry reached up and grabbed Emile's hand. With soft, pleading eyes, Terry looked up at his old friend and boss, and said, "Cat, we've been through so much together, so many good moments. This would be a helluva way to go out. Damn it, we've come back before and we're going to make it this time, too."

"You bet your aching old butt, we are. Don't even think about losing this one," the Cat replied.

A team of four doctors awaited Terry's arrival. Terry, despite feeling weak, was able to give the admitting intern a complete oral history.

The next morning, Saturday, May 30, a celiac arteriogram was performed to visualize the blood vessels of the upper abdomen. This intricate new test showed the extent of trauma and bruising the injury had caused. The arteries in the liver's right side or lobe had been stretched and straightened, and this lobe had been pushed up and turned. Yet the test concluded that the main damage seemed to have been done to the left lobe of the liver and to its artery which is supposed to supply it with blood. Bruising, bleeding, and poor blood supply to the liver itself was noted in the left liver lobe. The findings indicated his worsening condition was critical.

Emile Francis recalls, "After that test, the doctors held a meeting with him. I was there and they told him he was in serious condition and that they'd have to operate right away. They said he had a fifty-fifty chance of coming out of this, that there were no guarantees, that if things didn't go well, school's out. Terry didn't flinch. He faced the situation head-on. After the doctors were done, and I'll never forget the look on his face, he just looked straight ahead and said, 'Get me a priest.'"

An hour later, Terry was wheeled into surgery. As they passed Emile Francis in the hall, Terry asked them to stop.

He made two requests of Francis in case he didn't pull through. Removing his 1955 Cup ring, he asked that it be passed to Jerry. Then he asked Francis to see that Jerry got a chance to become a pro goalie.

"Hey, consider it done," Emile said to his goalkeeper. "Don't you worry, those things'll happen. And you're gonna be fine."

Terry thanked and shook hands with the man who had been with him steadily for the past few days and months.

Dr. Frank Glenn, assisted by Doctors McSherry, Tiedeman, and Eisenmenger, performed the long, complex, and intricate operation to solve the problem of Terry's bleeding liver. Dr. Glenn found a large area in the right lobe that had blood clots. Clots stop the blood flow to parts of the liver, thus much dead tissue had to be removed as well. After removing some 600 grams of blood clot and dead liver tissue, the bleeding that had plagued Terry resumed. Now knowing the source, Dr. Glenn secured the bleeding arterial vessels in the right lobe with sutures. The surgeons then watched the area for three quarters of an hour. The bleeding had ceased. After conferring, the doctors agreed that they had rectified the problem. Dr. Glenn was very optimistic as they closed Terry up. His colour and blood pressure had stayed constant throughout.

It is interesting to note that never did Dr. Glenn mention encountering what could be termed an "alcoholic" liver. In the extensive report Glenn filed, only the bleeding and clotting were noted to be abnormal.

In fact, despite having been a hard drinker for more than twenty years, Terry's liver continued to have an amazing capacity to "clot." Alcoholic livers usually have a tendency not to produce adequate amounts of clotting factors and thus they promote bleeding. Terry's liver was functioning very well, clotting well, perhaps too well. It was another amazing facet of the life of Terry Sawchuk.

Afterwards, Glenn told a waiting, concerned Emile Francis that things had gone well, but that the next forty-eight hours would be critical. He told Francis to go home and get some rest.

At ten p.m., Terry was moved from the recovery room into intensive care. His blood pressure and temperature were slightly elevated. His condition was now critical but holding. At eight the next morning, as he was being turned in bed, Terry suddenly, without warning, gasped for breath. His eyes rolled up and he went into respiratory arrest, quickly followed by cardiac arrest. A medical team poured into his room and extensive attempts to resuscitate him, lasting almost two hours, could not bring him back.

At 9:50 a.m., on Sunday, May 31, 1970, the greatest goalie who ever lived was pronounced dead. Cause of death was suspected to be a blood clot to the lungs, but only an autopsy could confirm that for certain.

At this time, Jerry was at the New York Hospital, in a room upstairs from his father's. He was completely unaware of the turn of events. "I was kept completely in the dark. I didn't even know why Dad was at the New York Hospital or why I couldn't see him. Then suddenly my Uncle Gerald comes into the room crying and he tells me Dad's gone."

The phone rang at the Francis home on Long Island. "They told me he had just passed away," recalls Emile Francis today. "I was in shock. I knew it could be touch and go, but . . . he was gone . . . Terry was gone."

"The phone rings and it's Joanie, Gerald's wife," Pat recalls. "And she says, 'Hello, Terry's dead.' Just like that. That's how she said it. I mean, wham! I just fell apart and then I had to go in and tell the kids and they fell apart. It was a shock. I sobbed and sobbed. I hadn't expected it. We knew nothing of his worsened condition."

"We were in the backyard by the pool in Toronto," Marcel Pronovost says, "celebrating my wife's birthday when the news flashed over the radio, 'Terry Sawchuk is dead.' I was stunned. I cried, I cried like a little baby. I didn't ever know he had been in hospital."

An autopsy performed that afternoon by Dr. Elliott Gross revealed that Terry really didn't have a chance. While the immediate cause of death was a large clot to both pulmonary arteries leading to the lungs, smaller clots were found in peripheral blood vessels. As well, large clots were found in the liver's hepatic vein and vena cava. These subsequent clots probably would have taken Terry sooner or later and were a direct result of his bleeding liver.

For Emile Francis, the long vigil was still not quite over. Before Terry's body could be released, it had to be legally identified. "They had moved Terry's body to a morgue on Second Avenue, fifteen minutes from the hospital. The people at the morgue didn't know who he was, didn't know who I was. So I had to fill out all these papers. Then this guy says, 'Follow me,' and we go down these two flights of stairs. When we got there, there were about thirty bodies all lying on the floor in these green body bags that looked like hockey bags, and there was Terry, in one of those green bags. I looked at him and I thought, 'Here's the greatest goaltender I've ever seen,' and I just couldn't believe that it should end this way."

As Emile signed papers and alternated between phone calls to Gerald and Pat, it became clear that Terry's brother and ex-wife disagreed as to who would execute funeral arrangements and arrange to transport the body back home to Union Lake.

Emile consulted with league president Clarence Campbell and lawyers in Detroit to determine who was legally responsible for Terry. In the end, brother Gerald, as legal next of kin, had authority.

Through all of this, the friend most involved in Terry's last year of life was in seclusion in Barrie. No doubt the death of Terry hit Ron Stewart like a thunderbolt. Initial attempts by the Rangers to reach him had been unsuccessful. At four-thirty p.m., when a reporter knocked on the door of his darkened apartment, Stewart opened the door a few inches. When asked to comment on Terry's death, he said, "No comment, nothing, sir, no," then quietly closed the door.

On Monday, June 1, when the headlines of Terry's death hit the newsstands, Nassau County homicide detectives re-opened the case and began door-to-door questioning of possible witnesses to the alleged fight and the earlier fight at the pub. District Attorney William Cahn, having received the full autopsy report, now awaited the police investigation before deciding whether or not to turn the case over to a grand jury. In the United States, any possible criminal charges must be examined by a grand jury, which hears evidence and then decides whether there is a possibility a crime has been committed. If so, then a person is charged with that crime. If these things came to pass, then Ron Stewart could be charged with manslaughter.

As the whole scenario spun out of control, the Rangers, who had hired noted defence attorney Nicholas Castellano to represent Stewart, were themselves at the centre of a controversy for having covered up the whole incident. As the rumours flew left and right, Terry's body came home to Michigan.

In their grief, Pat Sawchuk and her father Ed Morey only added to the rampant speculation. On the day after Terry's death, they knew no more details than what they'd read in the paper and their frustration showed. "There's something here that's being hidden and I want to find out what it is," Pat told Dan Shafer of the *Pontiac Press*. "I'm willing to do whatever is necessary to get to the bottom of this."

Ed Morey took issue with the autopsy. "No simple 'horseplay' could have caused internal injuries sufficient to require extensive surgery and result in his death. The reports in the newspapers, that Terry and his teammate got drunk and fought about something, leave his kids with a stigma they'll have to live with the rest of their lives."

But it was true. The problem was, the initial police investigation and interview with Terry were cut and dried. It was an accident, therefore no formal police report was ever filed at that time. Now with his very public death, the whole mechanics of justice had to come forward.

That same night, Monday, June 1, both Emile Francis and Ben Weiner appeared in front of police for a three-hour question-and-answer session, attended by Stewart's lawyer and representatives of the DA's office.

The next day, June 2, as Ron Stewart flew down to New York, William Cahn announced that he would send the case to the grand jury on June 8. With the public brouhaha about the case, Cahn almost had no choice, despite the overwhelming evidence that the injuries to Terry were a simple accident.

Then Dr. Gross, who performed the autopsy, clouded the air

with these printed comments: "There was a trauma or blunt force injury to Terry's liver, but the exact cause of death was a blood clot that travelled from a vein in a pulmonary artery. But forty-year-old men don't just get pulmonary embolisms." They could if a liver bleeds for a month, he should have added.

On Wednesday, June 3, an upset and nervous Ron Stewart appeared in front of Cahn in Mineola, New York, to be questioned. Stewart was accompanied by Rosemary Sasso and Castellano, his lawyer. Afterwards, Cahn told reporters that Stewart was "very cooperative."

The same day, Castellano agreed to let Stewart be interviewed by the *New York Post*. Intended to clear the air, the lengthy interview demonstrated how distraught Stewart was over Sawchuk's death.

"Terry just kept coming after me," Stewart said. "He fell on me, that's for sure, but all his lifetime, Terry took much worse falls on the ice and he always bounced back . . . and then he trips on top of me and suddenly his life is ended. It doesn't make sense. A fall like that, just like a thousand he's taken on that hard ice, and nothing ever happened to him. And this thing happened and Terry is gone. It's all like a bad dream when I look back now."

Stewart went on to explain how much Terry still loved Pat.

"You don't know how much Terry loved that woman. He was crazy about her. And his heart just melted over those kids of his. They had seven of them. Terry was brokenhearted. You've got to understand the guy. You got to know him the way I did to realize how badly he felt. He was very sensitive and, as tough as he might have been on the rink, he was really soft where it counted – in the heart.

"I can't tell you how sorry I am that I didn't turn away. When I think of it, I'm ready to go out of my mind."

"Ben Weiner called and explained the whole story to me," Pat said, "everything that happened. And I cried some more. And I know a part of me was crying because of the stupidity of it all, and the wasting of a life. I was angry because of that stupidity; my children now didn't have a father and their children would not have a grandfather. All these things were going through my mind. And of course, I thought of Terry, and . . . what a week that was. I wondered how we were all going to get through it."

The funeral was delayed so as to allow time for relatives to arrive from Western Canada. As the week ended and friends, relatives, and representatives of the hockey world arrived to bid Terry goodbye, a criminal investigation hung over the proceedings. Controversy had dogged Terry in his life. It seemed certain to mark his passing.

20

A WAKE TO REMEMBER

"RON Stewart was very concerned about going to the funeral," Emile Francis says, and I said, 'Ron, you're going to the funeral and you're going with me.' I knew for him to go on, to carry on with his life, he had to go through this. It was a tough, awful situation for him, but he came."

For Pat Sawchuk, the delay of the funeral was agonizing. Although, because of the divorce, she had been spared the trauma of making the funeral arrangements, she nonetheless wished that Terry's children had been consulted, at least Jerry, now fifteen years old.

"Terry's brother, Gerald, made all the arrangements," Pat recalls. "Why he didn't ask the kids, even Jerry — he was the man of the house now as far as I was concerned — give them some say about it all was puzzling. Little did I know it was an indication of things to come."

Terry's wake consisted solely of a Thursday afternoon and evening viewing, followed by a funeral mass on Friday morning.

"The morning of the wake was awful," Pat continues. "I had to get these seven kids ready for something that they didn't know anything about. They were sad, and they were scared. I've always found funerals and wakes barbaric . . . I mean, to drag families and young kids through something that tears them apart is awful. When we got in the car to go, I had a little talk with them. I told them, 'Dad's in heaven. He had the priest, he had confession, he's in heaven. If you don't want to go up front to look at him, you don't have to. If you don't want to look at your Dad, you don't have to. You don't have to do anything you don't want to do, okay?'"

Uncle Nick Maslak had arrived early at the funeral home in Royal Oak, Michigan.

"I went to Terry's wake with my brother Pete," says Uncle Nick. "I had said to Pete, 'I want to go early, to see Terry, while it's quiet, before later on, people coming and everything.' So we went early, all alone. Nobody was there, just me and Pete. The hall was empty. I knelt down and said a little prayer for him, for my Terry. It was hard to believe, let me tell you. Then Gerald came in and we sat around and talked a little bit and everything was fine. Then when Pat came and the kids, Gerald, well he kind of lost his senses and everything."

Pat continues the sequence of events.

"The kids and I got inside, and we went up to the kneeler, the kids all with me, and I bowed my head and said a prayer. The kids all knelt and bowed their heads, too. I never looked at Terry. I couldn't look at him in the casket. I wanted to remember him as he was.

"Then I stood up and the kids stood up. I took Terry Jr. and Mike by the hand and we went to a little anteroom off to the side, and I got them settled down.

"After a while I had them calmed down, and I thought they were all right. I said to them, 'I'll be right back,' and I went back out into the parlour, then went to Aunt Lena and Aunt Jessie, and Uncle Nick, of course, and then went back to sit with the kids. My first priority was to get the kids through this.

"Well, Gerald comes into the room, angry. He said Terry and I were divorced, that I shouldn't have made such a display, that my actions kissing Terry's family didn't look right, that the kids should come out and sit by Terry's casket, but that I should stay in this anteroom and keep myself scarce.

"I said, 'No, Gerald. My kids stay with me. If you want them to go sit by the front, I go and sit with them. If I sit in here, they sit with me.' Gerald then left in a huff."

Gerald's next thoughts turned to crowd control.

"He took hold of some chairs and put them from the head of the casket, around to Terry's feet," Uncle Nick recalls. "I said to Pete, 'Now, could you tell me what this guy is doing? Is this something new, that they make round, to sit the family around or something?' That's what I had in my mind.

"So I ask Gerald, 'What's this? Is this something new, Gerald?'"

"No, Uncle Nick," Gerald answered. "I'm going to put these chairs here in case the people come in and they rush the coffin." Uncle Nick was flabbergasted. Never one to hold his tongue, Nick set his nephew straight.

"Who told you this? Where did you come from? I can see you never were at a funeral before. When your mother died, did they have chairs like this? Around her? You're making a mockery out of this. You're not going to have it this way!"

Nick took the chairs away from the casket and put them over to the side.

"Now leave the chairs like that. Ain't nobody gonna bother Terry. Me and Pete are gonna stand right by Terry."

Gerald stomped away. Nick turned to Pete. "Let him get huffy! What do I care? My sister is gone, my nephew is gone. Soon my brother-in-law will go. I'm not gonna go to Detroit no more. Certainly not to see Gerald!"

Soon, as hundreds started packing the funeral home, many asked for Pat and soon there was a line of people going to the anteroom to give Pat their condolences. Again Gerald's nose got out of joint.

"Gerald came back in and said I'd been there long enough and that I should leave, that it didn't look right, people coming to see me," Pat says. "So I left the kids with either Rose Jollie or the Hanlans and I went out to the car. I was really upset by Gerald. Out at the car I had a good cry.

"Then Auntie Jessie came out and she asked, 'What's going on?' and I told her. She hit the ceiling. She said, 'If any person in this world deserves to be inside, girl, you do!' She went inside and I got in the car and drove around for a bit then came back to the parking lot. Then Uncle Nick came out."

Uncle Nick continues, "After a while, I say, 'Where the hell is Pat?' Finally I go out to the parking lot and I see her. 'What's the matter, Pat?' And so she told me. I say, 'Who the hell is he! You come with me inside, to be with the kids.' I brought her in and I brought her to those chairs I had moved before, near Terry. And I say, 'Sit right down here where you belong, on this seat. They belong to you and your kids. You do it!'"

Gerald came over to protest. Nick was again having none of it.

"I don't know nothin'. All I know, she belongs where she is and that's her husband. And she could do what she wants with him. You have no say in it!"

Gerald finally relented, leaving Pat alone for the duration of the wake. But, Uncle Nick was not quite finished helping out people in awkward situations.

"There was this guy outside and he kept looking in the window, and I said to Pete, 'Isn't that the guy that Terry had the argument with the night he got hurt?' And Pete said, 'Ya, ya, that's what's his name, Ron Stewart.'"

Uncle Nick went out and approached Stewart, who was worried about an unfriendly reaction if he went in. "You come to see your friend," Nick said. "You lived with him, you played hockey with Terry. Ain't nobody gonna tell you anything. You come, pay your respects."

From all walks of life, they came to pay their respects. "All the old gang, the old Red Wings, we all went to the funeral parlour," Lefty Wilson says. "God, you know what I remember? He looked so good lying there in the coffin — well shit, he was only forty years old — that I thought he could just get out of there and put the pads on, you know."

"There was a bunch of us back at the hotel," Emile Francis recalls, "everyone in hockey, but I specifically remember Punch Imlach and I sitting down for two hours together and talking about Terry, the great games he'd played, what a great goalie he had been. We all did that, sat down, had a few drinks and reminisced about Terry the night before the funeral."

Marcel Pronovost remembers seeing his best friend for the

last time. "You know, before they closed the casket, I reached in and put my hand on his hands, those big paws he had, and said goodbye. All I could think of is, 'Terry, it's much too soon for you to leave.'"

The funeral mass took place in Gerald Sawchuk's parish church, at Our Lady of La Salette Catholic Church in Berkley, Michigan, outside Detroit. On the day of the funeral, the animosity continued between Gerald and Pat. Again Uncle Nick had to intervene.

"Gerald did not want Pat to ride in the limousine with the kids, you know, behind the hearse. I told Gerald, 'What? That's what the limousine is there for. It was hired for her and the kids to go with the family.' She went, but he didn't like it."

Jimmy Skinner remembers being profoundly touched at the funeral mass. "You know, I consider myself a pretty strong person, but when I saw all of Terry's children come into church, some so young, come in behind Terry's coffin, I couldn't stop the tears. And around me everyone was the same way."

The funeral mass was presided over by Reverend E. A. Vecchio, assisted by Terry's good friend, Father John Gordon. Father Vecchio reminded the congregation that this was a time of expectation and triumph, not of mourning. Death was merely a door to a happier life with God.

As the mass ended and the procession filed from the church, Father Gordon approached Pat and hugged her.

Michigan State Troopers escorted the cortege of 150 cars as it slowly wound its way to Mount Hope Cemetery in nearby Pontiac. Louis Sawchuk, still in a body cast from his car accident, hadn't been able to go to the funeral home, so it was arranged for the cortege to make its way past Pontiac General Hospital.

At last Terry came home to be buried with his mother, in Pontiac. Terry's pallbearers included Marcel Pronovost; Bob Kinnear, the old Red Wing scout; Ranger goalie Ed Giacomin; Emile Francis; and Ben Weiner, Terry's New York buddy.

Also representing the hockey world at Terry's funeral were Ron Stewart, who stoically stood by Terry's gravesite; league president Clarence Campbell; Punch Imlach; Red Kelly; Sid

Abel; Tommy Ivan; Vic Stasiuk; Johnny Wilson; Maple Leaf president Stafford Smythe; Leaf director Harold Ballard; Wings' owner Bruce Norris; players Bernie Geoffrion, Jean Ratelle, Rod Seiling, Johnny Bower, George Armstrong, Gary Bergman, Frank Mahovlich, Dean Prentice, Roger Crozier, Busher Curry, and Doug Barkley.

Also in attendance at the cemetery were Jimmy Skinner, Lefty Wilson, Art Krass, and Terry's family, friends, and fans. Gordie Howe had attended the funeral mass.

"Later, Jerry felt guilty that he hadn't stepped in when Gerald was giving me such a hard time. But really, he behaved most like a man by not making a scene. There was nothing he could do. He was fifteen years old. It still bothers him, but it shouldn't."

"You could really see the tension that there was between Terry's brother and Pat," Emile Francis says. "And, you know, it made a sad event even sadder because at a time like that, the family needs to be together. It only made things worse and that was too bad.

"And, you know, there was no time to mourn." Indeed, Ron Stewart, Ben Weiner, and Francis had to head back to New York, where on Monday they were scheduled to appear before the grand jury.

Amid much sensation, nine witnesses appeared before a grand jury in the Mineola, New York, courthouse. Besides Weiner, Stewart, and Francis, those called to testify included Rosemary Sasso; Dr. Nicholson, who first saw Terry; barmaid Margaret Wilson, who had served Sawchuk and Stewart drinks; Joe Crane, who had also served the two men drinks; Detective Conrad Kessler of the Nassau County police department; and Dr. Elliott Gross, the medical examiner who conducted the autopsy.

Testimony lasted a mere three and a half hours, and half an hour later it was decided there was no evidence of any wrongdoing. District Attorney William A. Cahn reported the grand jury's findings: "There was no evidence by any of the eyewitnesses that any blows were struck . . . It was mainly a verbal argument and while a lot of pushing and shoving took place at the bar and the home, and although some blows may have been attempted, none was struck." Cahn pronounced the case closed.

Still, at an impromptu press conference after the decision, Emile Francis was under pressure to explain why Terry's hospitalization was kept a secret for so long. Francis said that Terry had had the best care, that the injuries he'd sustained were a complete accident. When a reporter asked him about the reason behind the fight, Emile had had enough and walked away from the microphones.

"Dad's death seemed almost natural," Jerry Sawchuk says today. "His hockey career was finished, and life off the ice had never been easy for him. You know, it was like, the play was over, the game had ended. It was like, the end of his time, you know.

"Our family has never blamed Ron Stewart for what happened. We know he's had to carry this around with him all of his life, and nobody can put themselves in his shoes, to know how much it may or may not have haunted him. Dad has the blame to shoulder and he paid for it with his life, plain and simple."

Detroit Free Press writer Joe Falls knew Terry Sawchuk as well as any newspaperman on the planet. Sawchuk often confided that he liked and respected Falls. In 1953, Falls, a greenhorn, had been waiting patiently in line to ask the great Sawchuk a question. The next thing he recalled was the scurrying of a photographer out of the Red Wing dressing room, and Sawchuk's skates slamming into the closed door behind him, as obscenities filled the air. Wisely, Falls saved his question for another day.

Seventeen years later, upon hearing of the death of "the greatest goalie I ever saw," Falls wrote a warm, elegant tribute to someone he called a "man of contrasts."

"Actually, the only time Sawchuk was happy . . . completely, totally happy . . . was when he was in those big, brown, bulging pads, with his legs dangling over the trainer's table and a cigarette dangling from his lips and he was exchanging insults with his teammates.

"I used to worry about Sawchuk. I knew that hockey was his

whole life, his whole being, his whole purpose for existing, and I'd wonder what he was thinking when he knew that it was starting to come to an end for him.

"I wondered how he'd take it when he realized they didn't need him anymore, that they didn't want him anymore.

"But I'd put these thoughts out of my mind because they got too grim even for me. Now I don't have to think about them anymore. The life he lived for, the life he needed, led to his ultimate fate."

21

NUMBER ONE

A S is the case with many legendary figures, Terry Sawchuk's public passing at such a young age only intensified the tributes paid to him by a stunned hockey world. In the weeks and months that followed, stories and articles graced sports pages and magazines, recalling his greatness.

On January 30, 1971, the Detroit Red Wing Hall of Fame committee announced Terry as a unanimous choice to be the twenty-sixth player inducted, and only the third goalkeeper to be so honoured. During on-ice ceremonies before the New York Ranger–Detroit Red Wing game on Thursday, February 4, former Red Wing defence great, Black Jack Stewart, presented the plaque to be displayed in the lobby of the Olympia to Terry's sixteen-year-old son, Jerry.

Emile Francis remembers that night well.

"Before the game, Jerry, Pat, and Terry's father — who was still in a wheelchair — came down to the dressing room and we had a nice visit. Jerry came into the room and all the players knew him, of course, and it was a warm time, a touching time. I was really glad that they had made a point of seeing us."

Nineteen days later, Terry was posthumously voted the 1971 winner of the Lester Patrick Memorial Trophy for outstanding service to hockey in the United States. Jerry went to New York to accept the award.

In June, voters for the Hockey Hall of Fame waived the usual three-year waiting period, and Terry was inducted in a ceremony at the Hall in late August, 1971. Jerry was on hand in Toronto to accept another accolade on behalf of his father. An AP wire photo of the ceremony shows a deadpan Emile Francis presenting the plaque to Jerry, who is looking down, biting his lip.

"You know, I have done a lot of eulogies and a lot of presentations at the Hockey Hall of Fame and elsewhere," Francis says, "but Terry's induction was the most emotional and difficult to do."

"But Terry's induction was a natural. He was in a class all his own really. I've seen a lot of the great ones, but Terry is still above the rest."

In November of 1974, Terry's hometown, Winnipeg, was celebrating its centennial. Terry, already a member of the Michigan Hall of Fame, was voted at this time a member of the Manitoba Hall of Fame, and was chosen the province's hockey player of the century.

On February 23, 1991, an arena in Terry's boyhood neighbourhood of East Kildonan was renamed in his honour. At the newly rechristened Terry Sawchuk Memorial Arena, a bronze plaque, photos, and four large banners depicting his career were unveiled by Winnipeg Mayor Bill Norrie and Terry's cousin, Robert Tatarnic. At the ceremony, Mayor Norrie added, "[The arena renaming] recognizes a very important and very significant contribution by a native son. It's a fitting tribute to a distinctive Canadian. Terry is someone we can all use as a role model."

Finally, on Sunday, March 6, 1994, all the old Red Wing greats assembled at Joe Louis Arena in Detroit to retire Terry's jersey number 1. In ceremonies before the Red Wing–Buffalo Sabres game, six of Terry's children looked on at centre ice, along with NHL commissioner Gary Bettman and Red Wing greats Gordie Howe, Alex Delvecchio, and Ted Lindsay, as Terry was honoured. A film clip of his life was shown on the scoreboard before Marcel Pronovost addressed the crowd.

"Terry didn't have too much to fear from the opposition," said his longtime friend. "He had more to fear from his own defence. I remember one night in Toronto when I accidentally scored three goals on him. I remember telling him after the game, 'I'm sorry, Uke, I beat you for three tonight.' And he said, 'Don't worry about it, you beat me clean on all three!'"

Jerry's loss for words was indicative of the overwhelming emotion of the moment. "I want to thank Mr. and Mrs. Ilitch [the owners of the Red Wings]. This is just, just marvellous . . . I just can't put it into words . . . thank you very much."

Finally, to the roar of the crowd of 21,000, Terry's banner was unveiled by his family and hoisted to the rafters alongside Gordie's number 9, Ted's number 7, and Alex's number 10.

"It was a great day for Dad and for us," Michael Sawchuk recalls. "But, you know, as I look back on it now, I'm glad that they didn't retire Dad's number for many years, because now, at the ceremony, we were all adults; some of us had our children with us on the ice. It meant much more to us because we could fully appreciate the moment. It worked out great."

Terry's equipment, donated to the Hockey Hall of Fame, was placed in a special display. The hall staff say the Sawchuk exhibit was one of the most popular and awe-inspiring during all the years that it was on display.

It seems that even those who didn't know him or ever saw him play are awed by his feats. As the Sabres' star goalie, Dominik Hasek, observed the afternoon of Terry's number retirement, "He had to be great. He had over a hundred shutouts!"

Terry continues to hold five NHL records: most seasons played in, twenty-one; most regular-season games played, 971; most victories, 435; most regular-season shutouts, 103; and most playoff shutouts in a single season, four (a record he shares with nine others).

He also remains the only player to win Rookie of the Year award in three professional leagues.

Unlike Gordie Howe, whose records have been surpassed by great Wayne Gretzky, Terry's records may well stand for all time. Besides his records, he has four Vezinas, the Calder Trophy, seven All-Star selections, and four Stanley Cups. His five NHL seasons with a goals-against average of less than 2.00 are untouchable, and his performance in the Stanley Cup play-offs of 1967 puts him in a class all of his own. He innovated the deep crouch. And he played through twenty-one seasons despite alcoholism, an endless series of injuries, and his troublesome elbow, which could easily have stopped his career at any time.

Terry played in an era when goalie equipment was small, archaic, almost dangerous to use. There were no goalie coaches, agents, nutritionists, physiotherapists, or physical trainers. The goalies of Terry's time learned alone, toiled alone, and excelled alone, on sheer talent and determination.

In eighteen seasons, Glenn Hall amassed eleven All-Star selections, won three Vezinas, and tallied eighty-three shutouts. He introduced the "butterfly" style of going down to the ice with legs spread apart to each side.

Jacques Plante came out of retirement to play seventeen seasons. He won seven Vezinas, was a seven-time All-Star, and helped win six Stanley Cups with Montreal in the late '50s. He introduced the face mask to the NHL on November 1, 1959. He also made goaltending into a "science" and was the first to truly teach it to others through his books and clinics.

Like Terry, Gump Worsley would toil in the NHL for twenty-one seasons. Remarkably, he did not don a face mask until his very last season in the early 1970s. He won the Calder as top rookie, won two Vezinas, made two All-Star teams, and won four Stanley Cups. His plump figure, brushcut, and acrobatic style made him a crowd favourite.

Johnny Bower won four Stanley Cups and two Vezinas, but his greatest contribution to goaltending was his development of the poke check. He played his last NHL game at the age of forty-five.

● ● ●

Terry would be very proud of his family today. Despite the anguish he caused them, they are all fiercely proud Sawchuks.

Jerry played Junior hockey for the Detroit Junior Red Wings, switching to defence from goal. He lives with his wife and two children in the Detroit area. In fact, his daughter, Maria, Terry's granddaughter, has taken up hockey with a vengeance and hopes one day to make the women's U.S. Olympic ice hockey team.

Daughter JoAnne lives in Bonita Springs, Florida, is married, and works in a house/apartment cleaning business. Her favourite memory of her father is from the age of eight when she and her girls' hockey team participated in a scrimmage between periods of a Red Wings' game. "I was so proud, especially when we were introduced to the crowd. I remember as I was getting ready for the face-off, I looked up and there was Dad standing at the bench smiling at me. Every time I watch a hockey game, I think of that moment and the grin Dad had on his face."

Kathy is divorced with one child and she too lives in Bonita Springs. Like her older sister, she is in the cleaning business. Kathy recalls, "I remember when Dad took JoAnne and me to the Olympia for one of his practices. After practice we were waiting for him to come out of the dressing room — he was always the last one out! When he came out, he took us to a back door but outside there was a group of fans and they came rushing towards us. Dad yelled, 'Run!' I know I ran as hard as I could to the car. We got in and locked the doors. The fans were all around us, as Dad gave autographs through his window. I felt very proud and special that day!"

Carol Ann is very happily married with one child. She lives near her other sisters in Naples, Florida. She too runs a cleaning business. Carol Ann reminisces, "I was only ten years old when Dad died, but I knew he was famous and I used to love reading about his victories. When my father was playing a game on television, the family would sit around and root for him. We were also able to meet other hockey players and this made us feel special. I used to see the fans grabbing at him, asking for his autograph. I sure wish I had one of his autographs now."

Debbie is married with two children and also runs a cleaning business in Bonita Springs, Florida. She recalls, "I can't remember much about my father. I was too young but I can remember him cooking breakfast — fried eggs and Canadian bacon. I also remember hiding out in the kitchen a lot with Mom."

Terrance Michael (Terry) lives in Colon, Michigan, and is now engaged to be married. He is a teacher and coaches many sports at his school, including his favourite, football. "I don't remember much about my father but someone every day tells me how great a goaltender he was or that they had met him once. I always feel extremely proud when this happens, although I regret never having the chance to get to know the man."

The youngest, Michael, recently married. He lives in Sturgis, Michigan, is a teacher, and is very involved in his school's athletic program. "I was only three when Dad died but today, I am extremely proud to be Terry Sawchuk's son."

Their mother, Pat Sawchuk Milford, remarried eleven years ago and lives with her husband Larry in Fort Myers, Florida. She is a proud grandmother of six. She continues to be close to all of her seven children.

"You know, it is truly tough to be married to someone who is in the spotlight, whether it be sports or entertainment. I wish, in my heart of hearts, that I could take all the bad memories and the hurt our kids have and are still going through. I wish I could make it disappear!

"If this book can help one person to get help, to live a normal life without abuse and spare their loved ones, the agony of watching someone you love destroy himself or herself and everyone around him or her, to save their children, then I know Terry would truly be happy knowing this. He would give this story his blessing. And he would be so proud of his children today.

"And we are all proud of his goaltending accomplishments. All these years later, anyone who says anything negative about the hockey career of Terry Sawchuk will have eight Sawchuks to contend with. In that respect he was and is number one. No doubt about it."

Terry would receive honours from the hockey world as recently as January 1998. An extensive hockey poll was conducted by *The Hockey News*, to rank the top fifty players of all time. Terry Sawchuk was chosen ninth overall, the highest-ranked goaltender on the list.

Twenty-eight years after his death, his memory has never faded.

Appendix I
THE GOALIES

	VEZINAS	HARTS/ CALDERS	REGULAR SEASON GAMES	ALL-STAR TEAMS	STANLEY CUPS	SEASONS	SHUTOUTS: REGULAR SEASON
THE FABULOUS FIVE							
Terry Sawchuk	4	1	971	7	4	21	103
Glenn Hall	3	1	906	11	1	18	84
Jacques Plante*	7	1	837	7	6	18	82
Gump Worsley	2	1	862	2	4	21	43
Johnny Bower	2	0	549	1	4	15	37
THE SINGLE BRIDGE							
Harry Lumley	1	0	804	2	1	13	71
THE FAMOUS FOUR							
Bill Durnan	6	0	383	6	2	7	34
Turk Broda	2	0	629	3	5	14	62
Frank Brimsek	2	1	514	8	2	10	40
Chuck Rayner	0	1	425	3	0	10	33
THE APOSTLES NINE							
Tony Esposito	3	1	886	5	0	16	76
Ken Dryden	5	1	397	6	6	8	46
Bernie Parent*	2	0	608	2	2	13	55
Patrick Roy	3	0	717	5	3	14	41
Ed Giacomin	1	0	610	5	0	13	54
Rogatien Vachon	1	1	795	2	3	16	51
Gerry Cheevers*	0	0	418	0	2	13	26
Grant Fuhr	1	0	806	2	5	17	23
Billy Smith	1	0	680	1	4	18	22

*played in the WHA

Appendix II

TERRY SAWCHUK'S SHUTOUTS

	DATE	VENUE	OPPOSITION	SCORE	OPPOSING GOALIE

DETROIT RED WINGS

1949–50

	DATE	VENUE	OPPOSITION	SCORE	OPPOSING GOALIE
1.	Jan. 15	New York	Rangers	1–0	Charlie Rayner

1950–51

	DATE	VENUE	OPPOSITION	SCORE	OPPOSING GOALIE
2.	Oct. 29	Detroit	Bruins	2–0	Jack Gelineau
3.	Nov. 12	Detroit	Canadiens	4–0	Gerry McNeil
4.	Dec. 6	New York	Rangers	9–0	Charlie Rayner
5.	Dec. 9	Detroit	Rangers	5–0	Emile Francis
6.	Jan. 4	Detroit	Black Hawks	1–0	Harry Lumley
7.	Jan. 7	Detroit	Bruins	3–0	Jack Gelineau
8.	Jan. 21	Detroit	Leafs	0–0	Al Rollins
9.	Mar. 7	Toronto	Leafs	3–0	Al Rollins
10.	Mar. 11	Chicago	Black Hawks	7–0	Harry Lumley
11.	Mar. 15	Detroit	Bruins	4–0	Jack Gelineau
12.	Mar. 25	Detroit	Canadiens	5–0	Gerry McNeil

1951–52

	DATE	VENUE	OPPOSITION	SCORE	OPPOSING GOALIE
13.	Oct. 11	Detroit	Bruins	1–0	Jim Henry
14.	Oct. 20	Detroit	Canadiens	3–0	Gerry McNeil
15.	Nov. 6	Boston	Bruins	0–0	Jim Henry
16.	Nov. 20	Boston	Bruins	2–0	Jim Henry
17.	Dec. 8	Montreal	Canadiens	3–0	Gerry McNeil
18.	Dec. 15	Detroit	Black Hawks	3–0	Harry Lumley
19.	Dec. 23	Detroit	Canadiens	4–0	Gerry McNeil
20.	Jan. 17	Detroit	Bruins	5–0	Jim Henry
21.	Jan. 19	Montreal	Canadiens	4–0	Gerry McNeil
22.	Jan. 27	Chicago	Black Hawks	2–0	Harry Lumley
23.	Feb. 10	Boston	Bruins	2–0	Jim Henry
24.	Mar. 16	Chicago	Black Hawks	4–0	Harry Lumley

	DATE	VENUE	OPPOSITION	SCORE	OPPOSING GOALIE
	1952–53				
25.	Oct. 16	Detroit	Black Hawks	7–0	Al Rollins
26.	Nov. 13	Detroit	Bruins	3–0	Jim Henry
27.	Dec. 6	Chicago	Black Hawks	2–0	Al Rollins
28.	Dec. 14	Detroit	Canadiens	0–0	Gerry McNeil
29.	Jan. 15	Boston	Bruins	4–0	Jim Henry
30.	Jan. 31	Detroit	Black Hawks	4–0	Al Rollins
31.	Mar. 7	Toronto	Leafs	3–0	Harry Lumley
32.	Mar. 11	New York	Rangers	2–0	Lorne Worsley
33.	Mar. 15	Chicago	Black Hawks	0–0	Al Rollins
	1953–54				
34.	Oct. 18	Detroit	Canadiens	4–0	Gerry McNeil
35.	Oct. 25	Detroit	Leafs	2–0	Harry Lumley
36.	Nov. 26	Detroit	Leafs	2–0	Harry Lumley
37.	Nov. 28	Detroit	Black Hawks	9–0	Jack Gelineau
38.	Dec. 3	Detroit	Rangers	4–0	Johnny Bower
39.	Jan. 3	Detroit	Leafs	0–0	Harry Lumley
40.	Jan. 21	Montreal	Canadiens	1–0	Gerry McNeil
41.	Jan. 24	Detroit	Leafs	2–0	Harry Lumley
42.	Feb. 4	Detroit	Bruins	5–0	Jim Henry
43.	Feb. 14	Chicago	Black Hawks	5–0	Al Rollins
44.	Feb. 17	Toronto	Leafs	0–0	Harry Lumley
45.	Feb. 22	Detroit	Canadiens	3–0	Jacques Plante
	1954–55				
46.	Oct. 9	Detroit	Rangers	4–0	Lorne Worsley
47.	Oct. 30	Detroit	Bruins	4–0	Jim Henry
48.	Nov. 7	Detroit	Rangers	1–0	Lorne Worsley
49.	Nov. 20	Detroit	Black Hawks	5–0	Al Rollins
50.	Nov. 21	Detroit	Black Hawks	1–0	Al Rollins
51.	Nov. 25	Detroit	Leafs	2–0	Harry Lumley
52.	Jan. 8	Detroit	Black Hawks	1–0	Al Rollins
53.	Jan. 13	Detroit	Bruins	1–0	John Henderson
54.	Jan. 16	Detroit	Rangers	3–0	Lorne Worsley
55.	Jan. 23	Detroit	Leafs	4–0	Harry Lumley
56.	Feb. 20	New York	Rangers	5–0	Lorne Worsley
57.	Mar. 20	Detroit	Canadiens	6–0	Jacques Plante

	DATE	VENUE	OPPOSITION	SCORE	OPPOSING GOALIE

BOSTON BRUINS

1955–56

58.	Oct. 12	Boston	Leafs	2–0	Harry Lumley
59.	Oct. 22	Detroit	Red Wings	0–0	Glenn Hall
60.	Oct. 29	New York	Rangers	1–0	Lorne Worsley
61.	Nov. 13	Boston	Red Wings	0–0	Glenn Hall
62.	Dec. 4	Boston	Leafs	5–0	Harry Lumley
63.	Jan. 20	Chicago	Black Hawks	3–0	Hank Bassen
64.	Feb. 19	New York	Rangers	3–0	Lorne Worsley
65.	Mar. 10	Montreal	Canadiens	4–0	Jacques Plante
66.	Mar. 13	Boston	Red Wings	4–0	Glenn Hall

1956–57

67.	Oct. 27	Montreal	Canadiens	1–0	Jacques Plante
68.	Nov. 29	Chicago	Black Hawks	2–0	Al Rollins

DETROIT RED WINGS

1957–58

					Julien Klymkiw/
69.	Oct. 30	New York	Rangers	4–0	Lorne Worsley
70.	Nov. 16	Chicago	Black Hawks	1–0	Glenn Hall
71.	Dec. 22	Detroit	Black Hawks	2–0	Glenn Hall

1958–59

72.	Oct. 12	Detroit	Rangers	3–0	Lorne Worsley
73.	Nov. 18	Detroit	Bruins	6–0	Don Simmons
74.	Dec. 4	Detroit	Bruins	4–0	Don Simmons
75.	Feb. 12	Detroit	Rangers	1–0	Bruce Gamble
76.	Mar. 17	Detroit	Black Hawks	2–0	Glenn Hall

1959–60

77.	Oct. 14	Chicago	Black Hawks	2–0	Glenn Hall
78.	Oct. 18	Detroit	Leafs	3–0	Johnny Bower
79.	Nov. 14	New York	Rangers	4–0	Lorne Worsley
80.	Dec. 9	Detroit	Black Hawks	3–0	Glenn Hall
81.	Mar. 8	Detroit	Canadiens	3–0	Jacques Plante

1960–61

82.	Oct. 20	Detroit	Bruins	5–0	Don Simmons
83.	Nov. 27	Detroit	Leafs	3–0	Johnny Bower

	DATE	VENUE	OPPOSITION	SCORE	OPPOSING GOALIE
	1961–62				
84.	Nov. 2	Detroit	Rangers	1–0	Lorne Worsley
85.	Nov. 12	Detroit	Canadiens	3–0	Jacques Plante
86.	Dec. 9	Detroit	Black Hawks	3–0	Glenn Hall
87.	Dec. 14	Detroit	Bruins	5–0	Ed Chadwick
88.	Jan. 24	New York	Rangers	3–0	Lorne Worsley
	1962–63				
89.	Oct. 13	Chicago	Black Hawks	0–0	Glenn Hall
90.	Oct. 23	Toronto	Leafs	4–0	Johnny Bower
91.	Nov. 1	Detroit	Rangers	4–0	Lorne Worsley
	1963–64				
92.	Oct. 13	Detroit	Bruins	3–0	Ed Johnston
93.	Nov. 7	Detroit	Rangers	1–0	Jacques Plante
94.	Nov. 10	Detroit	Canadiens	3–0	Charlie Hodge
95.	Jan. 18	Montreal	Canadiens	2–0	Charlie Hodge
	(broke George Hainsworth's Record)				
96.	Feb. 6	Detroit	Black Hawks	4–0	Glenn Hall

TORONTO MAPLE LEAFS

	DATE	VENUE	OPPOSITION	SCORE	OPPOSING GOALIE
	1964–65				
97.	Nov. 21	Toronto	Black Hawks	1–0	Glenn Hall
	1965–66				
98.	Feb. 9	Toronto	Rangers	3–0	Ed Giacomin
	1966–67				
99.	Feb. 25	Toronto	Red Wings	4–0	Crozier-Gardiner
100.	Mar. 5	Toronto	Black Hawks	3–0	Denis DeJordy

LOS ANGELES KINGS

	DATE	VENUE	OPPOSITION	SCORE	OPPOSING GOALIE
	1967–68				
101.	Jan. 28	Philadelphia	Flyers	0–0	Doug Favell
102.	Mar. 14	Quebec City	Flyers	2–0	Bernie Parent

NEW YORK RANGERS

	DATE	VENUE	OPPOSITION	SCORE	OPPOSING GOALIE
	1969–70				
103.	Feb. 1	New York	Penguins	6–0	Al Smith

Bibliography

Batten, Jack. *The Leafs*. Toronto: Key Porter, 1994.

Beliveau, Jean. *My Life in Hockey*. Toronto: McClelland & Stewart, 1994.

Bock, Hal. *Save*. New York: Avon, 1974.

Boucher, Frank, and Trent Frayne. *When the Rangers Were Young*. New York: Dodd, Mead & Company, 1973.

Brewitt, Ross. *Clear the Track: The Eddie Shack Story*. Toronto: Stoddart, 1997.

Camelli, Allen. *Great Moments in Pro Hockey*. New York: Bantam, 1971.

Cole, Stephen. *The Last Hurrah*. Toronto: Penguin, 1995.

Cruise, David, and Alison Griffith. *Net Worth: Exploding the Myths of Pro Hockey*. Toronto: Penguin, 1991.

Dryden, Ken, and Roy MacGregor. *Home Game* Toronto: McClelland & Stewart, 1989.

Esposito, Phil, and Tony Esposito. *The Brothers Esposito*. New York: Lancer, 1971.

Geoffrion, Bernard, and Stan Fischler. *Boom Boom: The Life and Times of Bernard Geoffrion.* Toronto: McGraw-Hill Ryerson, 1972.

Harris, Billy. *The Glory Years.* Scarborough: Prentice Hall Canada, 1989.

Hunt, Jim. *The Men in the Nets.* Toronto: McGraw-Hill Ryerson, 1972.

Hunter, Douglas. *A Breed Apart.* Toronto: Penguin, 1995.

—. *Open Ice: The Tim Horton Story.* Toronto: Penguin, 1994.

Imlach, Punch. *Hockey Is a Battle.* Toronto: Macmillan, 1969.

Inside Sports. Hockey. Detroit: Visible Ink Press, 1998.

Irvin, Dick. *In the Crease.* Toronto: McClelland & Stewart, 1995.

—. *Now Back to You, Dick.* Toronto: McClelland & Stewart, 1988.

Kendall, Brian. *Shutout: The Legend of Terry Sawchuk.* Toronto: Penguin, 1996.

Leonetti, Michael. *Hockey's Golden Era.* Toronto, Macmillan, 1993.

Liss, Howard. *Hockey's Greatest All-Stars.* Scarborough: Prentice Hall, 1972.

Macskimming, Roy. *Gordie: A Hockey Legend.* Vancouver: Greystone, 1994.

McFarlane, Brian. *50 Years of Hockey.* Winnipeg: Greywood Publishing, 1969.

—. *The Leafs.* Toronto: Stoddart, 1995.

—. *The Lively World of Hockey.* Toronto: Signet, 1968.

The Official NHL Stanley Cup Centennial Book. Toronto: McClelland & Stewart, 1992.

Orr, Frank. *Greatest Goalies of Pro Hockey*. Toronto: Random House, 1973.

—. *Hockey's Greatest Stars*. Toronto: Longmans Canada, 1970.

—. *The Story of Hockey*. Toronto: Random House, 1971.

Pagnucco, Frank. *Heroes: Stars of Hockey's Golden Era*. Scarborough: Prentice Hall, 1985.

Smythe, Conn, and Scott Young. *If You Can't Beat Them in the Alley: The Memoirs of the Late Conn Smythe*. Toronto: McClelland & Stewart, 1981.

Index